The Tapestry of Jewish Time

296.43
C

Cardin, Nina Beth.

The tapestry of
Jewish time.

$24.95

DATE			

The Tapestry of Jewish Time

A Spiritual Guide to Holidays and Life-Cycle Events

Rabbi Nina Beth Cardin

Illustrated by Ilene Winn-Lederer

BEHRMAN HOUSE, INC.

Book and cover design by Howard Levy Design

Book and cover illustrations by Ilene Winn-Lederer

Copyright © 2000 by Nina Beth Cardin

Published by Behrman House, Inc.
11 Edison Place
Springfield, NJ 07081
www.behrmanhouse.com

Library of Congress Cataloging-in-Publication Data

Cardin, Nina Beth
    The tapestry of Jewish time: a spiritual guide to holidays and life-cycle events / by
Nina Beth Cardin.
      p. cm.
    Includes index.
    ISBN 0-87441-645-0
      1. Fasts and feasts—Judaism. 2. Life cycle, Human—Religious aspects—Judaism.
      3. Spiritual life—Judaism. I. Title.

BM690 .C36 2000
296.4'3—dc21

                                            99-088876

Manufactured in the United States of America

לאמי, מורתי,   To my mother, my teacher,

שושנה בת שריה וחנה   Shoshana, daughter of Sraia and Hannah

כשושנה בין החוחים,   Like a lily among the thorns,

כן רעיתי בין הבנות.   So is my beloved among the daughters.

שיר השירים ב:ב   Song of Songs 2:2

Acknowledgments

This book is the inspiration of David Behrman. Once upon a time and long ago, David proposed that I write about time and sacred stories and children's dreams. He introduced me to the magic of the House of Behrman and to its warmth, professionalism and caring. So it was that our relationship began, and I have been pleased and honored to work with the Behrman family ever since.

I have learned much from Behrman House about how an idea becomes a book. If I am a better writer now than before, it is in large measure due to the wisdom of my early guides, David Behrman and Adam Siegel.

Midway through this project, Gila Gevirtz joined Behrman House and took over as my editor. I cannot imagine a greater gift. Gila is a talented artist and writer in her own right who brought to this project endless vision, creativity and energy. Every page of this book is touched by her wisdom and grace. I cherish her partnership.

I am grateful to all those who generously shared with me their stories and learning, much of which can be found in these pages. My thanks go also to the many people who read early drafts of the manuscript, either in whole or in part, especially Rabbis Debra Reed Blank, Joel E. Soffin, Richard Hirsh and William Cutter. Your comments and suggestions were invaluable.

And most of all, I thank my extended family, my children and my husband for allowing me to talk about them in the pages of this book. You, in truth, are my best and dearest teachers. You fill my days with love and joy and meaning.

May the tracings of our family's weavings be a blessing for our people and all humankind.

Generations

The Family and Friendship Tree of:

_____

"These are the generations…" The story of Creation begins this way (Genesis 2:4). So does the story of Noah, and Abraham and Sarah, and Isaac and Rebecca, and Jacob and Rachel and Leah. To introduce the record of our lives with these words is to link us forever to the ones who came before and to the ones we hope will follow. The lines on these pages are here for you to record your name and the names of family members, teachers, friends and mentors who framed your views and guided your steps. May each name be a blessing to the children and students who carry life forward.

NAME	RELATIONSHIP
_____	_____
_____	_____
_____	_____
_____	_____
_____	_____
_____	_____
_____	_____
_____	_____
_____	_____

NAME

RELATIONSHIP

_____

_____

_____

_____

_____

_____

_____

_____

_____

_____

_____

_____

_____

_____

_____

_____

_____

_____

_____

NAME   RELATIONSHIP

_____   _____

_____   _____

_____   _____

_____   _____

_____   _____

_____   _____

_____   _____

_____   _____

_____   _____

_____   _____

_____   _____

_____   _____

_____   _____

_____   _____

_____   _____

_____   _____

_____   _____

_____   _____

_____   _____

Special Events
and Dates to Remember

DATE   EVENT

_____   _____

_____   _____

_____   _____

_____   _____

_____   _____

_____   _____

_____   _____

_____   _____

_____   _____

_____   _____

_____   _____

_____   _____

_____   _____

_____   _____

_____   _____

_____   _____

_____   _____

Table of Contents

Prologue
A Union of Weavers

WE JEWS ARE A UNION of weavers. Interlacing our traditions and languages, our rituals and laws, with fibers gathered from the cultures around us, we each weave a personal shawl of Judaism. Some shawls are open and loose, allowing the currents of other cultures to flow in and out easily. Others are fine and tight, holding much of Jewish culture in and foreign cultures out.

The world of Judaism is filled with shawls of different weaves, from loose to fine, filtering the larger world in or out to a greater or lesser degree. Each adds its flair, its strength, and its warmth to the sacred garment of the Jewish people. Our choice of weave determines where we worship, what we eat, where we live, how we pray, whom we marry, what we do in our spare time, and how we educate our children. And every now and then we add a thread or two of a new hue and a new texture that serves to enrich and extend our wardrobe.

Sadly, sometimes we derogate one another's craftsmanship. It is true that with too loose a weave the cloth loses its integrity and ceases to be. And it is also true that with too tight a weave the body underneath smothers and dies. But most of our shawls fall somewhere in between. They complement one another, reflect in their similarity of form one another's authenticity, preserve the secrets of the different weaves for one another and for future generations, which is very good, for no one shawl can suit every Jew. And yet while we weavers differ, we should acknowledge that we all work on the same loom, with the same warp holding tight our differing patterns of weft. And that, if nothing else, should unite us.

CHAPTER 1
Entering the Story

I T HAPPENS EVERY NOW AND THEN as I sweep the kitchen floor of fallen debris from hurried breakfasts or groceries unpacked after an early-morning supermarket run. The sun streams through my eastern window, and there they are—shimmering particles of dust, high-riding renegades floating aimlessly, leisurely, in the air about me, kicked up by the vitality of life the morning has witnessed.

I have two thoughts about this dust, one common, the other ethereal. The common thought is this: If the dust is floating now, it will come down later. My kitchen will once again be dirty.

A more noble, enduring, even transforming thought pushes that mundane thought aside: The dust, of course, is always there, but I do not always see it. It takes a certain light, a certain attentiveness and a certain moment of stillness to see it. How many of us would have passed right by that burning bush in the desert thousands of years ago, giving it a wide berth, simply thinking "Man, that is hot" when in fact it would have been wiser to say "God, is that you?" If seeing what is evident requires attentiveness, stillness, even faith, how much more is required to see what is hidden.

What do we need to sense the love, caring and kindness that swirl around us? What do we need to imagine the desire of God? Can we know, see, feel holiness all around us? From what wellspring do the motivations for our everyday deeds flow—from the pools of selfishness or selflessness or from the place where those deep, pulsing waters converge?

This book tries to answer those questions. It is about reaching toward meaning through the everyday, about how Judaism structures time and about how time well framed can open us to the sacred. It is about pauses and preparation, birthdays and holidays, weddings and pilgrimages. It is a book about days and weeks and years, about hoping and remembering, about public times and private times. For every moment in time involves a choice: Do I stay or go, rest or act, buy or forgo, keep or give away, forgive or take revenge?

A Legacy of Stories

To speak of time is to enter the language of stories. "Once upon a time..." "In the beginning was the big bang." "When God began to create the heaven and the earth..." Whereas the present opens itself to action, yesterday and tomorrow lie solely in the realm of stories. Action and stories enliven each other, give birth to each other: Action is the grist for stories, and stories—whether of deeds past or dreams for the future—motivate us to act.

Stories endure across time and space, through war and oppression. Stories are what we can best bequeath to our children. For eventually everything else can be taken from us, even our lives. But not our stories. For a people without a home for 2,000 years, on the move, chased from one country to another, whose possessions

The first stories of the Jewish people are recorded in the Torah, the Five Books of Moses. We study them in community with others and read them from the Torah scroll in synagogue.

were targets of looting and destruction and loss, our stories are our legacy. They pack easily, travel well and fill the hearths of our new homes.

To tell stories is to tame time, to frame time, to press it into the service of meaning. Because we can't see time, because we can't color it or hold it or buy it or control it, we tend to believe we are at its mercy. But we have the power to plan, to declare a holiday, to celebrate a birth. Time is as much at our disposal as we are at its.

Our stories give calendars and life cycles a context, and context gives them meaning. Through stories, an autumn day turns into the birthday of the world, a family trip to Israel becomes a pilgrimage to the Holy Land, a wedding becomes a metaphor for God's love for us. Stories build a structure from the deeds of our lives. They hold the key that unlocks the portal to the heavens, allowing the sacred to pour out and fill our earthly space. When the sliver of the New Moon reflects the story of our monthly renewal, when a 50th wedding anniversary is celebrated under a quilted canopy made from the fabrics of a half century of love, these moments become sacred. And these moments are then woven into the ever-unfolding story of the Jewish people.

Stories allow an event to live again and again, transcending the hegemony of time. A story might have been told to me by my teacher or my grandmother, but it becomes mine the moment I begin to tell it. Perhaps that is why Jewish tradition tells us that every Jew ever to live—past, present, future—was standing at Sinai, witnessing God, receiving the Torah. When we *tell* the story of our people at Sinai, we enter the story, and the story enters us. Stories are the medium that sets our memories and holds them fast. They are more than what we own; they are a bit of who we are.

This book contains two sections. The first is about the Jewish people, all of us, all together, as told through the stories of the calendar. The second is about Jews, one by one, as told through the celebrations and the rituals of our lives. In reality, the two sections are intertwined. We celebrate our birthdays or mourn our losses in the week before Ḥanukkah or on the 13th day after Passover as happenstance demands. These occasions form the spiritual helixes of our lives, and we are the products of those interwoven strands of time.

The stories, dreams and prayers of our people belong to the entire community. The man on the right is signing the Torah reading service.

The Uses of Metaphor

Throughout this book, two characters appear: the people Israel and God. Israel comprises everyone who came forth from Abraham and Sarah, the motley group gathered around Moses to flee slavery and meet God in the wilderness, and every individual who has joined the march of the Jewish people throughout the ages.

It is harder to define God. For some, God is the Grand Storyteller; the Author of the Torah; the Giver of the Commandments; the God of Abraham and Sarah, Isaac and Rebecca, Jacob and Leah and Rachel; the Worker of Miracles; the Creator; the Rock. For others, God is the One who cares about the people Israel and all the world we live in, who inspires us and seeks us and pursues ways to meet us but who leaves the storytelling and the lawmaking to us. And for still others, God is not deity but power, the enduring, exalted legacy and wisdom that was born of, lays claim to, and enriches the Jewish people among all people of faith and goodness around the world.

All those beliefs speak of holiness. All locate that source of holiness somewhere in the interaction between the self and the Jewish people as lived under the canopy of "God." All use the medium of the story—along with the rituals and the deeds that flow from and give rise to stories—to bring meaning into their lives.

And all—to greater or lesser degrees—use metaphor to speak of God. From King Solomon to Maimonides to the mystic kabbalists, Jews have proclaimed that God is beyond speech, beyond our comprehension, beyond worldliness. Yet King Solomon built a temple for the presence of God, Maimonides wrote volumes about God and God's will, and the kabbalists developed spheres of divinity cast in human form.

That is because humans cannot help but speak about God, our loss of God, our search for God, our disappointment in God, our love and need and desire of God. When our hearts are bursting with joy or relief, when they ache from loss or hurt or anger, we want to speak to God and speak of God. And we do it in the most human of terms, untrue though they be, bound as we are by the limits of our language. Does God truly have arms that can hold us? A mouth that can kiss us? Does God cry with us in our pain, laugh with us, become angry? So when we speak of God, we have a

choice: lies or silence, metaphor or distance. Most of us seek close-
ness to God and therefore seek metaphor. Throughout this book, I
will use metaphor to speak of God—God as creator, God as father,
God as mother, lover, judge, warrior, friend, counselor, goad,
teacher—just as Jewish tradition does. To speak this way of God, as
if God were a person, allows us to draw closer to God. It allows us
to believe that we can reach toward holiness.

*Jewish tradition teaches that
visiting the sick is a holy act.
Our caring presence can help
revive the spirit of one who
is ill.*

> Said Rabbi Ḥamma, the son of Rabbi Ḥanina: What does it
> mean, "Follow Adonai your God"? (Deuteronomy 11:22). Is
> it possible for a human to literally follow God? Rather, this
> means that you should follow in the ways of God. Just as God
> clothes the naked, so should you clothe the naked; just as
> God visits the sick, so should you visit the sick; just as God
> comforts the mourner, so should you comfort the mourner.
> (*Sotah* 14a)

But that manner of speech also holds a danger in that we will
forget we are using a metaphor. We may believe in and cherish our
language as much as we believe in and cherish the God that our
language is reaching toward. We may forget the limits of metaphor
and draw conclusions that are misplaced. Jewish tradition offers a
safeguard by creating competing, even conflicting metaphors and
bids us to hold on to all the images at once. God is both merciful
and just, warrior and lover, forgiving and exacting, male and female.

As you read this book, remember the strengths and the limits of
metaphor.

Truth and Meaning

A word, too, about truth. There is no such thing as cyberspace
or La-La Land. Romeo and Juliet never lived; neither did Paul
Bunyan nor his ox named Babe. There is no tooth fairy, nor are there
little people. And George Washington did not chop down the cherry
tree. Yet each one of these myths is a bearer of truth. Many of us
meet others more frequently in cyberspace than at the supermarket.

To capture their truths, cultures create and gather up bundles of
symbols and store them in their treasure trove of myths. Myths are
not untrue: They are the garments of truth, what truth wears in

Moses and Aaron perform miracles before Pharaoh. Each Passover we join our friends and family around the seder table to retell and reenter the story of the Exodus. ❧

earthly existence. Americans possess myths of their coming to the free world, of the bravery and the suffering they endured, of their friendship with the Indians, of their triumph in having made it through the first winter. Nations possess myths of their noble beginnings (often expressed in national anthems) and the values that they hope become ingrained in the souls of their citizens. Every society, every culture, has its myths.

For me, the question to ask about the stories in the Bible and in our tradition is not Did they happen? but What do they mean to us? Why did our ancestors savor them, preserve them and teach them diligently to their children? What lessons did our fathers and our mothers find in those stories? What truths do these stories possess for us? What questions do they answer? When we speak to our children, will we tell them these stories? Other stories? After all, the stories we give them will be the legacy of our lives.

All Jews answer these questions in their own way. I love the stories of my tradition. I don't agree with them all; I am not proud of them all. But I keep them anyway. Some I keep to feel close to my past. They are my only heirlooms from family long gone. They bear the souls of my past within them; they are my substitute for an ancestral trunk, a trunk that exile and oppression denied me. But most of all, I keep those stories because they keep me. They are my counsel, my identity, the wisdom that guides me as I make my choices every day.

Authenticity and Change

Here is a story about change: From the earliest weeks of my marriage, I listened to my husband sing Friday-night Kiddush, the blessing over wine. He sang the melody, he said, that he learned from his father, who in turn learned it from his father before him. For years, I listened to that tune, believing I was hearing a faithful rendition of a generations-old song. And then my in-laws came to visit for Shabbat. We invited my father-in-law to make Kiddush. I began to hum along, confident in the rhythm, the pace and the melody of the prayer. Not eight words in, I faltered. His was not my husband's melody. It had a different pace, different notes and a slightly different rhythm.

I cast a glance at my husband. He seemed not to notice. He was hearing the melody of his youth, the melody he thinks he sings. It was a lesson in cultural transmission. Why would I ever imagine that a song would behave as the printed word behaves, unchanged by time or by those who give voice to it? And why, by extension, would we ever expect a dynamic tradition like Judaism to clone itself—unyielding to change and mutation—generation after generation?

In the very process of preserving our past we often unwittingly change it. One day, the Talmud tells us (*Menaḥot* 29b), God allowed Moses to return to earth to visit the academy of the early rabbis. Moses slipped in and sat in the back. After listening to a lesson by the famed Rabbi Akiva, he became distressed, for he could not follow what the rabbi was saying. A student rose and asked Akiva, "Master, from where did you learn this?" And Rabbi Akiva replied, "It is a law given to Moses at Sinai."

The most authentic Judaism is a Judaism of change. The only vibrant Judaism is a Judaism of change. This book of Judaism could not have been written 12 months ago. And it is not the same book I would write a year from now. By then, new stories, new traditions, new insights, will have melded themselves into our common text. Knowingly and unknowingly we create new traditions wrapped in the language of the old. Out of the deeds of our daily lives, new ways are born, new ways that lead us back to our roots.

"Let the old become new and the new become holy." So said Rav Abraham Kook, a mystic and the first chief rabbi of modern Israel. So it is when each of us weaves the sacred into our lives. May this book help make that happen.

When we study our sacred texts we enrich the Jewish tradition, and when we develop our own stories and interpretations we enlarge it.

Throughout this book I have used a kind of shorthand to present the most common practices of contemporary Judaism. I may indicate that Conservative synagogues celebrate this way, Orthodox that way, the Reform another way and the Reconstructionists their way. And, for the most part, that is true—but not always. For variations exist even within the denominations. Tradition, local custom, the birthplace of a synagogue's founders, desired length of service, use of Jewish camp traditions brought home, aesthetics and politics all affect how any one synagogue, and any one Jew or family, will choose to express their Judaism.

PART ONE

The Jewish Holidays

CHAPTER 2
The Story of Time

Judaism claims that the way to nobility of the soul is the art of sanctifying time.

—Rabbi Abraham Joshua Heschel

TIME IS THE MEDIUM OF OUR LIVES, the durable surface on which our deeds are etched.

And yet time remains largely invisible to us. We can see its tracings when it has passed:

when we need a haircut, when our vacation is over, when our children have grown and we have

not. Sometimes we notice time, too, when it has not yet come: while waiting for the bus to arrive

or the movie to begin or the test results to come back. We often imagine time, in these circumstances, as complicitous with the enemy. Either it moves too fast, or it moves too slowly. It is something apart from us, working upon us or against us. But if time is our medium, we can be its artists. Its texture and its quality are in our

The stories of the Torah are woven into the fabric of Jewish prayer services.

A Calendar of Sacred Time

The first commandment given to the Jewish people at the moment of the Exodus was: "God spoke to Moses, saying: This month shall be unto you the beginning of months…" (Exodus 12:2). Of all the laws that would be given to the Jews, why start with that law? Because freedom means being the master of your time, organizing it as you wish, naming it as you wish, and creating the sacred days that hold your precious memories. With the Exodus, the Israelites' time was no longer Egyptian time. Their new lives could only be charted by a new calendar.

hands. We can shape it and mold it with our deeds, fashion it even as it fashions us. At any given moment, we can fight or forgive, be generous or stingy, grateful or disgruntled, noble or nattering. And the artwork that we make with time becomes the masterpiece of our lives.

What helps us decide? What helps set our direction, guide our mood, chart our course? As Jews, we are heirs to a treasure map of wisdom drafted on the scroll of time. The map is drawn from the stories of Torah, the ways and days, prayers and rituals, of the Jewish people. Spread across the map, punctuating the time and the terrain of the everyday, are the holidays.

Each holiday is a place in time and space, with its own story, its own message and its own rituals. If we allow, it enters our homes with decorations and spirit and finds a way to enter our hearts. Each holiday is a guide to a different leg of life's journey. On Yom Kippur, we learn the gift of apology, to forgive and allow ourselves to be forgiven, to claim responsibility for our actions, to believe that we are not branded by our past mistakes. On Sukkot, we are reminded that the most secure and essential possessions in our lives are not the houses in which we live, the money we have, or the objects we own. Our most secure and most essential possessions are the love we give to others, the communities we build, the promise of our faith, and the stories we leave behind. On Passover, we learn that freedom is conferred on us as part of our dignity, that we are to seek out a partnership with God, and that we deserve freedom most when we place it at the service of others.

That map of time helps us see where we—or at least our people—have been and where we might yet go. It is well worn, yet ever renewed. And in its presence, we know that we do not travel this world alone.

When Time Began

The stories of the Jewish people begin with the creation of the world, for they offer a universal, not merely a parochial, message. The opening chapter of the Torah says that in the beginning the universe was dark and cold. There was no order. There was no breath. There was no light.

Then God said, "Let there be light." And there was light. With a word, light shot from one end of the universe to the other, flooding the skies, flowing everywhere. Light warmed the air and readied the heavens for life. And God saw the light and said, "It is good." And there was evening, and there was morning, a first day.

Light gave the world the means for sight, warmth, growth—and time. Light and darkness became daytime and nighttime. Together they constitute a day.

The Structure of Time

The first day presented no management problems. It was all there was. But then there were two. They had to be ordered. When there were more, they needed to be named, labeled, cataloged. Eventually people created calendars. Calendars help us bundle time in finite packages, segmenting the infinite in ways we can comprehend. They give us a way to plot our location in this endless sea, telling us what to call today, how to count to tomorrow, and how to speak of one particular yesterday.

The ner tamid, or eternal light, hangs above the Holy Ark in the synagogue sanctuary. Its constant light is a reminder of God's eternal presence. ❧

The Days of Creation

Yom Eḥad	Day 1	Creation of light
Yom Sheni	Day 2	Creation of heaven and earth
Yom Shlishi	Day 3	Creation of dry land and sea, grass, vegetation and fruit trees
Yom Revi'i	Day 4	Creation of the sun and the moon
Yom Ḥamishi	Day 5	Creation of fish and birds
Yom Hashishi	Day 6	Creation of bugs, land animals and humans
Yom Hashevi'i	Day 7	Shabbat: Day of rest

Calendars not only help us name time. They also help us mark time in unison. They help us agree on what day today is, when the World Series will be played, how old we are. Time may belong to the heavens, but calendars are the work of humans—and cultures. Each calendar reflects the stories and the beliefs of the people who created it. Each community and culture imposes its particular story on the universal experience of time. Throughout the course of history, there have been hundreds of different calendars. Today the

What Is It That Unites All Jews?

Jews are fundamentally united by four things: *Torah*—the laws, ways, traditions and stories of the Jewish people; *Sinai*—our Covenant with God and one another that gives us a common identity and common mission; *Israel*—our spiritual homeland and our people; and the *calendar*—the way we organize, name and mark time.

world shares one coordinated, global calendar. Not surprisingly, as our calendars merge, so do our national stories. Wars, treaties, business contracts, stock transactions, international travel schedules—all encourage our common counting of time and contribute to our increasingly common culture. Yet as Jews, we also mark time according to our own reckoning.

Living in Two Worlds

Cultures create holidays, and holidays create cultures. As North American Jews, who live with two calendars, we have a heightened sense of living within two cultures. Sometimes these cultures collide, as when the World Series falls on Yom Kippur, or popular fashions worn at a bat mitzvah celebration fall outside the strictures of proper synagogue dress. Other times they work well together, as when Passover falls during spring break or cyberspace links formerly isolated Jews to one another.

How we choose to interlace these two worlds, with their preferred values, achievements and ways of conduct, determines to a large extent the kinds of Jews we elect to be. The different patterns form the distinctions that constitute our major denominations: Conservative, Orthodox, Reconstructionist, Reform. Judaism is the loom upon which all the threads of our lives can be worked. The colors and the textures of our days may come from the infinite variety in the life around us. But they are held fast and given form and shape by the bonds of Judaism.

The Gregorian calendar was created more than 400 years ago (according to its own reckoning), in the year 1582. It is designed to begin on January 1 and end on December 31. The Gregorian calendar is a solar calendar; it is tuned to the earth's rotation around the sun. That journey, of course, takes 365 1/4 days. Because calendars measure whole days, the Gregorian calendar is 365 days long, except every four years, when one day is added to make up for the four quarter days that were lost. That year is called the leap year. The number of days in a year, according to the Gregorian calendar, is roughly divided into 12 months, each with 30 or 31 days (except, of course, for February).

The "modern" Hebrew calendar, a lunar calendar, was created more than 2,000 years ago. It is tuned to the moon's rotation around the earth, which takes 29 1/2 days. So a Hebrew month is counted as either 29 or 30 days. Twelve of these months make one year.

But now a problem of reconciliation arises. Twelve lunar months add up to approximately 354 days; that is 11 days short of a solar

We Are Our Memories

The Jewish calendar is the scrapbook of our people. Without it, we would lose our collective memory. Elie Wiesel says, "Memories, even painful memories, are all we have. In fact, they are the only thing we are. So we must take very good care of them."

year. If we didn't adjust the Hebrew calendar to match the solar calendar, Rosh Hashanah and all the other Jewish holidays would end up wandering around the solar year. They might be in winter one year and in summer a few years later. That would be a bit awkward, especially since several of our holidays are harvest holidays and therefore tied to the seasons of the Land of Israel. It would not do to celebrate the fall harvest (Sukkot), for example, in early spring.

To solve the problem, the lunar calendar must occasionally be adjusted. Only instead of adding one day in its leap year, as the solar calendar does, the Hebrew calendar adds a whole month. That additional month is called Adar Bet, that is, the second Adar, for it is inserted after the regular late-winter month of Adar.

The Hebrew leap year also occurs more often than the solar leap year. The rabbis calculated that it must come seven times within a 19-year cycle to align regularly with the solar year. That averages out to about one leap year every two or three years. Whereas in any given year the lunar calendar will be either a bit longer or a bit shorter than the solar calendar (which is why we say the holidays are either "early" or "late"), everything evens out within a year or two.

With the lunar calendar as our map and our family and friends as our companions, we can travel well through the years of our lives, gathering lessons and wisdom and love as we go. And the tracings we make with our deeds will one day become part of the eternal record of the Jewish people.

The Face of Time

Not too long ago all watches were analog watches, with faces and hands that travel around the dial, pointing to the time of day. Such watches foster a sense of expectation, of passage, of context, of where we come from and where we are going. They allow us to see the distance time must travel before a loved one returns or the arc of time traversed as we linger over coffee.

Nowadays many watches are digital, with numbers divided by a colon that separates the hour from the minutes. Digital watches tell us what time it is now. They give us a sense of precision and control and a pride in knowing the correct time to the second. But they also give a hint of urgency, with the display often blinking at us. They elicit the discomfort of disconnectedness: In which direction is the future? What happened to the past? They give us nothing but the ever-present present.

I do not own a digital watch.

Counting the Days

In the Gregorian calendar, days begin at midnight. In Judaism, days begin at sunset. As it says in the Bible, "And there was evening, and there was morning, a first day." What is the difference? Midnight is a concept made by people; sunset is a moment made by God.

Fattening the Year

Why is the extra month added after Adar? According to one reckoning, Adar is the last month of the year. Where better to add than at the end? The leap years come in the following years of the 19-year cycle: 3, 6, 8, 11, 14, 17, 19.

Festival Dates

In biblical times, when the new moon was seen in Jerusalem, a new month—Rosh Ḥodesh—was proclaimed. Special fires were lighted all over Israel to announce the new month. But it took longer for the news to reach Jews living outside of Israel. Concerned that they might begin the month on the wrong day, and thus celebrate holidays on the wrong day, too, they added an extra day of celebration to the three festivals on which they made a pilgrimage to Jerusalem: Passover, Shavuot and Sukkot. This way they were assured that one of the days had to be right. This is a tradition that Orthodox and Conservative Jews living outside of Israel continue to this day.

The Jewish Holiday Calendar

Tishre

1–2	Rosh Hashanah	Jewish New Year and the birthday of the world
3	Fast of Gedaliah	Commemoration of the assassination of the last Jewish governor of Judaea, by Jews who opposed his cooperation with the Babylonians following the destruction of the First Temple, in 586 BCE
10	Yom Kippur	Day of Atonement
15–21	Sukkot	Holiday of Booths and celebration of the end of the autumn harvest
21	Hoshana Rabba	Last day of Sukkot
22/23	Shemini Atzeret and Simḥat Torah	Autumn's last hurrah and celebration of the end and the beginning of the annual cycle of the reading of the Torah

Ḥeshvan

1	Rosh Ḥodesh	New Moon

Kislev

1	Rosh Ḥodesh	New Moon
25–30	Hanukkah (days 1–6)	Festival of Lights celebrating the rededication of the Holy Temple, in 165 BCE

Tevet

1	Rosh Ḥodesh	New Moon
1–2	Hanukkah (days 7–8)	
10	Fast of the 10th of Tevet	Commemoration of the beginning of the siege of Jerusalem by the Babylonians, in 588 BCE

Shevat

1	Rosh Ḥodesh	New Moon
15	Tu B'Shevat	New Year of the Trees

Adar

1	Rosh Ḥodesh	New Moon
13	Fast of Esther	Commemoration of the fast that was held as Esther prepared to petition the king to save her people
14	Purim	Celebration of the Jews' deliverance from mass destruction in ancient Persia, in the fifth century BCE
15	Shushan Purim	Day the cities of Israel that were walled in ancient times celebrate Purim

Nisan

1	Rosh Ḥodesh	New Moon
14	Fast of the Firstborn	Remembering the tenth plague in which the firstborn of the Egyptians died, but those of the Israelites were saved
15–21/22	Passover	Celebration and retelling of the Exodus from Egypt
27	Yom Hashoah	Commemoration of the six million Jews who died in the Holocaust

Iyar

1	Rosh Ḥodesh	New Moon
4	Yom Hazikaron	Commemoration of all those who gave their lives for the modern State of Israel
5	Yom Ha'atzma'ut	Celebration of the establishment of the State of Israel, in 1948
18	Lag Ba'omer	33rd day of the counting of the *omer,* a day of relief and celebration in the midst of a semimournful period
28	Yom Yerushalayim	Celebration of the reunification of the city of Jerusalem, in 1967

Sivan

1	Rosh Ḥodesh	New Moon
6/7	Shavuot	Celebration and reenactment of the giving of the Torah and celebration of the spring harvest festival

Tammuz

1	Rosh Ḥodesh	New Moon
17	Fast of the 17th of Tammuz	Commemoration of the breaching of the walls of Jerusalem by the Babylonians, in 586 BCE, and by the Romans, in 70 CE

Av

1	Rosh Ḥodesh	New Moon
9	Tisha B'Av	Day of mourning for the destruction of the Holy Temples in Jerusalem, in 586 BCE and 70 CE

Elul

1	Rosh Ḥodesh	New Moon
	Seliḥot	Period in which early morning penitential prayers are recited. Ashkenazim (Jews from eastern Europe) begin reciting the prayers on a Saturday night before Rosh Hashanah. Sephardim (Jews hailing largely from Portugal and the Mediterranean countries) begin the first of Elul and recite them for 40 days (until Yom Kippur).

CHAPTER 3

The Blessings
of Everyday

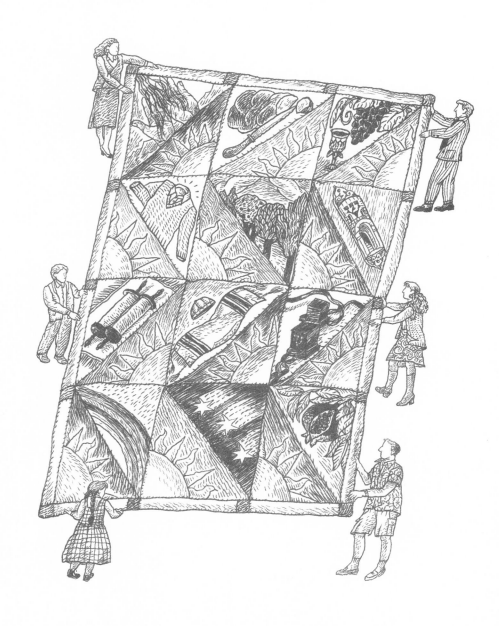

Soon after the death of Rabbi Moshe of Kobryn, Rabbi

Menachem Mendel of Kotzk asked one of his disciples,

"What was most important to your teacher?"

The disciple thought and then replied, "Whatever he

happened to be doing at the moment."

—Martin Buber

I F TIME WERE A NECKLACE, holidays and birthdays would be its jewels, and the everyday would be the strands on which they rested. The special days would cast their luster forward and back, illuminating our daily lives. And although our eyes might be drawn to the glistening jewels, it is in the common days that most of life is lived.

Judaism cares about how we behave in the everyday. Of the six major divisions of the Talmud, the premier compendium of rabbinic law and lore, five occupy themselves with our lives on common days. Only one focuses on the observance of the holidays. Of the Ten Commandments, only one speaks of a special time. The rest speak of deeds we must do or avoid doing every day.

Most of us are taught the manners, traditional foods, dress code and at least some meaning of the holidays. But how are we to behave on the days on which we just slip into our jeans? What vision inspires us on the day whose date we don't know until well into the afternoon?

What about the days that burden our lives? Whether because of our boss, our job, our health, the enormity of the world's needs or our own limitations, we begin to grow tired, give up, cut corners, lower the bar. Or maybe because of the noise in our lives—from the streets, the TV, the radio, the microwave, the refrigerator, the fax, the cellular phone—we use up all our energy and senses deflecting the onslaught of the world. We are overwhelmed and so numb to the beauty we long to see. It is like being in a bakery too long: The smell is still there, but we no longer notice. If only we could move through our days with a five-year-old at our side who would point out to us all the important things we miss: the bugs on the sidewalk, whose turn it is to sit in the front seat, the color of the M&M candy that tastes best.

Too often, we approach days of indistinction as time we wade through on our way to something important, moments we push aside to get to the real thing. But that is a tragic view of time. Rabbi Abraham Joshua Heschel, a 20th-century theologian, scholar, mystic and civil rights activist, once wrote that we should live our lives as if they were works of art. Every act is like a brushstroke and every thought a color. Over time, we create out of our daily affairs the masterpieces of our lives. They are built not only by our dreams and our big plans but also out of the trips to the cleaner's, the visits to our aunt, the tzedakah—gifts of philanthropy—we give, the umpteenth Little League game we watch, the temper we hold in check when we come across socks yet again tossed on the floor.

Each of us has a masterpiece that is constructed of our deeds, reflecting the ways we move through life. It can be imagined as a painting, a building, a garden, a sculpture. But no matter what the image, we do leave behind a legacy as real and as tangible as a piece of art. The awareness of ourselves as artists endows us with the ability, the imperative, to build our lives mindfully.

A Life's Weave

I like to imagine my masterpiece as a garment continuously woven from my actions, words, intents and dreams. It reveals the times I have pulled the threads too tightly, closing myself off from the world around me, and the times I have been too lax and too loose, threatening the fabric's integrity and mine. My cloth has woven into it the faces and the gifts and the hurts of the thousands of people who have touched my life. It is honest, sometimes brutal. But mostly as it grows day by day, it comforts and inspires me.

Judaism offers three interwoven strategies to help us remain conscious of the artistry of everyday living, three ways for us to open ourselves to the holiness of the everyday: prayers, blessings and sacred deeds. Prayers and blessings are the verbal pauses we insert in the course of our everyday, words that focus our awareness and our appreciation, words we say before or after an act or a moment of discovery. Sacred deeds are moral, ritual or social acts that anchor and secure our masterpiece.

Mitzvot

In his book *God in Search of Man*, Rabbi Abraham Joshua Heschel said:
[A symbol serves] as a *meeting place* of the spiritual and the material, of the invisible and the visible. Judaism too had such a meeting place—in a qualified sense—in the Sanctuary. Yet in its history, the point of gravity was shifted from space to time, and instead of a place of meeting came a moment of meeting; the meeting is not in a thing but in a deed.
Today, the mitzvot are the meeting place of Jew and God.

Formal Prayers

A person can pray alone—at home, at school, at work, at an airport. But a soulful minyan helps bind spirit to spirit and gives lift to those who feel alone, or whose words to God feel heavy.

Formal Prayers

To immerse ourselves in the prayers of the everyday is to shed the perspective of self that might restrict us and enslave us. We are invited to don the cloak of community that enlarges us and encompasses us. As sociologists and psychologists tell us, the surest and most satisfying way to self is through the corridors of community. "It is within society, and as a result of social processes," Peter Berger writes in *The Sacred Canopy*, "that the individual becomes a person, that he attains and holds onto an identity, and that he carries out the various projects that constitute his life." Liturgical prayer, especially conducted within the context of community, is one place where self becomes.

Perhaps that is part of my romance with the tallit, the prayer shawl that adult Jews drape around themselves during morning prayers. When I put on a tallit, even when I am alone, I place myself in the folds of my people. Donning the tallit is a daily, visual symbol of my identity, reminding me to whom I belong as I begin my day's journey. It protects me, shields me and defines me. Falling around my shoulders and arms, the tallit provides me with a secure

The warm embrace of this tallit is enhanced by its atarah, or decorative collar. It was made by transferring onto fabric pictures of a family's matriarchs and bat mitzvah celebrant.

Tefillin—two small black leather boxes attached to black leather straps—are worn by many Jewish adults while reciting the morning prayers, except on Shabbat and festivals. A parchment with verses from Exodus and Deuteronomy is stored inside each box. The tefillin are strapped around one arm and around the forehead as a symbol of our faith in God. ❧

awareness of my body and its boundaries. I am not lost there, but found. Others are outside, I am inside, but we are one. I fill up my tallit. No matter my size, I always will. And it is in that fullness that I am counted as a member of the congregation.

These two domains—the personal and the communal—are not distinct; rather, they meld into each other. I cannot be who I am without my community nor can my community be what it is without me. Rabbi Arthur Waskow tells how the tallit is a symbol of this melding: The corners of the tallit are not sharp and precise but edged with *tzitzit,* the fringe mandated by the text of the Torah. The fringe, the woolen threads, represent how the boundaries of the community and those of the individual open themselves to one another every day.

Some of our prayers are formal, with words set by the hand of tradition. You can find them in daily and holiday prayer books. We say those prayers at designated times, either alone or with a minyan (a group of at least ten adult Jews). Those formal prayers weave together the needs and the dreams of the Jewish community with those of its individual members. Whatever our personal needs, we are always also members of the Jewish people, sharing in our people's joy and pain. So three times a day every day of the year it is the tradition of some Jews to say those prayers on behalf of ourselves and our community, the people Israel.

The Liberating Effect of Liturgy

A Christian woman seeking to rediscover her faith spent nine months in a Benedictine community. While there, she recited psalms the way observant Jews recite prayers. She discovered that the act of immersing herself in the discipline of daily recitation "frees one from the tyranny of individual experience." To commit oneself to the regular recitation of the words of the liturgy is to gain an enriched perspective of self.

"I learned that when you go to church several times a day, every day, there is no way you can 'do it right.' You are not always going to sit up straight, let alone think holy thoughts. You are not going to wear your best clothes but whatever is not in the dirty clothes basket. You come to the [prayers] through all the moods and conditions of life, and while you may feel awful, you sing anyway. To your surprise, you find that the [prayers] do not deny your true feelings, but allow you to reflect on them."

—Kathleen Norris, "Why the Psalms Scare Us," *Christianity Today*

The three daily prayers are the morning service (shaḥarit), the afternoon service (minḥah) and the evening service (ma'ariv). Whether we are happy or sad, busy or bored, traveling or at home, we are to say them.

In the face of modernity's inviolable values of autonomy and individualism, standardized liturgy can appear tiresome, meaningless and burdensome. We instinctively ask, If I can choose to pray, why say words that are not of my choosing and that do not represent what I feel? Why should I interrupt my daily routines, lose precious moments in the rush of morning, to pray at all, much less just that way at just this time with just those words? If I want to pray, why can't I pray when and where and how I want?

We can—and do. Judaism has a rich history of private prayers. But private prayers do not replace liturgy, for the discipline of saying words set in time by tradition opens up parts of ourselves that we, on our own, cannot unlock.

Every prayer service is built around a text so central to our liturgical tradition that the ancient rabbis called it *Hatefillah,* The Prayer. We call it the Amidah or the Shemoneh Esrei.

In the morning and evening services, we recite the Shma, our central affirmation of faith, before the Amidah. In the morning, we add prayers that speak of renewal and hope, and in the evening, we speak of rest and peace.

On Saturday afternoons, Mondays and Thursdays, we chant a short segment of the weekly Torah portion. The full Torah portion is chanted on the following Shabbat. The rabbis explain that the Torah is like water, nourishing and refreshing. Just as we cannot go more than three days without water, so we cannot go more than three days without Torah.

SHMA

The Shma is perhaps the most famous of all Jewish prayers. It is traditionally recited every morning (during *shaḥarit*) and every evening (during *ma'ariv*) and there is also a version of it to be said just before going to sleep.

The Shma, which is named for the first word of the prayer, includes three passages from the Torah. It begins: *"Shma Yisrael,*

Jewish law prohibits us from destroying anything with God's name on it. The tradition is to place worn or damaged ritual objects, such as prayer shawls and tefillin, and sacred books and Bibles, in a storage room called a "genizah," or to bury them in a cemetery with the same care and dignity accorded a person who has died.

This burial of sacred books and objects was held in a Jewish cemetery in Los Angeles.❧

The Importance of Community

Certain prayers can only be said when we pray in a minyan. Two such prayers are Kaddish and Kedushah. Their names come from the Hebrew word *Kadosh,* meaning "holy." When we recite these prayers, we are reminded of the importance of coming together as a community to live as holy people, *am kadosh.*

Inside the case of a mezuzah, the ritual object that is affixed to the doorposts of Jewish homes, is a parchment containing the first two paragraphs of the Shma.

What Is the Soul?

The soul is the part of us that can feel but cannot be felt, that can see but cannot be seen. It is the breath of life that God blew into us at the dawn of Creation. It is that which makes us holy.

Prayers of the Amidah

The Amidah begins and concludes by praising and thanking God for protecting us and caring for us now and forever. In the middle, it asks God for health and strength, for a strong Jewish nation and a rebuilt homeland, for justice to reign and peace to prevail.

Hear, O Israel, Adonai is God, Adonai is One" (Deuteronomy 6:4).

This is a call to attention and intention for all Jews, every one of us. The Hebrew word *shma,* meaning "hear!" is singular, *not* plural. Through this call, each of us is asked to hear the message of our people according to our own abilities and our own wisdom and each of us is asked to respond.

The primary message is straightforward: We have only one God, to whom we are utterly devoted. There is not one god for me and another god for you. We are all made in the image of the one God. We are all of equal value and of equal worth. As our God is One, so we are one.

The three paragraphs that follow the opening of the Shma express other core tenets of the Jewish faith. The first speaks of loving God with all our hearts and with all our souls and with all our might. It asks that we teach our children the ways of God and our people (Deuteronomy 6:5–9). The second calls us to honor and observe the word of God (Deuteronomy 11:13–21). The third reminds us of the mitzvah of *tzitzit.* The *tzitzit* is said to serve as a reminder of all the other mitzvot (plural of *mitzvah*) we are asked to observe as Jews (Numbers 15:37–41).

AMIDAH

The Amidah is the other central formal prayer in Judaism. *Amidah* means "standing," and that is how we recite that prayer. Its other name, Shemoneh Esrei, means "eighteen," for it had 18 blessings in its weekday version when it was created, almost 2,000 years ago. Sometime in the Talmudic period (200–500 CE), one blessing was added, so now there are 19, but we continue to call the prayer Shemoneh Esrei anyway. (We have similarly anachronistic terms in English, such as "blackboard" and "phone dial.") The Shabbat Amidah has fewer blessings than the weekday Amidah, for most of the prayers of petition—prayers that ask God to answer our pleas—are not included. Shabbat, after all, is a time of completion, *shleimut.* In our prayers and in our rituals we act as if all were already given, and the world were at peace.

The Amidah's opening and closing paragraphs remain the same on weekdays, Shabbat and holidays. It is only the middle sections that change, depending on the nature and theme of the day.

Personal Prayers

As much as we are members of a community, we are also individuals who live our lives according to our own pace, passions and schedules. We have our own needs and our own dreams; we feel sad or awed, happy or hungry, careful or daring, strong or needy. Sometimes we want someone to pay attention just to us—to us alone. Sometimes we want to throw down our pain before the gates of heaven and defiantly say, "God, take this all back. I do not want it anymore." Sometimes we want our singing to be heard above all others, to declare the news of our deepest joy.

Throughout the ages, Jews have offered personal prayers that are not tuned to the time of day and do not speak to the Covenant of the Jewish people. Rather, they focus on the destiny of a single Jew. Those prayers, fashioned out of our own words and in response to our own needs, are directed toward the moment, toward what we are doing and what we are feeling. All we have to do is open our hearts and mouths and pray.

A Prayer from the Heart

The holiness of the Hebrew language notwithstanding, our tradition respects the authenticity of all heartfelt prayer.

There was a young cattleman who was unable to recite the Hebrew prayers. So he prayed the only way he could, in his own language, in his own way: "Sovereign of the universe! You know that if You had cattle and gave them to me to tend, though I take wages for tending from all the others, from You I would take nothing, because I love You." (Sefer Ḥasidim)

The Talmud records pages and pages of private prayers that the rabbis of old would say. One rabbi asked that God keep him far from trouble; another asked that he might be kept from saying anything mean or hurtful; still another, a teacher, asked that he not lead his students astray. The Bible likewise is full of personal prayers: Abraham asks for God's kindness and mercy; Abraham's servant seeks help in finding Isaac a wife; Rebecca seeks help in childbirth; Hannah asks that she might have children. The Book of Psalms is a stream of personal prayers.

Women especially had a tradition of personal prayers, some of which were recorded and preserved. They had prayers to carry them through the long hours of childbirth, to say when their child's first tooth came in, on their children's wedding day, when their husbands were away and at their family's graves. One Yiddish prayer even asks that God watch over the baking of the Shabbat kugel (pudding), so that it would rise nicely and not fall.

We, too, today can turn to God whenever we choose. As parents, we may pray that we learn how best to care for and raise our children, that we live to see them blessed with strength, health, courage and wisdom. As children, we may pray that we bring pride and comfort to our parents and wisdom and prosperity to our community. As colleagues or friends, we may pray that God help those dear to us through difficult times and help us manage both success and failure gracefully.

Sometimes, however, when we want to pray, the words do not come. But that does not mean we have no prayers. It simply means our words are too small to hold the message of our hearts. At such times, we may shun words altogether, and our tears may carry us to God. The rabbis tell us, though all the other gates to heaven may close, the gate of tears is always open.

Or we can turn to the words of others, to the psalms and the liturgy and the phrases of the tradition. When we take leave of a mourner and are at a loss for words, we are taught to say "May the One who is everywhere be with you as a comfort and with all those who mourn in the house of Israel." When loved ones are sick, we are given words that ask God to heal them, strengthen them and restore them to vigor, both in body and in soul, along with all others who are in need of healing. What better words could we find to say?

Blessings of the Moment

Blessings, *brachot,* are short, formulaic prayers that traditionally begin "Blessed are You, Adonai, our God, Sovereign of the universe, who..." There are three kinds of *brachot:* those we say in our liturgical prayers; those we say as a prelude to specific acts, such as reading Torah or eating; and those we offer in response to an awareness, such as seeing a rainbow or hearing sad news.

The latter two are blessings that emerge from the moment. Together, they keep us open to the world around us. They help us

The Sheheḥeyanu

Perhaps the most famous of the blessings we offer in response to an awareness is the Sheheḥeyanu. We recite the Sheheḥeyanu on the occurrence of a notable event, thanking God for sustaining us so that we might wear new clothing or usher in a particular holiday or celebrate a moment we thought would never come.

live with awareness, calling on us never to take things for granted. A blessing is an act of transformation. Through our words, the world is brushed with a tincture of the sacred.

> ## Noticing the Wonders of the World
>
> The wonder of wearing new clothes is something we often take for granted. Yet when we think of those who cannot afford a brand-new shirt, and when we think of the work that went into financing, designing, drawing, weaving, cutting, stitching, folding, ironing, packaging, moving, displaying and selling that one garment we now put on for the first time, we realize that it is truly a wonder. So just before we cut off a tag from a new article of clothing, we might pause and say the Sheheḥeyanu.

Most of our daily tasks are not endowed with a designated blessing. But that does not mean they are totally relegated to the secular domain. Rabbi Irving Greenberg teaches that if properly performed, almost every act can become a doorway to holiness. Learning from Franz Rosenzweig, an early-20th-century German Jewish philosopher, Rabbi Greenberg tells us:

> Some day, as religious insight broadens, a mother's recipe for gefilte fish will be passed on in the family, bearing with it the same sense of tradition as do formal commandments or customs. Every act of social justice…every act of human socializing and dignity will become a secularized *halachah* as Jewish religious insight deepens and sacred dimensions of the profane are uncovered.
>
> —*In the Name of Heaven*, CLAL: The National Jewish Center for Learning and Leadership

The Task of Everyday

In addition to prayers and blessings, Judaism gives us mitzvot as everyday acts that help us build our life's masterpiece. There are two kinds of mitzvot: those between God and us (*mitzvot bein adam lamakom*) and those between us and someone else (*mitzvot bein adam l'ḥavero*).

The first kind of mitzvah includes all the rituals we observe because God and our tradition ask us to, mitzvot that have spiritual, but not necessarily moral, value: blowing the shofar on Rosh Hashanah, keeping kosher, affixing a mezuzah on our doorposts,

Our morning prayers remind us that the obligations of parent to child and child to parent are sacred matters in Jewish tradition.

Tzedek and Tzedakah

The Hebrew language interlaces the words *tzedek*, meaning "righteousness," and *tzedakah*, meaning "philanthropy." Tzedakah differs from charity. In the realm of Jewish values, tzedakah is not an act of beneficence or largesse, but one of propriety. It is not something you choose to do; it is something you must do. The philosopher Maimonides identified eight levels of giving, each of which fulfills the mitzvah of tzedakah. At the highest and most gracious level, the benefactor welcomes the needy as a business partner or helps the person become self-sufficient. At the lowest level, the benefactor gives grudgingly. One may be more gracious and more enduring than the other, but they both fulfill the rudiments of the mitzvah.

eating matzah during Passover, lighting the Shabbat candles. These are the mitzvot that mark us as Jews. Together they translate into a language of action that forever reminds us of who we are, why we are here, and what is expected of us. They are actions that shape our days and our souls.

The second kind of mitzvah includes all those acts of fairness, justice and lovingkindness that we do for one another. Those mitzvot, also commanded by God, have both spiritual and moral value. Every morning we recite a passage based on a text from the Talmud, reminding us of these mitzvot:

> These are the deeds that earn you a reward both in this world and in the world to come: honoring your father and mother, [raising a child in the ways of Torah,] performing acts of loving-kindness, going early to the house of study both morning and evening, caring for the homeless, visiting the sick, making a wedding for someone in need, attending to the dead, praying with feeling, restoring peace between friends and between husband and wife, and the study of Torah leads to them all. (Based on *Shabbat* 127a)

How common these tasks are! We don't have to be wise or rich or talented to do them. When loved ones are in pain, we can sit with them, listen to them, hold them when they cry. If loved ones are sick, our visits (or calls or letters) can bring them comfort. If our children or friends have had a hard day, if they have achieved a goal that is important to them, we can give them a hug to share their pain or their pride. For pleasure is like pain: It is too big to be experienced alone.

We can volunteer at a homeless shelter, become a counselor of victims of domestic violence, help our neighbor who has difficulty getting to the store. Each one of these is an act of lovingkindness. Each helps us mend this broken but reparable world. And when we do these things, we fulfill our calling to live as partners with God.

These acts may seem small, but our lives are lived in the details of the everyday. Taking a co-worker to lunch for a job well done, writing to praise a company for its stance on the environment, thanking a teacher for an inspiring lecture, showing good humor and patience with those around us while waiting in line—each of these brings a bit more goodness into the world. Every day is made a little better because of them. They are the keys to the storehouse of holiness.

It is in the performance of these humble deeds that we become more. For humans become what they do. "Man [sic] cannot be conceived of apart from the continuous outpouring of himself into the world," Peter Berger tells us. "Human being, or being human, cannot be understood as somehow resting within itself, in some closed sphere of interiority, and then setting out to express itself." Rather, being human happens through doing, through our interaction with the world. We become a teacher by teaching, a builder by building, an actor by acting. So, too, we become who we are by doing. The mitzvot of everyday build the full measure and the full value of our identity and our life.

Kavanot

To heighten their awareness of the sacred in the routine, the mystics developed the technique of reciting *kavanot. Kavanah* (singular of *kavanot*) means "orientation," "focus" and "direction." Before performing a mitzvah or another specific act, the mystics would recite words of focus and intent designed to concentrate their attention and infuse the task with cosmic significance. A Hasidic teaching tells the story of Enoch, the cobbler. "With each stitch he sewed he would say, 'Even as I now join the upper and lower soles of these shoes, so may these stitches join together the Holy One, blessed be He, and the Shechinah.'"

We, too, can infuse our daily routines with greater, if not mystical, significance. Choose a part of your day or your work, and imagine what you might say to enrich the way you approach it. Pause for a moment before beginning the task, and imagine the deeper purpose and power it possesses.

Shira Ruskay, a hospice worker, once told me that when she visits a patient at home, she pauses on the doorstep, turns her face and palms upward, and says, "God, fill my hands with what I need to prepare me for what I find on the other side."

Bedtime

On any given day, many things happen. Some, perhaps even most occurrences, make us proud or satisfied or at least not ashamed. But some may have hurt us or hurt others, angered us or angered others. Often at night we compulsively replay the day and relive the hurt. But neither peace nor sleep comes easily when we feel angry or hurt or, worse yet, vengeful. Therefore, Judaism created a bedtime prayer that helps us to unload the events of the day, to shake out our anger or feelings of vengeance, and to seek to do better, to forgive the other and ourselves. It is a prayer that helps heal the part that hurts.

> Sovereign of the universe, I hereby forgive any who have angered me or spoken against me or hurt me, whether intentionally or by accident, in word or in deed. Please do not punish them for my sake. And please, God, keep me from doing any harm to others. Forgive me, too, all that I have done against You.

This prayer reminds us that every night is like a little Yom Kippur. It reminds us that before God can forgive, we must forgive the one who offended us. And lest we unduly withhold forgiveness, the prayer reminds us that only when we let go of our anger and forgive do we merit God's forgiveness.

Once we are released from the battles of the everyday, our next prayers tend to the demons we may harbor within. Tradition gives us the words to ask that God help us "to lie down in peace" and the words to declare our defiance against all that would rob us of tranquility, shelter and hope. Those words form a declaration of solidarity with the Jewish people, with God and with ourselves.

We follow those prayers with the Shma. Some Jews who know no other prayers know the Shma. It is often the first prayer we learn as children, and it is the prayer we are asked to recite with our last breath. And each night as we set our bodies down to sleep—releasing our hold on consciousness, our most precious possession—it reminds us that all is well, for we know where we belong. Our people and our God are with us. Now and forever we are not alone.

One Hundred Blessings Every Day

Judaism teaches that we should recite 100 blessings every day, among them the blessings that speak of the wonders of nature.

On hearing thunder: "Blessed are You, our God, Sovereign of the universe, whose power and might fill the world."

On seeing a rainbow: "Blessed are You, our God, Sovereign of the universe, who remembers the Covenant, is faithful to it, and is certain to keep the promise."

On seeing wonders of nature like a sunrise, or a mountain range, or a shooting star: "Blessed are You, our God, Sovereign of the universe, who daily performs works of creation."

On seeing the ocean: "Blessed are You, our God, Sovereign of the universe, who made the great sea."

On seeing a creature of beauty: "Blessed are You, our God, Sovereign of the universe, for there being such in this world."

On hearing good news: "Blessed are You, our God, Sovereign of the universe, who is good and who grants goodness."

On hearing bad news: "Blessed are You, our God, Sovereign of the universe, the judge of truth."

On returning to a place of rescue or wonder: "Blessed are You, our God, Sovereign of the universe, who made a miracle happen here for me."

The Talmud

The early rabbis composed the Talmud over the course of 500 years (roughly from the beginning of the Common Era until the 500s). It contains the Mishnah, the earliest rabbinic legal code, which was created over a period of 200 years and finalized (in oral form) around 200 CE, and the Gemara, the rabbinic commentary on the Mishnah, comprising an encyclopedic assortment of rabbinic wisdom: legal discussions, stories, Torah commentaries, healing potions, prayers, rituals.

The Talmud is massive: 6 volumes (called orders, organized around the topics of agricultural laws, holidays, women, torts, Temple sacrifices and purity), comprising 63 books, more than 2,700 pages. On each page, there are not only texts of the Mishnah and the Gemara but also the all-star commentaries that open and unpack them. In effect, each page of the Talmud is a visual intergenerational dialogue, appearing as if all voices were talking at once. Readers must break into the conversation and lay a claim to a spot on the page. The reward for this work is that once in, new worlds unfold, and each reader's voice merges with that sacred sing-song of the ages.

Each page of the Talmud has a schematic structure. The oldest portions of the conversation are placed in the middle, surrounded by the voices of later generations.

The Tallit

The prayer shawl that is draped over our shoulders can be imagined as if it were the wings of God. "Gather me close, beneath Your wing," the modern Hebrew poet Ḥayyim Naḥman Bialik wrote, "like a mother and sister when I despair. Your lap is a refuge for my head, a resting place for my rejected prayers." Some Jews begin their daily prayers by wrapping the tallit over and around them, from the top of the head to as far as the shawl will fall, covering themselves as if they were children hiding in the drapes or in the flowing skirts of a loving mother. And why not? What better way to begin a day than enfolded by images as big and as safe and as soft as these?

CHAPTER 4

Shabbat

The Palace in Time

Even more than the Jews have kept Shabbat,

Shabbat has kept the Jews.

—Aḥad Ha'am

E VERY SEVENTH SUNSET, Shabbat comes. Whether heralded or not, welcomed or not, on the seventh day Shabbat comes. Brushed with the dew of Creation, Shabbat is dif-

ferent from the other Jewish holidays. It does not mark a historical event or a seasonal harvest.

It is not dependent upon the phases of the moon, and it existed even before there was a Jewish

people. Shabbat is, as it were, God's holiday, the eternal seventh day of Creation, the day of completion and rest.

"There is a realm of time," writes Rabbi Abraham Joshua Heschel in his classic book *The Sabbath,* "where the goal is not to have but to be, not to own but to give, not to control but to share, not to sub- due but to be in accord." Shabbat is that time, an antidote to that

A Treasured People

Just as all children should feel special in the eyes of their parents, just as all friends should know they give something no other friend can give, so the Jewish people speak of themselves as treasured and chosen. We believe we have a unique but not exclusive relationship with God. To be treasured is to be loved. One of life's paradoxes is that the bigger the family, the less sibling rivalry; the larger the circle of friends, the less jockeying for position. Just as there is room for all children in the heart of a parent, there is room for everyone in the heart of God. Being treasured is an honor and a comfort, but it is also a calling. Like love, it lays claim to our time and our desires. To be a Jew is to learn what we are called upon to do, for God and for all humankind.

Having set aside our weekday distractions, on Shabbat we can devote ourselves fully to the blessings and goodness in our lives.

which hardens our hearts. "The higher goal of spiritual living is not to amass a wealth of information but to face sacred moments."

Shabbat is the first of all sacred moments, the first aspect of Creation to be called holy. This holy day was given as a gift to the Israelites on the day we became God's people at the foot of Mount Sinai. Ever since then Shabbat has been called an *ot*, a sign, an eternal reminder that God is our God and we are God's treasured people.

How can we describe Shabbat, for—like all meaningful holidays—it is not so much a day as an experience. Heschel calls Shabbat "a palace in time." It is a magical, holy place that opens its doors to us once a week, inviting us to enter. Six days of the week we live in our world, occupying ourselves with the tasks of jobs, school, home and play. Sometimes in this world we can feel the touch of God. It may happen when our love comforts a child, when we linger after a meeting to tend to the concerns of a colleague, when we pause to thank those who helped us, or when we strive to see the image of God in the face of the other.

Sometimes we are aware of these feelings of godliness. But it is difficult to hold on to them in the midst of the hustle and bustle of our everyday world. Shabbat is a weekly dose, a megadose, of holiness. For on Shabbat, we are invited to enter God's dream for our world, a place of wholeness and fullness, a place of caring and peace. We wish each other Shabbat shalom, a day full of the peace we hope one day to find.

In our world, work is essential because Creation is incomplete. Needs abound. There is much to do and much to achieve—so many roads to pave, so many houses to build, so many mouths to feed, so many things to discover, so many people to tend to, so many toys to make. "For six days you shall do your work," the fourth commandment tells us. "Fill the land," God says as a blessing to the first man and the first woman. "Make it fruitful, and tame it." According to the Torah, God made the earth "very good." It is up to us to keep it that way. Perhaps to make it better.

Work, then, is the fulfillment of our earliest covenant with God, an expression of our legacy as creatures made in the image of God. Work is what we are called upon to do. And yet we must beware, for it is ever so easy to slip across that line that separates *fill* from *overrun* or *tame* from *vanquish*. It is ever so difficult to know when to say "when." Just as we need white spaces to define the borders of the written, just as we need silence to set off the sound of a musical note, so we need stillness to silhouette the contours of our work.

If we never stopped working, task and goal, need and desire, would be blurred. Instead of money serving as a tool with which to make products, products would become a tool with which to make money. Growth and greed would be unchecked, the earth's resources would be ravaged to sate never-ending appetites. Like the saltcellar that churned and churned and turned the seas salty, like the brooms of *The Sorcerer's Apprentice* that could not stop carrying water, we would begin to believe that what we are doing is more important than *why* we are doing it. If that should happen, we will destroy both the world and the human spirit.

Learning the Way of Menuḥah

Every seventh day, therefore, our tradition asks us to stop work-ing, to mimic God as it were, who rested on the seventh day. Setting aside quiet time and space gives definition to the work of creation. Shabbat is the quiet that defines our work.

The Hebrew word for this quiet is *menuḥah*. It conjures up the sensation of restfulness and stillness, the way we feel when the race has been won, the store secure and locked up for the night, the last dish put away. It speaks of completeness and satisfaction, when there is no more to do, for it has all been done. And it has all been done not *for* us but *by* us. *Menuḥah* refers exclusively to the rest of Shabbat. Although work is forbidden on many other holidays, that rest is not called *menuḥah*.

An Open Invitation

Shabbat is not just for Jews; it is for everyone. The whole world is invited, indeed deserves, to celebrate this day of *menuḥah*, Jews and non-Jews, old and young, poor and rich, bosses and laborers. In God's world, everyone is equal, and everyone can share in the vision.

For most of us, Shabbat is an acquired awareness, something, paradoxically, we must work at learning. Many of us seek to be in control always, to do, to fix. We pride ourselves on our ability to get the job done: Plan the work, and work the plan. We measure

Tzedakah

For generations, just before Shabbat, families have had the tradition of putting tzedakah, money for the needy, in a collection box known in Yiddish as a *pushke*. They put in pennies, nickels, dimes or quarters. When the *pushke* is full, the family members count up all the money and decide where it should be sent.

Twice a year—in the week before Passover and in the week before Rosh Hashanah—it is traditional to be extra generous in the giving of tzedakah. Today those holidays can become the times of your semiannual family distributions. A month before the distribution, older children can research their favorite causes. You might also want to share with them solicitations that come in the mail and help them begin to manage the requests that will one day be addressed to them. They can set their priorities and then present the options to the whole family so that you can make the decision together.

How Many Candles Do We Light?

Although the blessing mentions only one candle, most households traditionally light two. Some families light one candle for each child. Other families light one candle for each member of the household.

Our weekday concerns are set to rest with the first glow of Shabbat. ❧

our worth and our identity by our profession. We turn to a stranger at a party and ask, "So, what do you *do*?" Surrendering to *menuḥah* is a hard-won skill. The ways of Shabbat show us how to achieve it.

Shabbat asks us to clear our calendars on Friday night and Saturday so we can spend time at home and in the synagogue, with our families and our friends. Shabbat asks that we take the time to return to ourselves, be with the ones we love, seek the pleasures of God's Creation. It calls us to sing and play and read and eat and talk and sleep and love. Shabbat asks that we not cook or shop, that we not build anything or fix anything or sew anything or grow anything. Shabbat is a taste of God's dream for our world. It is a world that, for a moment, is fulfilled.

Through a Magic Portal

When the sun goes down on the sixth day and we light the Shabbat candles, we open a portal in time and space. We stand before the candlesticks, circling our hands above the flames three times, gathering, collecting, immersing ourselves in their light. We cup our hands as if scooping up their glow. Cradling it, we carry the light gently toward our eyes. We recite the traditional blessing: "Blessed are You, our God, Sovereign of the universe, who has sanctified us through Your mitzvot and commands us to light the Shabbat candles."

We take our hands away. "And there was light." Everything is bathed in this radiance, borrowed from the first light of Creation so long ago. We have walked through the portal, into time eternal.

Ushering in Shabbat

On Friday night, *erev* Shabbat, the seventh day is escorted into the synagogue with a service called *kabbalat Shabbat,* the welcoming of Shabbat. At home, Shabbat enters with the lighting of the candles. Traditionally, *kabbalat Shabbat* begins at or just before sunset and lasts about an hour. However, to accommodate those who return home from work late or eat dinner with their families first, some synagogues begin *kabbalat Shabbat* at eight o'clock. The prayers of the service speak, or more accurately sing, of the wonders of God as Creator, of the promises that God makes to Israel and of the wondrous gift of Shabbat. Sometimes, especially after late Friday night services, the congregation sponsors an oneg Shabbat in an adjacent room. There, congregants and visitors gather for refreshments, camaraderie and relaxed conversation.

Shabbat Dinner

Shabbat is the only day of Creation to receive a blessing, "and God blessed the seventh day" (Genesis 2:3), and so it has become a day full of blessings. Shabbat dinner is bounded by blessings. It begins with wine, a symbol of happiness and riches, leisure and luxury. Kiddush, the prayer that speaks of the holiness of the day, is accompanied by the drinking of the wine.

The Choreography of Kiddush

Kiddush can be made in many ways. In some homes, one adult (or one child) recites the Kiddush for everyone. In others, each person around the table who so desires recites the Kiddush, one after the other. In still others, everyone sings the Kiddush together.

In some homes, everyone begins the meal with a cup filled to the brim. In others, the leader holds a broad, full cup and after Kiddush pours a bit from the cup into the others' cups. Richard Siegel, Executive Director of the National Foundation for Jewish Culture, sees in that act a metaphor for the fluid creativity of American Jewish life: "Each drop that has been poured" may have diminished the leader's cup, but it has successfully "been caught in another vessel." He further notes that "to some the central organizations of Judaism may appear to be diminishing. But perhaps their wine is simply being poured into different, younger vessels."

In other homes, there is one Kiddush cup from which everyone drinks, signifying that we all drink from a common tradition.

The words of the Kiddush recall the very first Shabbat, described in Genesis:

And it was evening and it was morning, the sixth day. The heavens and the earth and all they contain were complete. On the seventh day, God completed the work that God had been doing; God rested on the seventh day from all the work that God had done. And God blessed the seventh day and made it holy, for on that day, God rested from all the work that God had intended to do. (1:31–2:3)

When Do We Recite a Blessing?

By reciting a blessing before we enjoy the goodness in our lives, we can enhance the experience and sharpen our appreciation of it. For example, we recite the blessing over bread before we eat. However, because Shabbat begins when we say the blessing over the candles and because it is forbidden to kindle a fire on Shabbat, we light the candles first and then recite the blessing, covering our eyes so that we do not enjoy the Sabbath light until after we have completed the blessing.

A Taste of Israel

Many people prefer to make Kiddush using Israeli wine. It reminds us of the special ties between our people and our homeland.

Ephraim and Menashe

Ephraim and Menashe were two sons of Joseph, who in turn was the son of Jacob, the son of Isaac, the son of Abraham. Why do we bless our sons in their names? Because it is written, "Jacob blessed his grandsons saying: In your name shall Israel invoke blessing, saying, 'May God make you like Ephraim and Menashe.'" And why did Ephraim and Menashe merit such an honor? Perhaps because they were the first brothers in the Torah to break the pattern of sibling violence.

Sarah, Rebecca, Rachel and Leah

Sarah, Rebecca, Rachel and Leah are our first matriarchs, the wives of our first patriarchs, Abraham, Isaac and Jacob. Rachel and Leah, who were sisters, along with their handmaids, Bilhah and Zilpah, are the mothers of the twelve tribes of Israel.

It is customary for parents to bless their children at the dinner table. They bless their sons by saying, "May you be like Ephraim and Menashe." They bless their daughters by saying, "May you be like Sarah, Rebecca, Rachel and Leah."

For both sons and daughters, parents often offer the blessing with which the priests blessed the Jewish people: "May God bless you and protect you. May God's glory shine upon you. May God be kind and gracious to you and grant you peace."

Some children bless their parents by saying, "May God bless our love for one another." And, not to leave out the guests who are seated around the table, the hosts may choose to include the guests in the priestly blessing and offer the blessing: "May you find peace within these walls and seek goodness far beyond them."

Why Is the Ḥallah Braided?

The simple answer is to make the ḥallah beautiful. But perhaps, as Rick Dinitz suggests, it is to remind us that the lives of all Jews are interwoven like the strands of the ḥallah. And like the braids of a ḥallah that dive deep, disappear, and then surface again, some truths of life are clear and visible, and some are hidden.

After the wine and the blessings, the dinner begins. In Judaism, meals traditionally start with bread, and the Shabbat dinner is no exception. Because this meal is no ordinary meal, however, the bread we eat is no ordinary bread. It is made from rich, golden dough brushed with egg or honey, and braided as if it were a bride's hair. It is called *ḥallah*, a word reminiscent of the baked goods that were given to the priests in the ancient Temple.

Some people don't cut the ḥallah with a knife; instead, they tear it with their hands as a reminder that Shabbat is a time of peace, when we dream that the nations will put aside their weapons of war.

In keeping with the richness of the meal, not one but two loaves of ḥallah are placed on the table. The rabbis of old teach that the two loaves remind us of the miracle that happened in the desert long ago. After the Exodus, when the Israelites were wandering in the wilderness, food was scarce and the people were hungry. They complained to God, who responded by giving them the gift of manna. A soft, doughy substance whose taste matched the desires of the one who ate it, manna was found on the ground six days a week, under the morning dew. The people were told to gather only as much as they could eat on one day, enough to satisfy them. Any excess would spoil.

No manna fell on Shabbat, however, for the Israelites were not allowed to work at gathering on the day of rest. What was to be done? God caused an extra measure of manna to fall on Friday and bade the Jews to collect two days' worth. That extra measure did not spoil.

As a reminder of how God fed the Jews in the desert and how the manna fell in double portions in honor of Shabbat, we begin the Shabbat meal with a double portion of ḥallah.

The meal ends as it began, with blessings and song. Poets throughout the ages have composed song upon song about the pleasures of Shabbat, the food, the peace, the tranquility, the joy. With nowhere to rush to and no work calling us away, family and friends sing these songs, share new tunes, and let their spirits rise with the melodies of the night.

Wine, in moderation, gladdens the heart and is part of every Jewish celebration. For those who prefer, grape juice can be substituted for wine.

Shabbat Day

Shabbat morning has a texture different from that of the night before. It is still soft and peaceful, but it is more structured. The synagogue beckons.

As with *kabbalat Shabbat,* the morning's prayers also speak of God's greatness, the majesty of Creation, and our limited ability—but also our endless desire—to sing of God's kindness. "If our mouths were filled with song as the sea or our tongues with joy like the countless waves, if our lips formed praises as endless as the skies,…still we could never fully thank You, God."

The peak of the morning service is the Torah reading. All personal celebrations happen around it; all prayers for healing are woven through it; the sermon or the study is linked to it. Every week, as determined by the calendar, a designated portion of the Torah is read. (The text of the Torah is divided into 54 portions that are read in sequence in exactly one year, with some portions doubling up in shorter years and standing alone in leap years.) A portion, called a *parashah,* is chanted from a handwritten scroll, just as it was thousands of years ago. The words on the scroll contain no vowels and no punctuation.

The Blessings Surrounding the Torah Reading

Every week we return to Sinai. We gather and stand at the foot of the mountain, at the ark where the Torah scrolls are kept. We open the ark in a grand gesture of revelation, announcing, "Here is the record of the legacy of Sinai." But the text does not sing itself, and it does not read itself. It is mute until we give it voice. Like Moses, who spoke the words of God to the Israelites, so we, too, are called up to stand and speak the words of God to the Jewish people.

The ritual procession in which the Torah is carried round the synagogue from the ark to the reading table, the ancient script, the text with no vowels, the chant so unlike the music of today —all add to the awe and mystery of the moment. Torah reading is where the eternal and the present converge, where all who are called up become priest and prophet, witness, teacher and advocate of our tradition. No wonder it is the ritual that signifies a child's coming-of-age. No wonder it is sometimes a moment of awe, sometimes of discomfort. But it is a moment we dare allow ourselves to experience.

No one can read from this scroll unprepared. Therefore, many synagogues have at least one official Torah reader. That person is called the *ba'al* (if male) or *ba'alat* (if female) *koreh*, the master reader.

On Shabbat, seven people are traditionally given the honor of sharing in the Torah reading, although most don't actually read. One by one they are called up to the *bimah,* the platform from which the Torah is read. The going up to the *bimah* is called an *aliyah.* (*Aliyah* is also what each section of the *parashah* is called, as in "Not only did the bat mitzvah chant the haftarah beautifully, but she also read the seventh *aliyah!*") Those honored with the *aliyah* recite a blessing before and after the reading of their section of the *parashah.*

Standing before an open Torah, we are witnesses to the extraordinary power of the writing. Black fire on white fire, the Jewish mystics called it. Look at the letters too long, and we can feel ourselves being drawn into them. Perhaps that is why the reader uses a *yad,* meaning "hand," a pointer fashioned in the shape of an arm and hand with the index finger extended to show the place. The *yad* not only serves to keep readers from having to touch the parchment with their fingers but also to anchor them on this side of the scroll, to hold them back from too intimate an encounter.

So it is at this special place, at this special time, that the Jewish people choose to offer their most personal prayers, prayers for those who are ill, for new parents and newborn children, for those who have returned home from a long journey, for those coming home from the hospital, for those soon to be married. When such prayers are offered, the Torah reading becomes not only a time when we hear about the stories of our ancestors but also a time when we learn about our neighbors and our friends. The stories of the past become mingled with the stories of the present, flowing into a single stream of sacred history.

As the most social part of Friday-night services is the oneg Shabbat, so the most social part of Shabbat-morning services is the kiddush. After the services, everyone gathers around tables of food and wine and drink. The blessings over the day, over the wine and, often, over the ḥallah are recited. And people shmooze. It is a weekly time for checking in: "How did your visit to the dentist go last week?" "Marsha is away visiting her family." "The baby is doing fine." You can hear about who is in the hospital, who has a new grandchild, what people think about the latest newsbreak, how your friend's child is doing at college. "Max goes to shul to talk to God," a Jewish saying tells us, "but I go to shul to talk to Max."

Each Shabbat, as we read from the Torah scroll, the words are formed and read exactly as they were centuries ago. 🐦

The 39 Rules of Shabbat

To help us keep Shabbat without slipping into the ways of the workweek, the rabbis of old listed 39 things that we should not do on Shabbat. They include lighting fires, building, destroying, tying permanent knots, carrying in public areas, hammering, cooking, farming, weaving or sewing, tearing, writing. For many of us, the minutiae of Shabbat observance can seem overwhelming, irrelevant, archaic. But in them lies the secret of Shabbat.

If you are curious about how Shabbat feels, try it, but keep things simple. Begin by selecting one Shabbat ritual and committing yourself to observing it. Start with the rituals whose beauty is self-evident: lighting Shabbat candles, making Kiddush, eating ḥallah, inviting friends, singing at the dinner table. Though it may feel awkward at first, try to stay with the ritual for at least one month, giving yourself the time to develop an emotional and a physical ease with the observance. As with so many other things, what we get out of Shabbat depends on what we invest in it.

Consider buying a prayer book, a siddur, to have on hand as well. It will give you the traditional Shabbat prayers to say, including Kiddush and havdalah, and it will help remind you that for thousands of years, Jews have been working to keep Shabbat, just as you are doing. (There are a variety of siddurim [plural of *siddur*]. Consult your rabbi, a friend or a salesperson in a Judaica shop to learn about the differences and to select the one that can best meet your needs.)

After the morning services, people return home to eat lunch, read, take walks, play pickup games of basketball or football, or gather in a park. They may go to a friend's and while away the afternoon or stay at home to enjoy a Shabbat nap. In keeping with the tradition of *bikkur ḥolim,* visiting the sick, some synagogues arrange for their members to visit patients in nearby hospitals or neighbors who are shut-in or convalescing, so that they may bring comfort and provide company on that day of community.

A light late-afternoon meal, called a *se'udah shlishit* (third meal) completes the formal eating for the day.

The Limits of Living "As If"

Judaism recognizes that no matter how much Shabbat is a vision of God's dream-world, it is still only a vision. People will still get sick on Shabbat, and they will still need others to help them on Shabbat. So great is the mitzvah of saving someone's life that it overrides the restrictions of Shabbat. So on Shabbat, if someone is very sick or has been in an accident and we can help, we must help even if it means breaking the laws of Shabbat. In Hebrew, this is called *pikuaḥ nefesh,* the imperative of saving a life.

Spices

There is only one rule regarding the use of spices, *besamim*: that there be more than one. It is easy to make your own spice container for havdalah. Choose a pretty box, cup or porcelain potpourri jar. Place within it your favorite spices (cloves, cinnamon and dried rose petals make a nice combination), close it up, and, voilà, a spice box. If the box doesn't have any holes, you can open it up to smell the spices. Flowers from the celebration of special occasions, like weddings, anniversaries, graduations and housewarmings, can be dried and added to your *besamim* collection.

Jewish tradition teaches that God gives us a second soul on Shabbat. On Saturday night we inhale the havdalah spices to find strength and comfort as our second soul leaves us until next Shabbat.

Havdalah

After the sun sets, when three medium-sized stars can be seen in the sky, Shabbat ends. It is escorted out with a special service called *havdalah* (separation). Just as we entered that sacred place through a portal of candlelight and accompanied by wine, so we leave it through a portal of candlelight and accompanied by wine. Using a tall, braided candle with two or more wicks, a bouquet of spices and a cup of wine, havdalah leads the way back to the workaday world that awaits us.

Why Are the Wicks of the Havdalah Candle Wound Together?

We tend to enter Shabbat with our souls unraveling, pulled as we are in so many directions by the demands of the week and the many roles we play. On Shabbat, we have time to weave together those disparate strands of our lives. We may begin the day like the Shabbat candles, apart, pieces of ourselves separated from one another. But through the peace of Shabbat, we emerge whole once again, woven together like the wicks of the havdalah candle.

The candlelight is reflected in the faces of our friends and loved ones as someone sings the ten lines that constitute this simple service:

Behold, God is my deliverance; I am confident and unafraid....
Blessed are You, God, the One above all, who created distinctions between holy and common, light and dark, Israel and other nations, the seventh day and the six days of work. Blessed are You, God, who creates distinctions between the sacred and the everyday.

The candle is extinguished. The lights come on. Our rest is over. We return to where we left off. Our clothes need washing; food needs cooking; presents need to be bought; meetings need to be scheduled. We work for another six days with God at our side, until the next Shabbat, when we reenter God's palace in time.

Themes of Separation

Because havdalah is a time of distinctions, some families are choosing it as the time to mark personal transitions. For example, rituals for a child going off to college, for families seeking healing after a miscarriage, and for those seeking healing from abuse are getting woven into the symbols of havdalah. Just as havdalah separates Shabbat from the workweek, so these rituals are designed to help families negotiate a necessary separation in their lives.

Remembering Shabbat

"I was 15 and my sister Edith was 17 when we were taken to Auschwitz," Alice Lock Kahana told me. "The Nazis took everything away—clothing, possessions, family. Fear was overpowering. Every day was a *Selektion*, a separating out of those who would be sent to work from those who would be sent to the crematoria. My sister and I were in constant fear of separation.

"One day, I decided with Edith to remember the Shabbat we celebrated at home, to alleviate our fears. On one Friday night, we started to talk about how the table was set—the plates, the silverware, the cups and saucers. Edith played Mother. She would reprimand me if I didn't shine the candelabra just so. We would remember the foods we ate—soup, fish, meat. I was always a finicky eater. Now, however, we were starving.

"One Friday night we were punished. We were always being punished. We were not allowed time for our simple bodily functions. We were permitted to go to the toilet only when the SS allowed. Most of us had diarrhea and bladder infections, so such a delay caused excruciating pain.

"We stood outside the latrine waiting our turn. I turned to Edith and said, 'Tonight we will celebrate Shabbat inside the latrine'—because when we talked about Shabbat inside the barrack, we just whispered to each other. But inside the latrine, where the SS wouldn't come because it was so awful, we could sing Shabbat songs, to make Shabbat even more real, more present.

"Shabbat in our house was always celebrated so beautifully. We had two big candelabras with five holders each. Grandfather made Kiddush and sat at the head of the table. After the meal, my aunts and uncles would come over. We would sing *z'mirot*, the songs one sings only on Shabbat.

"So here, outside the latrine, it was now getting dark. 'How about tonight we celebrate inside and sing *z'mirot*?'

"Edith said it was sacrilegious to sing *z'mirot* in such a place. I said, 'Let's go away from the door, into a corner, and sing "Shalom Aleichem."' So we found a corner as far away as we could and began to sing. There were lots of other children there who did not speak our language, for we were brought to the camp from many countries. But as soon as we began, a group of children encircled us, and we all sang songs of Shabbat.

"From then on, we celebrated Shabbat every Friday night in the latrine, singing. And the children would form a circle around us.

"I always thought the angels were coming and listening to us."

—Personal conversation between the author and Alice Lock Kahana

It Is Not Good for a Person to Be Alone

Celebrating Shabbat alone can be daunting, especially for those new to the experience of the day. For many, young and old, veterans and novices, it can be lonely. Yet in our society, where privacy is highly valued, it is hard to invite ourselves to others' homes and say, "Show me how you celebrate Shabbat," or, "Let me share in your celebration." And novices may be uncomfortable inviting others to join them for Shabbat.

What's to be done? Call your rabbi to say that you would like to share Shabbat with someone. Be sure to mention special needs you may have, such as dietary requirements or wheelchair accessibility.

If you belong to a synagogue, be certain that it offers and *publicizes* home hospitality for others in the community. Encourage those who live alone to invite family and friends; encourage families to open their homes to others; reach out to the elderly and offer to accompany them to your home and back. Anytime of the day is good for visiting—for meals, in the afternoon or for havdalah. The celebration of Shabbat with others can revitalize the sense of home and family for those who are newly divorced or widowed.

CHAPTER 5

Rosh Ḥodesh

The New Moon

God, grant us a long and peaceful life,

A life of goodness and blessing,

A life of achievement and strength of body,

A life of decency and dignity, free from shame and full of honor,

A life filled with Torah and love for You.

—FROM THE BLESSING ANNOUNCING THE NEW MOON

SINCE THE EARLIEST OF EARTHLY TIMES, the sun has eclipsed the moon as the premier heavenly body, both in its radiance and in the human imagination. The sun was the symbol of strength and power. The pharaohs were children of the sun, not the moon. But the Israelites were partial to the moon. No matter how many times the moon was vanquished by the demons of the night, it always reemerged—in the heavens and in our stories—as a symbol of hope and renewal. Every month the moon would wane until it completely disappeared. Then, just after the darkest moment, the moon would give birth to itself, begin to re-form itself, and grow into a luminous, soothing orb.

A waning moon right before Rosh Hodesh ✦

The Jews saw in the moon a reflection of themselves. No matter how many nations were greater than they, no matter how often they were oppressed, like the moon, the Jews would always come back, shining bright, not in fire or vengeance, but in renewal, confidence and joy.

The Jews have a story, a midrash, that says that at the end of time the moon and the sun will no longer be rivals. Rather, the one will become like the other in size, and they will reign in the sky together, in peace, one light that warms and one light that cools, one light that excites and one light that soothes. And so it shall be with the Jews. At the end of time, the Jews will share the world with all who may now appear stronger. All will offer their complementary strengths. And no one shall be oppressed.

The Measure of Time

Besides providing romance and serving as a symbol, the moon has also played a practical role for the Jews, as an instrument of keeping time. Monitoring the changes in the cycle of the moon was a chief way in which the ancients measured the months.

Two thousand years ago, there was no published Jewish calendar. The birth of the New Moon (the first sliver of light to be seen after the old moon fades completely), which marks the beginning of the new month, had to be witnessed before the new month could be declared. The Jewish leadership's knowledge of astronomy and ability to predict the New Moon had not yet displaced the tradition of witnessing. Given the moon's rotation, the new month could begin on either the 30th or the 31st day after the previous New Moon. Knowing of this uncertainty, the Jewish people would await the authorized declaration of the New Moon. Only then could they reckon the correct time to celebrate the holidays that occurred in that month.

Keeping the calendar was a sacred, public task, for the determination of the holy days rested upon it. During the Temple period, calculating the calendar was one of the major responsibilities of the Sanhedrin, the supreme court of the Jews, located in Jerusalem. Only with the declaration made by the Sanhedrin did the Jews know when to gather for the Passover seder, when to sit in the sukkah, when to mark the New Year of the Trees.

Sanhedrin

The Sanhedrin was the supreme political, religious and judicial body that governed the Jews before and after the destruction of the Temple. It is said that it was composed of 71 men drawn from both the priestly class and the ranks of the rabbinic (that is, Pharisaic) scholars. While the Temple stood, the Sanhedrin sat in Jerusalem. Once the Temple fell, the Sanhedrin moved with the rabbis as they established their first academy in Yavneh. After Yavneh was destroyed in the wake of the failure of the Bar Kochba rebellion (132–135 CE), the Sanhedrin moved to the Galilee. It functioned there until the early 400s.

Any people who wish to remain united need a common calendar and a common timekeeper. Today the world is united by Greenwich mean time. Air travel, international communications and market transactions would be exceedingly cumbersome if every place in the world did not count time the same way. In the biblical and Talmudic periods, the Jews set their calendars by Sanhedrin time.

How did the members of this high court know when the new month began? On the 30th day of the month, they would sit in session in a courtyard in Jerusalem and wait for testimony to be presented. Witnesses who had seen the light of the New Moon would run to the Sanhedrin to announce it. They would be questioned by the court about the color of the moon, its height in the sky, the direction the arc of light faced, and more. If the judges were satisfied that the testimony of at least two of the witnesses was reliable, they would declare that the month had been 29 days, and the new month had begun.

A shofar was then blown, and bonfires would be lit from mountaintop to mountaintop to let people far and wide know that the New Moon and the new month had been proclaimed. Within hours, the nation of Israel would be synchronized in their count.

If there were not at least two reliable witnesses, or the evening was cloudy, the New Moon was declared for the following day. When the Samaritans began setting bogus bonfires, the Sanhedrin instituted a system of runners. Those who lived outside that circle of communication would observe Rosh Ḥodesh on the 30th day of the month. That method of declaration continued until the middle of the fourth century, when the rabbis established a permanent calendar.

Diaspora Jewry and the Calendar

While the Jews of the Diaspora, far beyond the reach of the bonfires and the monthly heralds, might not have known the precise day of the New Moon, they did know that it had to be one of two days. Thus, they determined that they would celebrate the pilgrimage holidays (Passover, Shavuot and Sukkot) on both of those days, for one of them had to be right. This is a tradition that Orthodox and Conservative Jews living outside of Israel continue to this day.

From the earliest of times, Rosh Ḥodesh has been celebrated as a semiholiday. In the biblical period, feasts would be held, and women, especially, would seek out the prophets for advice and help. Today

The First Light of the New Moon

According to the reckoning of the rabbis, the old month yields to the new month when the sun, moon and earth—in that order—are perfectly aligned. That is called, appropriately enough, the *molad,* or birth. Six hours after this birth, the first light from the New Moon can be seen.

Shabbat Mevorchim

The Shabbat before the New Moon—Shabbat Mevorchim —was also a special time for women. Even women who would otherwise stay home from the synagogue would go on this particular Shabbat. When the ark was opened, when the Torah was raised, they would offer prayers from their hearts, asking God to care for their families, and they would invoke the memories of the matriarchs and of family long gone, asking for their intercession on behalf of their loved ones.

Hallel

Hallel, a series of psalms praising God, is recited during the morning service on Passover, Sukkot, Shavuot, Ḥanukkah, Yom Yerushalayim, and Yom Ha'atzma'ut, as well as on Rosh Ḥodesh. The name Hallel comes from the very first word in Psalm 113, *halleluyah*, which means "praise God." The psalms that make up Hallel are Psalms 113, 114, 115, 116, 117 and 118.

Women's Rosh Ḥodesh groups can provide opportunities for cross-generational sharing and celebration. 🌿

it is celebrated as a day of joy, when Hallel—a collection of psalms of praise and rejoicing—is recited and a special portion of the Torah is read. Rosh Ḥodesh is a time for new beginnings, a time to test new skills, to dare to make changes in our lives. Some people set Rosh Ḥodesh as the day to embark on new hobbies, or start on a new course of study, or begin taking better care of themselves. Rosh Ḥodesh is our perpetual new beginning, sanctioned and encouraged by the memory of so many other beginnings pursued over thousands of years.

The Texture of Time

Each month of the Jewish calendar has its own personality. Some months are joyous, like Adar, for the raucous redemption of Purim occurs in it. Some are subdued, like Ḥeshvan, for it has no holiday at all except for the semiholiday of Rosh Ḥodesh. Some are tragic, like Av, for we remember the destruction of the Temple and the loss of thousands of Jewish lives. But regardless of the historic texture of the month, Rosh Ḥodesh—the first day of the month—is always joyous. It reminds us that our lives are always full of new possibilities, that we should not think of ourselves as prisoners of the past or as prisoners of the circumstances around us. For just as the moon is relentless in its pursuit of renewal, so we can be.

Both the light side and the dark side of the moon serve as our teachers. The light of the New Moon slicing through the darkness teaches us that small successes can rip holes in the dark cloth that sometimes threatens to bind us. Rosh Ḥodesh symbolizes the idea that the darkness of life will undoubtedly reassert itself now and then but it need not overwhelm us. The New Moon teaches us that there are ways to take advantage of the darkness—whether welcome or not—when it enters our lives. The darkness, after all, allows us to see the stars, by whose light we can set our bearings, and it allows us to trace the pale outlines of our dreams. It reminds us that those sights become clear only when we achieve a certain patience, openness, familiarity, and trust in gazing into the darkness.

It is no wonder we choose the moon to comfort us in our times of sorrow, for the sun never sees the darkness and cannot know the fear of being swallowed up by it. But the moon lives in the darkness. It is a worthy and wise companion.

How We Celebrate

The celebration of Rosh Ḥodesh begins the week before the new moon and continues up to 14 days afterward. The Shabbat before Rosh Ḥodesh is called Shabbat Mevorchim, the Sabbath of Blessing. After the Torah reading, the congregation rises. The Torah is lifted by the cantor, or other person leading the service, who begins to chant a special blessing (a portion of which is found at the beginning of this chapter) on behalf of the congregation and all Israel. It is a prayer as tender as a parent's wish for a newborn, with a tune as soft and as embracing. It is a prayer full of hope and the power to overcome fear. A proclamation is then made, telling everyone when the New Moon will appear, down to the very hour. The congregation repeats the proclamation to reinforce the news.

Because the day of Rosh Ḥodesh is a semiholiday, we read from the Torah, Numbers 28:9–15, in the synagogue in its honor. (When Rosh Ḥodesh falls on Shabbat, we read that portion along with the regular weekly reading. A special haftarah, Isaiah 66:1–24, which speaks of hope and rebirth, replaces the haftarah that would otherwise accompany that Shabbat's *parashah*.) Hallel, the psalms of praise and rejoicing, are recited. Tefillin—the black boxes and leather straps that Jews wrap around their arms and heads during weekday-morning blessings—are removed for the latter part of the morning prayers as a sign of the New Moon's holiday status.

Rosh Ḥodesh is a holiday for everyone, but women have a special attachment to the day. For at least 2,000 years, Jewish women have celebrated the appearance of the New Moon in their own way, most notably by refraining from sewing, spinning, weaving or doing any needlework. It was a day on which women were free of family chores, a one- or two-day vacation they honored every month. In some communities, women would gather to light candles (perhaps recalling the bonfires of Israel), tell one another stories, enjoy one another's company.

Many societies associate women's bellies with the moon. In Judaism, the rabbis offered the following explanation for the special relationship between women and the new moon: After the Exodus, while Moses was on Mount Sinai receiving the Torah from God, the

Tracking the Moon

The weather section in your local newspaper can tell you when the different phases of the moon will occur. You can also find the information in a Jewish calendar, which you can get at a synagogue or a Judaica shop. So that you remember to celebrate, mark the dates in your calendar, the one you refer to most regularly, just as you would other special days. You may want to stock up on candles of different colors—and perhaps of different scents— for the different moods of the months. The ambitious may want to learn to sing a new portion of the Hallel each month. By the end of the year, you will know the entire Hallel.

Tefillin

God spoke to the Israelites saying, "Bind my words as a sign upon your hands, and they shall be like jewelry between your eyes." Eager to ritualize that symbolic statement, the rabbis of old created a sacred ornament of black leather straps and boxes to hold and bind the words of God upon their bodies. To this day, traditional Jews, both men and, increasingly, women, conduct their everyday morning prayers wrapped in the lengths of the tefillin straps. Tefillin, holy adornments, are not worn on Shabbat and holidays, those being special days considered adornment enough.

Miriam's Cup

Even as Moses led the men of Israel out of the land of Egypt, so did Miriam, the prophetess, Moses' sister, lead the women. As the women crossed the Sea of Reeds, Miriam led them, timbrel in hand, in their song of victory and jubilation, singing, "This is my God, whom I will praise." We can imagine that Miriam also led the women in their refusal to give their jewelry to make the golden calf.

As a reminder of Miriam's prophetic role and the roles of other remarkable women both hidden and known throughout the ages, some women choose to purchase or designate a special cup of Miriam for their Rosh Ḥodesh Kiddush.

This etching, done in 1682, shows a Jewish community celebrating the renewal of the moon.

Israelites, impatient and worried, succumbed to idolatry. They pooled their gold and made the golden calf. But in this case, the rabbis tell us, "the Israelites" means only the men. The women refused to participate; they refused to offer up their gold and jewelry for such an abomination. Yet when the time was right, they proved themselves generous, for upon Moses' return and the building of the Tabernacle, they gave abundantly of their mirrors and other prized belongings to help make the sacred instruments of the Temple. God rewarded the women for their devotion and their generosity by granting them the New Moon as their holiday.

In the 1970s, Jewish women around the world began to reclaim Rosh Ḥodesh. Once again women are celebrating the day, alone or together, as they light candles afloat in pools of water in crystal bowls. They sing songs, share stories, study Torah, comfort one another in response to recent losses, or rejoice at one another's successes and pleasures, large or small. It is a time of caring and connecting, of knowing that they belong. And for some, it is a moment of reconnecting to a tradition that they had thought had no place for them.

The celebration for Rosh Ḥodesh—for both men and women—continues with the *kiddush halevanah,* the sanctification of the New Moon, on the first or second Saturday night of the month. After the evening service, if the skies are clear and the moon can be seen, the congregation goes outdoors. Congregants turn their faces skyward and say:

> Halleluyah. Praise God from the heavens, praise God from the heights…. Blessed are You, God, Sovereign of the universe, who with but a word created the heavens and who said to the moon that she will be renewed as a crown of splendor for all God's children, just as they are destined to be renewed like her.

A private prayer for those in need of healing or seeking to have a child is sometimes inserted here.

Kiddush halevanah cannot be said after the moon has reached its zenith. That time belongs to next month's New Moon.

Do Not Turn Back a Witness

Traveling to Jerusalem to serve as a witness for the new moon could be a burden as much as an honor. We can imagine an overworked farmer finally settling into his easy chair during the week, gazing at the land and the sky, catching a glimpse of the moon, and saying, "No, I'm too tired to go." What if the New Moon fell on Shabbat, when both the distance traveled and the method of travel were restricted?

But so important was the keeping of the calendar that the prohibitions against traveling on Shabbat could be suspended to allow one to travel to Jerusalem. And no matter when the New Moon was sighted, all witnesses had to believe that their testimony could be the one that would make the difference.

The story is told *(Mishnah Rosh Hashanah* 1:5) about the one month when more than 40 pairs of witnesses traveled to Jerusalem. As they passed through Lod, Rabbi Akiva stopped them, telling them to go home, for not all of them were needed. Upon hearing this, Rabbi Gamliel, the head of the Sanhedrin, sent word to Rabbi Akiva, saying, "If you continue to turn people back, you will dissuade them from coming altogether, for they will say, 'Surely someone else has gotten there by now.'"

Those who made the effort were feted and thanked with a grand banquet laid out in a courtyard of Jerusalem. Perhaps if they were treated graciously and honorably, it was thought, they would choose to make the journey again.

Women's Prayers

Throughout the ages, women have crafted complex prayers to be recited in honor of the New Moon. This one, whose author is unknown, appears in English and Yiddish in Susan Berrin's book *Celebrating the New Moon: A Rosh Chodesh Anthology.*

I beseech You, blessed God, who generously provides food and clothing to all creatures, give me my sustenance and provide food for my household and a decent living for all *Yisro'el* [Israel], with contentment of spirit and not with sorrow, with honor and not with indignity, so that I may not be ashamed. May all our endeavors bring good results, with blessing and success. Shield us from darkness and give us light. Be a protector to me and to my household and to all *Yisro'el,* and shield me from all kinds of trouble and sorrow this year and in all years to come and in all months and weeks and in all hours and in the time it takes to blink the eyes. Protect me from all confusion and from all the ominous fears of my heart. May we hear good tidings, true and righteous. Forgive the sins and misdeeds that I have committed....

Yehi rotson [may it be Your will], God, my God and God of my ancestors, that You grant me grace and compassion and joy and happiness and bring good luck to me in all my endeavors and may I merit grace in Your eyes.

Illumine my children's eyes through the study of *toyre* [Torah], and may they not forget what they have learned. May You give clarity, beauty, felicity, and grace to my speech, and may

everything that I request come to pass and bring good results....

Dear God, may my feet walk to *shul* [synagogue] to praise You and may I walk in Your path. May my breasts nurse children who will be strong. I beg of You, dear God, may violent death not overtake them. May there be no tears in my eyes because of worry, and may there be no sound of wailing or mourning in my household. May we not have to be fed by others, and may we merit to see salvation and consolation.

Favorably fulfill all the requests of my heart, for You are a God of mercy. May the words of my mouth and the meditations of my heart be acceptable to You, O God, my Rock and my Redeemer. *Omeyn* [amen].

Foods for Rosh Ḥodesh

Women who gather in celebration of Rosh Ḥodesh often bring foods symbolic of new beginnings and hope: lentil soup or salad, bagels or other round breads, nuts and fruit, cheese wheels and hard-boiled eggs.

For More Information About Celebrating Rosh Ḥodesh

Celebrating the New Moon: A Rosh Chodesh Anthology by Susan Berrin is an excellent resource. Of particular interest is Berrin's geographically arranged, annotated directory of Rosh Ḥodesh groups and materials for celebration. For more information, ask your rabbi or local chapter of Hadassah or Jewish Women International about programs in your area, or check your local Jewish newspaper.

CHAPTER 6

Rosh Hashanah

The Birthday of the World

1–2 TISHRE

Today is the birthday of the world.

—FROM THE HIGH HOLIDAY PRAYER BOOK

AFTER WORKING FOR SIX DAYS, fashioning form from chaos and life from darkness, after finishing the heavens and the earth and all that was in them, the Torah tells us that God looked at the brand-new world and declared, "It is very good." That is hefty praise from the Source of all—and great comfort, too. For if the One who is the measure of all goodness finds goodness in the world and in us, shouldn't we?

Yet, as we look about, we note that the world is awash with diverse possibilities: laughter and tears, bounty and famine, sickness and health, companionship and loneliness. Sometimes the bad matches, if not outweighs, the good, begging the question, "How could God—or the authors of the Torah—have judged the world as good?"

On Rosh Hashanah the Torah reading includes verses from Genesis 24 and Numbers 29. Numbers 29:1 instructs us to hold a holy gathering on the first day of Tishre (Rosh Hashanah): "It shall be your day of sounding the shofar." ❧

Dressing the Torah

In most synagogues throughout the year, the *sifrei Torah* (Torah scrolls) are draped in colorful and elaborately embroidered or brocaded sheaths or covers. On the High Holidays, however, the Torah scrolls are dressed all in white, a symbol of the freshness, purity and newness the season offers.

God's Prayer

The rabbis imagined that not only do humans pray but that God prays as well. What does God pray? Mar Zutra bar Tuvia said in the name of Rav, "God prays as follows: 'May it be My will that My mercy vanquish My anger and that I deal with My people in love and understanding'" (*Brachot* 7a).

Perhaps the Torah means to teach us that good is not a commodity, like bricks or sugar, that we should measure simply by stacking all the good and all the bad in piles, seeing which is higher. Good and bad are not to be compared pound for pound or inch for inch. To recognize the world as very good is to see goodness as an ever present promise, a constant possibility, a ray of light that can cut through the thick of darkness just as a ray of joy can brighten a roomful of pain.

The Torah's declaration that the world is "very good" is not so much a divine observation as it is a divine prayer from God to us. "This world may not be perfect, but it has so much of value," we can hear God saying. "It was born with blemishes. It may always have faults. Sometimes the deepest fault seems to lie between you and Me, hiding us, dividing us, from one another. But even so, do not forget that the world can be very good. See that it is so."

Rosh Hashanah, the Jewish New Year, is our annual celebration of that first and everlasting belief in goodness. On Rosh Hashanah, we are reminded of the possibilities of eternal renewal; that the past is a launching pad for the future; that even though our past resides in us, we do not reside in our past. As the world can be renewed each year, so can we.

In Search of Renewal

Yet floating through our awareness in this dewy air of Creation is the sobering knowledge that renewal takes work, that for us to move forward, we must tend to our accounts. Rosh Hashanah affords us the time to review our past year. It offers us time to reflect on our achievements and weave them proudly into our story, the epic that will be our life. It offers us time to regret our mistakes, extend our apologies where we should, forgive ourselves our indiscretions, and accept our limitations. That, too, we then must weave into the story of our selves.

According to tradition, we do not have to travel the road toward renewal alone. We have two partners in our journey: the Jewish people and God. There is comfort in knowing that around the world and for thousands of years, Jews have spent that time of year learning and pursuing the lessons of renewal. And for those who believe, there is an added incentive and perhaps an urgency in knowing that the Almighty, in love and in justice, watches over that personal accounting.

We can imagine that along with desiring to witness our regrets and our intentions to do better, God delights in the recounting of our achievements, and in our declaring our hopes for the future. For perfection belongs to the realm of the heavens. Here on earth, we must settle for lesser goals.

Francis T. Vincent, Jr., former commissioner of baseball, could have been giving a High Holiday sermon when he said, "Baseball teaches us how to deal with failure, that failure is the norm in baseball—that those who hit safely in one out of three chances become star players. I also find it fascinating that baseball, alone in sport, considers errors to be part of the game, part of its rigorous truth."

Seeing Our Goodness and Our Potential

One grand lesson of Rosh Hashanah is not that we have to be perfect but that we are, and can continue to be, very good. It is sufficient if we strive to achieve our potential. It is only when we fail to be the fullness of who we are that we are held accountable. Rabbi Zusya said, "In the world to come, they will not ask me, 'Why were you not Moses?' They will ask me, 'Why were you not Zusya?'"

The language of our prayers imagines God as judge and king, sitting in the divine court on the divine throne of justice, reviewing our deeds. On a table before God lies a large book with many pages, as many pages as there are people in the world. Each of us has a page dedicated just to us. Written on that page, by our own hand, in our own writing, are all the things we have done during the past year. God considers those things, weighs the good against the bad, and then, as the prayers declare, decides "who shall live and who shall die."

In order to make sense out of the conundrum of life and death, many Jews of old came to believe that death is a punishment for our sins. Others came to believe that death not only punishes—for what value lies therein?—but also atones for our wrongdoings. After the atonement, we greet the afterlife pure and cleansed, ready to enter the garden of Eden, paradise.

Greetings

During the weeks before Rosh Hashanah, we greet one another and send cards with this wish: *L'shanah tovah tikateivu* (May you be inscribed for a good year). Between Rosh Hashanah and Yom Kippur, we make this wish: *G'mar ḥatimah tovah* (May you be sealed in the Book of Life).

Sending homemade New Year's cards and personal notes can add special meaning to the holiday.

This theology of punishment and atonement held sway for centuries and is preserved in much of our liturgy. It is easy to understand why, for that belief brings order and meaning to the world. Many people find it preferable to believe that we are responsible for our own suffering than to imagine that suffering is random and meaningless. It is tempting to choose a world of guilt and punishment over a world of capriciousness, in which there is no apparent moral relationship between our actions and our suffering or our rewards.

Nonetheless, while classic rabbinic theology promotes belief in sin and punishment, it takes every opportunity to soften that belief. The best punishment is the one that is averted. That is, the goal of the theology of retribution is not to punish but to redirect. "I set before you life and death," God says in the Torah. "Therefore choose life" (Deuteronomy 30:19). That is why, according to the ancient rabbis, the rules of God's court are different from those of a worldly court. In a worldly court, the task is to discover the facts about the case and mete out justice. In God's court, the task is to explore the goodness that dwells inside each person, and to help it grow.

Self-Assessment

Even those of us who wonder about the nature and the existence of God can find a place for ourselves in the rhythms and the texture of Rosh Hashanah. For it is not only God who judges us. In private moments of contemplation, often without prompting, we judge ourselves—when we lie in bed at night, unable to sleep; when we drive long distances with little to distract us; on vacation, when we sit alone, gazing at the stars. It is good to capture those moments, to harness them and channel them into more than passing speculation or the regrets of "if only." Those moments of awareness can mark turning points in our lives. Such is the gift of Rosh Hashanah. Safe in a community busy with self-assessment and turning, we are encouraged to make an honest assessment, too.

When we look carefully, we often find that the texture of our lives is an enlarged pattern of the little things: the times we lost our temper and the times we held our peace, the times our friends could count on us and the times we weren't there, the times we did

Days of Awe

Aseret Y'mei Teshuvah (The Ten Days of Repentance) is one name for the period from Rosh Hashanah through Yom Kippur (The Day of Atonement). Another name is Yamim Nora'im, Days of Awe. The days between Rosh Hashanah and Yom Kippur, although not holidays, carry the atmosphere of solemnity and seriousness, of self-searching and return. The work we do not finish on Rosh Hashanah we can carry into those days as we head toward Yom Kippur.

what was right in our workplace and the times we looked away. We recall the times we took too much, drank too much, spent too much, cared too little; the times we acquiesced when we should have fought back, when we fought hard but for the wrong reason.

Rosh Hashanah is a day set aside for such remembering. We ask God—and we ask ourselves—to see our goodness, understand our frailties, accept our regrets, deepen our wisdom and strengthen our resolve to weave new threads of goodness into the fabric of our lives.

We also ask God to forgive us when our offense is both against God and against another person. What is an offense against God? Is it when we reject God's rituals? Yes, for it is as if we reject a gift given to us lovingly and expectantly. But even more, it is when we reject God's ways. "What is good and what is it that God wants of you but to do justly, pursue kindness and walk humbly with your God" (Micah 6:8).

When we fail in our task as the partners of God, which we all do at times, we can seek God's forgiveness. But when we hurt others, we must seek them out for forgiveness. God can forgive us only after we seek the forgiveness of those we wronged. They own the hurt. They deserve and are owed the first apology.

A family praying at High Holiday services.

Preparing for Rosh Hashanah: The Month of Elul

Certainly we can and should ask forgiveness any time of the year. But the month before Rosh Hashanah, the month of Elul, is an especially good time for this. It is not always easy to approach someone we love or, even more, someone we do not particularly like and say, "If I have hurt you this past year, I am sorry. Please forgive me." Elul, the month of reconciliation, gives us the encouragement and the opportunity to do that.

Some people seek forgiveness face-to-face. Some find it easier to write a letter. Others may want to give the aggrieved a gift or do them a favor, all in the context of apologizing and making amends. Asking forgiveness may take many guises. But its one common element is that it must be intentional. Both parties must be aware of what is at stake. There is no such thing as accidental or casual forgiveness.

Elul is not only a time set aside to ask others for forgiveness; it is also a time when others ask that we forgive them. Sometimes it

Forty Days

From 1 Elul to 10 Tishre (that is, Yom Kippur) is a 40-day period of reflection and renewal. Tradition connects these 40 days to another 40 days long ago, when Moses went back up the mountain after the incident with the golden calf, after he broke the first set of tablets on which the Ten Commandments had been written. He went up Mount Sinai seeking God's forgiveness for the weakness of the Israelites. God forgave them and gave them a second set of tablets. The shards of the first tablets were laid beside the intact stones of the second tablets in the ark that traveled with the Israelites in the desert. And so it should have been. We all carry within us the pieces of our past, essential parts of our whole selves. The relationship of the two sets of 40 days allows us to hope that just as God forgave the Jews of long ago, so will God forgive us.

is easy to forgive—for small infractions harmlessly incurred. But at other times, it is hard. How can we release others after ugly words or demeaning acts have shamed or hurt us? How can we be certain that they are truly sorry, that they have earned our forgiveness, that they merit such kindness on our part? Rosh Hashanah teaches us that just as we ask God to trust that we are worthy of forgiveness, so we must be open to the worthiness of our offenders. All too often we are so full of anger and hurt, so unsteady in our recovery from pain, that we hold on to a grudge. Sometimes we even lean on it. Yet to hold on to our grievances, to hold tight to our identity as victims, is to chain ourselves to the past and to the one who aggrieved us. To forgive is to let go. We need to release our sense of having been offended, to open our hands and let it go.

Forgiving and being forgiven are of a piece. If we seek to be trusted in our contrition, if we present ourselves as worthy of forgiveness, so must we trust—cautiously and courageously—that the other is worthy of forgiveness as well.

Three Steps to Forgiveness

How do we merit the forgiveness of others? How do we convince ourselves that we are worthy of our own forgiveness? And if we are unrepentant for our deeds, how can we begin to soften our hearts when anger, hurt or hatred causes us to be defiant? The prayers of Rosh Hashanah present three strategies: *teshuvah* (acts of repentance), *tefillah* (prayer) and *tzedakah* (philanthropy).

TESHUVAH

Teshuvah means "returning." It means realizing that we are not stuck, that our mistakes are not irreparable, that we can turn around and find a way out of the mess we made. The process of *teshuvah* begins when we acknowledge that we were wrong, that we did wrong. It continues when we seek forgiveness from the one we wronged (including ourselves) and when we strive with honest intention not to repeat the wrongful act.

Teshuvah is both strategy and goal, act and attitude. It manifests itself when we genuinely feel that we have done wrong and are truly motivated to rectify the wrongdoing. But sometimes we are so angry or hurt that we cannot acknowledge our part. And then the question is, How do we do *teshuvah* when we do not feel repentant? The answer is, We start with the acts of *teshuvah*. We go through the motions, not to fool the other person, not to be duplicitous, but, rather, to open ourselves to the feelings of *teshuvah*.

It is popular to believe that feelings should precede and motivate our actions, but that is not always so. More often than we acknowledge, actions coax out hidden feelings. We get dressed up and *then* feel elegant. We whisper and *then* feel conspiratorial. We eat out of fellowship and *then* realize that we are hungry. So, too, with repentance. Often we do not realize the extent of our regret until we face the one we offended and say out loud, "I am sorry."

Repentance, then, can be discovered in the deed as much as in the intent. We need not wait until we are ripe for apologizing; done well, with openness and hope, apologizing can make us ripe for repentance.

The word *teshuvah* itself reveals a belief in this strategy by hinting at the fundamental goodness of each of us. To value returning is to value our beginnings. *Teshuvah* is a cheer for who we are at our root. We needn't seek our better selves abroad; we need not fear that who we ought to be is beyond our reach. Our better selves are the impulse and the spirit with which we are born. On the High Holidays we are asked to shed the crust that forms around our hearts as we are hardened by the fires of life, to scrape away the patina that we might think seasons our lives but in reality just dulls the brilliance beneath.

As this bulletin board with the Hebrew words "teshuvah," "tefillah" and "tzedakah" illustrates, we must teach our children that Judaism is more than a series of holiday rituals. We must teach them that there is a Jewish way to gain forgiveness, to prepare and eat a meal, to enjoy a rainbow, and to mark the beginning and end of each day. Indeed, there is a Jewish way to move through all time and space.

TEFILLAH

Through acts of *teshuvah,* we create patterns of a renewed self. Through acts of *tefillah,* prayer, we blend those patterns into an extended tapestry of self, God and community. The holiday prayers found in the *maḥzor,* the prayer book created especially for Rosh Hashanah and Yom Kippur, speak of God's goodness and righteousness, of how God cares for us, all of us, and seeks our renewal. We remind ourselves that when all is said and done, our lives are in God's hands: "For we are the clay, and You are the potter; we are the sheep, and You are the shepherd; we are Your people, and You are our God." We place ourselves within the community of Israel and, buffered and bolstered by our community, we pray that God will strengthen our resolve, accept our repentance, forgive us our misdeeds and continue to care for us. As we repeat those familiar words, we turn and return to ourselves to find the freshness and the innocence that life has encrusted.

Sometimes as we pray, we want to say things not found in the prayer book. Sometimes we seek to pray from the heart. One of the most beautiful and most forgiving personal prayers in Jewish history is the one Moses recited for his sister, Miriam, when she was afflicted with leprosy as divine punishment for challenging his authority. Moses pleaded, "Please, God, please. Heal her" (Numbers 12:13). He did not need a book; he did not need a synagogue. He needed only the desire to pray. On Rosh Hashanah, we pray both from the book and from our hearts.

TZEDAKAH

Judaism teaches that every person is made in the image of God. That means that being godly, every person has the right to a life of dignity, and every person has the obligation to treat others with dignity. People in need make claims on us, our time, and our belongings. Giving tzedakah, gifts of money, is one way we meet that obligation.

Tzedakah boxes come in many sizes and shapes. Some are made of ceramic, others of wood or metal, and yet others of glass or plastic. But all tzedakah boxes remind us to give generously and regularly to those in need.

Checking Your Accounts

Rabbi Irwin Kula teaches that "during the ten days of repentance, it is a sacred custom for people to look over their checkbooks to review how they have lived their lives. How much money has been spent on leisure, tzedakah or rent? What are the active values of our lives?" (*In the Name of Heaven*). After dinner one night between Rosh Hashanah and Yom Kippur, alone or with the family, gather your financial records, look through them carefully, and discover the narrative of your life that they tell. A financial accounting, *heshbon mamonim*, can lead us toward our spiritual acounting, *heshbon hanefesh*.

Tzedakah is not a penalty for our wrongdoing, or a fine or penance. It is also not a bribe or a bargaining chip. Rather, tzedakah—rooted in *tzedek*, righteousness—gives back to the world some of the goodness that we, with our less than noble acts, have taken out. It sets our hands to tasks that are good. It reestablishes the world's equilibrium. And it reminds us that our own fortune is tied to the fortunes of our fellow humans and to all Creation.

How We Celebrate

The season of the New Year begins 30 days before Rosh Hashanah, on Rosh Ḥodesh Elul, the first day of the month of Elul. From that day until the day before Rosh Hashanah, the shofar, the hollowed-out ram's horn, is blown every morning. In ancient times, the shofar was used for many reasons: to announce the new month, to alert the Israelites to danger, and to assemble them for war. Today the shofar is commonly used to declare that the Day of Judgment is approaching. Everyone should prepare.

Psalm 27, which says, "God is my light and my salvation, of whom shall I be afraid?" is added to the morning and evening prayers. It speaks of our trust in the Holy One, and reminds God that the Judge of Judges is also our champion and protector.

Beginning with the last week of Elul, additional prayers, called Seliḥot, are added to the morning service. Seliḥot are prayers that speak of our sorrow for whatever wrongs we have committed. Seliḥot is also the name of the midnight service held at many synagogues, usually on the Saturday night before Rosh Hashanah. Some synagogues turn the evening into a community event, with special activities for adults, children, teens, families and singles. With Seliḥot, the energy carrying us toward the New Year kicks into high gear.

The eve of Rosh Hashanah begins with candlelighting and a blessing: "Blessed are You, Eternal One, who commands us to light the holiday candles."

On Rosh Hashanah, as on all other holidays except Shabbat and Yom Kippur, cooking for the household's immediate needs and carrying in the public domain are allowed. Special foods are prepared. The ḥallah, the sweet, golden, braided bread we eat on Shabbat and holidays, is now round instead of long. Apples are dipped in honey to symbolize the sweet year that we hope lies ahead. As we eat the apples, we say, "May the new year be full of sweetness and goodness."

It is customary to wear new clothes on the second day of Rosh Hashanah and to eat a fruit we are unaccustomed to eating. Those

One or Two Days?

The Bible (Leviticus 23:24) tells us to observe 1 Tishre as a holy day. But, for the same reason that a day was added to the pilgrimage holidays (see the sidebar "Festival Dates" on page 17), a second day was added to Rosh Hashanah.

This second day is celebrated by Jews in Israel as well as by many Jews outside of Israel. Some Reform congregations, however, retain the biblical practice of observing only one day.

The sweet pleasure of ḥallah dipped in honey on Rosh Hashanah is the stuff of childhood memories. 🐦

customs give us additional reasons to celebrate and to say the Sheheḥeyanu, the prayer that thanks God for bringing us to a special occasion: "Blessed are You, Eternal One, who has given us life, kept us in health and brought us to this moment."

A Rosh Hashanah Seder

Passover is not the only holiday with a seder, or ritual meal. Traditionally, Sephardic Jews (those hailing largely from Portugal and the Mediterranean countries) embellish their Rosh Hashanah meal with a modest New Year's seder. They set out plates with special foods that—because of a play on words or a folk belief associated with them—symbolize health, long life, fertility and security. An appropriate prayer is recited before each food is eaten. For example, karah is a squash, and the word sounds like the Hebrew word for cutting or revoking. So as the squash is eaten, the participants recite, "Revoke our harsh sentence, and recall our merits."

American Jews continue a hint of this tradition when we dip the apple in honey and say, "May this coming year be a year of sweetness and goodness for us, Israel and all the earth."

You can create your own Rosh Hashanah seder for the first night of the holiday. Fish often symbolizes fertility; round objects (like the High Holiday ḥallah) symbolize life; pomegranates can symbolize love and plenty; olives can symbolize peace. Feel free to make your own selections and draft your own complementary prayers (keeping them to one line is usually appreciated). Invite guests to choose a food and offer their own wishes. The seder foods can serve as the appetizer. Or each course can be introduced with another symbolic food.

A Shofarless Holiday

Despite the fact that the shofar is the main symbol of Rosh Hashanah, it is not sounded in Conservative and Orthodox synagogues when the holiday falls on Shabbat. The rules of Shabbat (which traditionally exclude the use of musical instruments—including the shofar) overrule the ritual needs of Rosh Hashanah.

The most familiar sound of Rosh Hashanah is the shofar. It is blown 100 times in the synagogue on each of the two days—100 blasts, three different voices that stealthily pierce our armor of confidence and blasé sophistication—*tekiah,* one long blast; *shvarim,* a series of three medium blasts; *truah,* a series of nine short blasts. Some imagine that the shofar mimics the imploring message of the day: an urgent call for help *(tekiah),* the sounds of protest or pain *(shvarim)* and the heartrending sound of sobbing *(truah).* It is as if the shofar became our throats and our mouths, crying for us in a way that decorum and dignity do not otherwise allow.

One tradition tells us that the shofar is the sound of Sarah crying upon hearing that her son, Isaac, had been taken by Abraham to be sacrificed. The *akedah,* the binding of Isaac, is the Torah story we read in the synagogue on Rosh Hashanah. Sarah stands for all who weep over their lot in life, and those who weep over their loved ones: those who are ill, those who are sad, those who are looking for a sign showing the way home. Perhaps the shofar is such a sign, the voice to follow when we lose our way.

But the shofar is not only a surrogate for our voices; it may also be a surrogate for God's voice. Perhaps through the notes, God is calling to us to take stock, to take care. Perhaps through its voice, we hear God crying for us and to us. Perhaps that is why it is so stirring and so disturbing.

A grand moment of drama in many synagogues on Rosh Hashanah occurs during the Aleinu. Throughout the year at the end of every service, this prayer is recited. It is a prayer that speaks of our need and our duty to praise God. It includes the words "We bend our knees and bow down and give thanks before God." Throughout the year whenever we read these lines, we slightly bend our knees and partially bow from the waist. On Rosh Hashanah, however, the prayer is said in the middle of the Amidah, and we do more than just bow from the waist. In many synagogues, the cantor and the rabbi, and sometimes the congregants as well, bow completely. They prostrate themselves, lie on the floor face to the ground, showing their—and our—humility before God. Jews can bow to no one else the way we bow to God. Only God deserves such honor and such submission.

The sound of the shofar is like a wake-up call reminding us of our potential to live with mercy and compassion as partners with God.

Divesting Ourselves of Sin

What do sins look like? The truth is, of course, that we can't see them. But if we could, if sins were something we could hold in our hands, we could capture them, bundle them up and throw them away.

World religions have always been fertile with imagination and are often eager to enact in ritual that which occurs in the realm of the spirit. So it was with the Jewish ritual of the scapegoat (a biblical ritual of cleansing and atonement on Yom Kippur). And so it is with a more modern Rosh Hashanah ritual, *tashlich*.

On the afternoon of the first day of Rosh Hashanah (or the second day if the first day is Shabbat, when traditional Jews don't carry in the public domain), Jews perform the symbolic ritual of *tashlich* (meaning "you shall throw or cast off"). The idea was inspired by a verse

A Ritual of Release and Relief

Although *tashlich* is designed to rid us of our sins, it can also serve as a ritual in which we shed past grudges and loosen the grip of painful memories. Whether performed during Rosh Hashanah or at another time of the year, a personal *tashlich* can be devoted to freeing us from feelings that linger too long and block our way to a better future, from memories of abuse or violence, from fears of past failure or from a relationship that simply must end.

The Rite Time?

As with other rituals, the traditions of *tashlich* continue to evolve. For example, some Jews have broadened the period when they may perform *tashlich* to include any time during the Ten Days of Awe.

Bread is passed out for the tashlich ritual. ❧

from the prophet Micah: "God will take us back in love; God will vanquish our iniquities and cast our sins into the depths of the sea" (7:19). Using stones or bread to represent our sins, we go alone or as a community to the shores of a lake, stream or reservoir; recite psalms of compassion and forgiveness; consider the magic of transference; and throw our "sins" into the water. *Tashlich* might not literally relieve us of our sins. Yet somehow we always feel lighter on the way home.

We return to our homes, to the company of friends and family, to a sumptuous meal of hope and renewal, grateful and exquisitely aware of all we have right now.

The Shabbat of (Re)turning

Shabbat Shuvah, or Shabbat Teshuvah, is the name given to the Shabbat that falls between Rosh Hashanah and Yom Kippur. It is taken from the first words of the haftarah, the prophetic reading for that Shabbat: "Return, O Israel, to the Eternal One, your God, for you have fallen because of your sin" (Hosea 14:2). It reminds us that the day of atonement and reckoning is fast approaching.

Sovereignty, Memories and Shofar Blasts

On Rosh Hashanah, the repetition of the Amidah, the central prayer that dominates every service, features three themes: *malchuyot,* (sovereignty), *zichronot* (memories), and *shofarot* (shofar blasts). As we consider the classic meaning of these concepts, we can imagine another level, one that urges us to a deeper understanding of self. For example, *malchuyot,* which speaks of God's kingship, leads us to wonder, What is worthy of our highest allegiance? What rules our lives, for better or for worse? What impostors try to lay claim to us? What ideal will inspire us to put aside self-interest and put another first?

Zichronot reminds us that memory is the beginning of self. We are who we are today because we carry the memories of our yesterdays. We often cherish our best friends because they can say with us, "I remember." If we approach Rosh Hashanah mostly as a day of reluctant and fearful self-disclosure, then God's memories, as well as our own, can be worrisome. But if we can see Rosh Hashanah as a day of reconnecting with someone who knows us well, whose memories remind us of who we are and what we can be, Rosh Hashanah can be comforting. God knows us, holds us

and safeguards the memories that form us.

Shofarot represents that clarion call that awakens us, that sacred calling that sets us on the right path. Sometimes the call comes in the shape of a boot: getting fired from a job we should have left long ago or being kicked out of a relationship we were too lazy to end. "The blare of the shofar grew louder and louder" —and magically a better path appeared before us, and we were free to take it. Sometimes the call is more subtle: It is that still, small voice or that ringing silence that follows a shattering noise.

When the prayers truly work, they are so much more than the words on the page. They are a lattice braced against our dreams that allows us to climb higher than before.

The Fast of Gedaliah

The day after Rosh Hashanah, 3 Tishre, is called Tzom Gedaliah, the Fast of Gedaliah. The fast commemorates the assassination of Gedaliah, the last Jewish governor of Judah, who was appointed by the Babylonians immediately after the destruction of the Temple in 586 BCE. The assassination, by a group of overzealous Jews, marked the end of Jewish self-rule. It is a daytime fast, beginning at sunrise and lasting until three stars can be seen.

Teshuvah, Tefillah and Tzedakah

"Repentance, prayer and giving avert the harsh decree." That is the usual translation of a line in the famous Unetaneh Tokef, the prayer that declares "who will live and who will die." But in fact the true translation should read, "Repentance, prayer and giving soften the harshness of the decree." What is the difference? The first translation seems to say that the triad of repentance has the power to erase all punishment, earn full pardon, whereas the second translation seems to say that although the punishment will stand, the severity will be softened.

Shira Ruskay, who was a hospice worker in New York City, taught another reading. The true understanding of this prayer, she suggested, may be that the triad changes not the decree but us. After all our efforts at repentance, prayer and giving, we may still have cancer; we may still suffer the loss of a loved one. And yet repentance, prayer and giving may bring us to a calm we had not known before or to an awareness and a connection with God and others that we did not have before. These gifts can surely soften the harshness of the "decree."

CHAPTER 7

Yom Kippur

The Day of Atonement

10 TISHRE

Is this not the fast that I have chosen: to unlock the shackles of injustice, to

loosen the ropes of the yoke, to let the oppressed go free...surely it is to share

your bread with the hungry, and to bring the homeless poor into your house; when

you see the naked, to cover them, never withdrawing yourself from your own kin.

—Isaiah 58:6–7,
RECITED ON YOM KIPPUR AS PART OF THE HAFTARAH

Our God and God of our ancestors, forgive us, pardon us, grant us atonement.

—REFRAIN FROM THE YOM KIPPUR PRAYERS

"I AM SORRY. FORGIVE ME."

These may be some of the hardest words to say. How often do we say instead, "I am

not responsible." "They started it." "It is not my fault!" We renounce responsibility and, there-

fore, ownership of the deed. Sometimes we simply deny that it was ever done.

Too often, we become self-righteous or angry and thus blind to our own wrongdoings. The months of Elul and Tishre offer us the opportunity to reflect on and take responsibility for our mistakes.

An Accounting of the Soul

Just as we review our personal finances for April 15, so we review our behavior for Yom Kippur. This task is called *ḥeshbon hanefesh*, the accounting of our soul. We begin with a simple tabulation of deeds and move to an assessment of our motivations, reactions, responses and goals. On Yom Kippur, we sign off on our accounting in the Book of Life, just as at tax time we sign off on our tax forms.

When We Are Not Forgiven

Our tradition teaches that after reasonable attempts on the offender's part at tendering an apology, God will be moved to forgive the offender with or without the offended one's consent.

The problem is as old as humankind. When asked by God whether he ate the forbidden fruit, Adam replied, "The woman you gave me, to be with me, she made me do it," implicating both God and woman in a single breath.

And when God asked Eve what happened, she said, "The snake made me do it."

Often we face temptations or pressures that seem irresistible and therefore, we argue, we should be absolved of guilt. "I can resist everything except temptation," Oscar Wilde said. But the fact is that Adam and Eve were responsible for their actions and were held accountable, and so are we. Birth, upbringing and experiences can explain much about our impulses and the emotional struggles we endure, but they cannot excuse our actions.

Yom Kippur is a time when we are reminded that we own what we do, that over a lifetime of actions we become the fullness of what we do. To acknowledge that we have commited a wrong is the necessary first step of *teshuvah*. For only by acknowledging our wrongdoings and claiming responsibility for them can we be truly repentant. And only then can we return to the selves we choose to be, the selves God called "very good."

Still, it is *so* hard to say "I am sorry." Our mouths may speak the words, but our hands fidget and our eyes look toward the floor. We say it in a very soft voice or shout it in discomfort and anger. The act of apologizing might not be so bad if only we didn't have to be there when we did it.

It is hard, but if we were never made to say "I'm sorry," we might never learn how much we hurt one another; we might never know the consequences of our actions and we might never care enough even to wonder about them. So the Jewish calendar sets aside one day a year—in fact, the holiest day of the year—as a time to focus on saying "I am sorry."

The Nature of Repentance

Judaism teaches that when we hurt one person, we really hurt three: the one we offended, God and ourselves. We must ask forgiveness from all three, but in a specific order. We must start with the one we offended. God cannot forgive us until the one we offended forgives us. And we cannot forgive ourselves until God forgives us. And then we must be as gracious to ourselves as we are to others and learn to forgive ourselves.

Certainly we don't have to wait for Yom Kippur to offer our apologies. When an appropriate occasion presents itself, we are wise to take it. But sometimes we just can't *find* or *make* the right time. So the Jewish calendar creates the time during the month of Elul and the Ten Days of Repentance.

Of course, apologies aren't magic, nor are they all that goes into making amends. They are not restitution for what was lost, nor do they automatically fix things. But they can put balm on an aching heart and begin to reconstruct bonds that have been broken.

Preparing at Home

In late afternoon an hour or two before the holiday, families gather to eat the *se'udah mafseket*, the last meal before the fast. We do not say Kiddush, for this meal takes place *before* the holiday begins. In fact, there is nothing at all special that we do at this meal, except perhaps to savor each bite a bit more than usual and to eat perhaps just a touch more than usual, hoping it will help get us through the coming day. (That meal, like the one to break the fast, is often dairy, lightly spiced, with plenty of carbohydrates.) Yet that meal, perhaps more than any other, marks the line between our old selves and our new selves. For we are about to embark on a journey of 25 hours of contemplation and imagination. We rarely leave Yom Kippur the same as we were when we entered it.

Just before we head for the synagogue, those who have close loved ones who have died—fathers, mothers, sisters, brothers, sons or daughters—may light a *yahrtzeit* (memorial) candle, designed to burn throughout the day. Any candle that can safely last through the night, all through the day and into the next evening, can be used. Scented candles, which recall the smells of the incense burned in the ancient Holy Temple, may buoy the soul and strengthen it for the intimate day's journey ahead.

Then we light the holiday candles. On other holidays, we say, "Blessed are You, Eternal One, who has sanctified us through Your mitzvot and commands us to light the holiday lights." But on Yom

A Day of Abstinence

Yom Kippur is the holiest day of the year, bar none. We are bidden not to cook or light fires or write on Yom Kippur. We are not to wear leather shoes (many Jews wear sneakers instead), for how can we speak of life when we wear the byproducts of death? We are not to bathe or shower or eat or drink or engage in sexual relations. Those are regulations that remind us—and God—of the needs and the frailty of the human body and of the ways in which we are given to temptation. With these restrictions, our senses are heightened, our understanding clearer. It is ever so difficult to be frivolous when we ache with hunger, ever so hard to be confident when our bodies are weak. And yet, to come through the day intact, to withstand the pains and the discomforts of self-deprivation, is to know that we have triumphed in a small way. We have withstood temptation; we have endured that which we did not choose. If we could do it today, we can do it tomorrow. That is why the break fast at the end of Yom Kippur often has an air of achievement.

When You Should Not Fast

The emotional rigors of the day are made even more stressful by fasting. Sadly, sometimes an elderly congregant must be escorted to an ambulance. The point of fasting is to sweep away earthly distractions, not to put us at risk. Some folks should not fast: the frail, those on certain medications, nursing mothers, children who have not reached the age of bar or bat mitzvah and diabetics. If you cannot fast, you can still participate in the spirit of the day by setting boundaries on what you will allow yourself to eat. Favorite foods, comfort foods, warm foods, foods in abundance, can all be avoided in the spirit of the day.

The stark formality of Kol Nidre sets the holiday's tone of awe and drama. ❧

Kippur we say, "Blessed are You, Eternal One, who has sanctified us through Your mitzvot and commands us to light the Yom Kippur lights."

At the Synagogue

A bit before sundown, while the day is still light, Yom Kippur services begin. The ark is opened and all the Torah scrolls are taken out. They stand before us as escorts and witnesses and perhaps as protectors as we approach God on this most holy of days. They support us and strengthen us in what we are about to do. And what we are about to do is to say two astonishing prayers, proclamations, really.

The first astonishing declaration says, "By the authority of the heavenly court and by the authority of the earthly court, with the consent of the One who is everywhere and with the consent of this congregation, we declare it permissible to pray with those who have done wrong."

> **To Fast or Not**
>
> During the Holocaust, the Nazis often added to the torment of the Jews in the camps by serving sugar and other delicacies only on Yom Kippur. Starving and depleted, the Jews had to decide whether it was a greater service to God to eat, despite the mockery of the Nazis, or to fast.

The images of a court and a judge, so prominent in the Rosh Hashanah prayers, assume center stage here through that declaration. And yet what role do I, the Jew who has come to pray, assume in the context of that declaration? Am I, as a congregant standing in the synagogue, granting transgressors permission to be admitted alongside me? Am I the transgressor who is being granted permission to take part? Am I the entourage of God's court, the emissary of the heavens who joins these earthly proceedings? The answer is that each of us is all three: the voice crowned with authority, the outcast and sinner, the one who is God's partner.

Mistakes, even sins, are part of our humanity. They do not remove us from the presence of God or from the presence of the community of Israel or from our place among our peers. Rather, it is how we respond to our errors, how we correct and learn from our mistakes, that reveal who we are and can become.

The High Cost of Education

A young investor—straight out of school—made a mistake and lost millions of dollars for his company. He was called into the president's office, expecting to be fired. As he stood on the threshold, the president waved him in and asked him to sit down. They spoke for a while about the investment, the promise, the expectation, and what went wrong. At the end of the discussion, the president shook the young investor's hand and returned to his work. Confused, the young man said, "Aren't you going to fire me?" "Fire you?" responded the president. "I just spent a fortune educating you."

The second astonishing declaration is the famous prayer called Kol Nidre, meaning "all vows." Recited three times by the cantor in traditional congregations, each repetition louder than before, this declaration states that all personal vows made between God and ourselves from now until this time next year will be null and void.

Why say such a prayer at the beginning of Yom Kippur? Why, at the time when we gather to promise ourselves and God that we will be better and try harder, do we recite a prayer that annuls those promises?

One popular answer is historical: During one period in our history, Kol Nidre offered a lifeline to some desperate Jews. In Spain in both the 7th and the 15th centuries, Jews were given the following choices: convert to Christianity, leave the country forever, or be killed. It was a horrible choice. Some chose death. Thousands ran away. Many went through the motions of conversion, offering their words but not their spirits. In fact, those *conversos*—called Marranos by the Spanish, meaning "pigs," and *anusim* by the Jews, meaning "those who were threatened and coerced"—secretly remained Jews. When "converting" to Christianity, they had to take an oath in the presence of a Christian court, declaring that they had renounced Judaism. For those Jews, the Kol Nidre prayer was a way to make their vows to Christianity empty and meaningless before God.

Another popular answer is the excesses of human nature. Who among us has never promised more than we could deliver? How many times has business called us away on a child's birthday or during a championship soccer game? How many times have we promised to call? to take time to visit? to exercise more? to be on

Kol Nidre

Traditionally, Kol Nidre is said while it is still light out, for court sessions must be held during daylight. In the Ashkenazic (eastern European) tradition, the declaration of annulment is for vows made between this year and next year. In the Sephardic tradition, the annulment is for vows made between last year and this year.

In the Days Before Thomas Edison

The only time the tallit is worn at night is on Yom Kippur—at Kol Nidre—which, after all, begins during the daylight hours. The last paragraph of the Shma—which speaks of the *tzitzit*, the ritual fringe that is put on the four corners of a tallit—says that you shall see the fringe. The rabbis of old argued that nighttime is not the time of seeing. So we wear the tallit only in the daylight. Once we have put it on for Kol Nidre, however, we take it off only after the *ma'ariv* service.

time? to volunteer? to do a favor? How many times, in our earnestness, do we overreach? How many times have our creations—in clay, ink, words, yarn, food—betrayed us, failed to match the vision of a gift we crafted so meticulously and flawlessly in our minds?

If that happens in our everyday lives, how much more could it happen on Yom Kippur, in our moments of boundless optimism or deepest fear, in those moments when we seek to please God, our families and ourselves. Kol Nidre may have been composed for the *anusim*, but it remains the prelude to Yom Kippur for all of us because it responds to our overreaching, our desperation and our frailty today.

Two more points are relevant. First, only promises made to God are nullified. Promises made to others are not nullified by this statement. They must be kept. Second, we can keep the voided promises anyway. Nullification is not prohibition. The prayer forgives rather than forbids.

When Kol Nidre is over, the Torah scrolls are returned to the ark. The sky has already darkened. We are warmed up, wound up, ready. Now the real work of the day begins. We pray that we can be open to that quiet voice within, honest with ourselves and God, forgiven for our past mistakes, cautious of new ones. We pray that we can become the person we want to be. More than at any other time of year, we are open to molding the future into our legacy and our legacy into a blessing.

We remain that way for the next 25 hours, accompanied by hundreds of pages of prayers, our families and our congregation, a willing heart and a compassionate God.

God as Judge, God as Creator

Throughout the day, the prayers of Yom Kippur depict God as Judge and Creator, Parent and Sovereign. Sometimes God is stern and demanding; at other times, God is loving and understanding. Different prayers express different beliefs and evoke different moods as the day weaves our story from the memories of our lives.

On Rosh Hashanah, it is written, and on Yom Kippur it is sealed: How many will pass away and how many will be born, who will live and who will die, who will become rich and who will be poor, who will become famous and who will be brought low.

This prayer is a call for purpose in the universe. It helps us proclaim, in structures and metaphors that we can understand, that our lives have meaning, that what we do matters, that we should care. The prayers go on to propose that God is not a stern bookkeeper mechanically toting up points for and against us. God is our creator, our teacher, our parent, our coach, who wants us to learn and live and succeed: "We are Your people, and You are our God. We are Your children, and You are our Father. We are Your flock, and You are our Shepherd. We are Your work, and You are our Creator. We are Your faithful, and You are our Beloved. We praise You, and You honor us."

As on Rosh Hashanah, on Yom Kippur the Torah scrolls are dressed in white.

Yizkor

On Yom Kippur, often in the morning, we recite special prayers in memory of our loved ones who have died. We ask that God care for their souls, that they be bound up in the bond of life. All congregants who have suffered a loss recite a private prayer for their loved ones. Then the cantor sings a closing prayer on behalf of all who are assembled: *Merciful God who dwells on high, grant perfect peace to the souls of our beloved who have gone to their eternal rest. Shelter them in Your Divine Presence among the holy and the pure whose radiance is as bright as the heavens. May their memory inspire us to live justly and kindly. May their souls be at peace, and may they be bound up in the bond of eternal life. And let us say "Amen."*

Often, children, even adult children, whose parents are alive leave the sanctuary for the duration of Yizkor.

We recite that prayer and are reminded of the many ways in which we are partnered with God. And God, as it were, is reminded of all the ways God is partnered with us. "We need each other," we are saying to God. "How can You be our Shepherd if you have no sheep? How can You be our Father if You have no children? How can You be our Creator if You have no creation?"

Those words of partnership and mutual connection remind God that justice must be tempered with compassion. We ask in our prayers that God move from the throne of justice on this Day of Judgment to the throne of mercy and from that perspective determine the year's decrees. And if we ask God to do that for us, so we must do it for others.

The Tradition of Partnership

Rabbi Shimon bar Yoḥai taught how God depends on us, as it were. "'This is my God, and I will glorify God' (Exodus 15:2). When I praise God, God is glorified. When I do not praise God, God is not, as it were, glorified. And so it says in Isaiah 43:12, 'You are My witnesses,' says the Eternal One, 'and I am God. When you are My witnesses, I am God. But if you are not My witnesses, I am not God.'"

In the Shelter of One Another

When we address God in these and other prayers, we speak in the plural: "*We* are Your people....*We* are Your flock." On Yom Kippur, Jews do not approach God alone. God may judge us one by one, but we go as a group. Why?

Jews are responsible for one another. We do not abandon one another in times of need. We are fearful of facing God alone. At the time of confession and trial, we stick together as a people, giving support and encouragement to one another. We share the guilt, and we share the blessing: Perhaps I have shone where you have faltered; perhaps your goodness can help offset my guilt.

Rabbi Lawrence Kushner teaches that each of us is born with the pieces of a jigsaw puzzle we are to assemble throughout our lives. Some pieces are missing, however, and some belong to other people. It is through our encounters with others—intimate as well as casual, appointed as well as by chance—that the pieces get redistributed and each person's puzzle takes shape. We need one another to complete who we are.

The rabbis put it this way: When a Torah scroll is sewn together, it becomes holy, and it is forbidden to erase even one letter. But when it is still in segments, it is permissible to make an erasure. That concept represents the souls of the Jewish people—when united, none may blot them out.

In this spirit, when we recite the alphabetic list of our sins on Yom Kippur, as we do so many times, we use the plural: *Ashamnu,* we are guilty; *bagadnu,* we lied; *gazalnu,* we stole; we spoke ill of others; we were stubborn; we gave bad advice; we acted badly, and we caused others to act badly.

Does this text imply that each of us is guilty of the entire list? Of course not. It means that each of us may have committed only one or two of these acts, but we are capable of committing all of them, and we may even be complicitous in their commission by another. We cover for each other. To punish any one of us, God must punish all of us. But in the wake of the Flood, God promised never to do that again.

The alphabetic confession is like any good performance review: It not only tells us what we did in the past but it also tells us what

Yom Kippur services for Jewish soldiers in Brussels, Belgium, during World War I. Our traditions and holy days connect the Jewish community across time and space.

we should avoid doing in the future. And it is an equalizer. It teaches us not to judge another's misdeeds more harshly than we would judge our own. We should not look over our shoulders or down the aisles and say to ourselves, "My mistakes are not half as great as theirs." To string this confession in one long alphabetic chain reminds us that we are not here to measure and compare one another. Judgment will come from somewhere else. But today we are to support and strengthen one another.

Yet another alphabetic prayer of confession is the rhythmically repetitive Al Ḥet: "for the sin that we sinned against You by the hardening of our hearts, for the sin that we sinned against You with foolish speech, for the sin that we sinned against You by eating too much and drinking too hard."

The Al Ḥet is a prayer that stretches on for pages. Yet even as we recite it, we may be tempted to say, "That is not all of it. There is yet more." And we begin to feel engulfed, surrounded, almost swallowed up by the looming presence of what we can do wrong, what we have done wrong. As we confess sin after sin, we wonder how we can ever rise above our past weaknesses, or ever again resist their temptation, for there are so many of them, and we are so small. Then, like a ladder reaching down to us from above, the prayer calls upon us to climb, hope and remember: Repentance, prayer and tzedakah mend the tears in our spirit and reweave the fabric of forgiveness.

Yom Kippur in the Bible

The command to observe Yom Kippur comes from the Bible. It is the day when, in ancient times, all Israel would gather at the Temple in Jerusalem to watch the high priest, the *kohen gadol,* perform the rituals and sacrifices for seeking God's pardon. In the time of the Temple, the high priest performed these duties on behalf of all Israel.

What did he do? First he prepared himself by studying and washing, so that his thoughts would be as pure as his body. Then he took two goats. One was designated the scapegoat, the goat upon which all the sins of Israel would be placed. On that goat's head would be tied a crimson ribbon, and then that goat would be sent into the wilderness.

Strikes Against Oneself

During the recitation of the confessional Ashamnu and Al Ḥet, Jews traditionally beat their breasts as a sign of sorrow and contrition. Because Judaism forbids the mortification of the flesh, we control any impulses we may have to punish ourselves physically for our feelings of guilt by creating a symbolic but significant expiatory act. We make a fist of our right hand (even if we are left-handed) and gently strike our chest above the heart upon the recitation of each verb in the Ashamnu prayer and with the recitation of each line of the Al Ḥet.

The Jewish way of life is, and has always been, varied and a blend of many cultures.

Shlugging Kapores, an Animated Tashlich

On the afternoon before Yom Kippur, some Jews take an animal (a rooster for a man and a hen for a woman), swing it around the head, and say, "This is my atonement, this is my offering, this is my substitute, This rooster/hen shall go to its death instead of me, and I will enjoy a long and peaceful life." The animal is then slaughtered and given to the poor for their holiday meal.

Today, most Jews who perform that ritual, *kaparah* (atonement), do not use a live animal. Instead, they use money, often wrapped in a handkerchief, and ask that the money, which will be donated to tzedakah, be received by God as an atonement for their wrongful deeds.

When Youth's Fancy Turns to Love

The Mishnah tells us that in the Temple period the afternoon of Yom Kippur was one of the most joyous times of the year. After the ritual of the goats and after the high priest exited the Holy of Holies, the thoughts of the young people turned toward earthly matters. The young women of Jerusalem would dress in borrowed white gowns: borrowed to avoid competition, white to avoid extravagance. They would go and dance in the vineyards. They would tease the young men, saying, "Choose from among us the one you like."

Now, we know—and the Israelites knew—that sins are not physical objects that can be bundled up in a kerchief and tied around an animal's neck. Still, it benefited all to see that mistakes and misdeeds could be symbolically cast away (much as we cast away our sins in the form of the bread crumbs of *tashlich*). It makes visible and external that which is invisible and internal and thus strengthens our belief that we, too, can free ourselves of the burden of our undesirable past.

The other goat was then sacrificed to God to atone for the sins of the entire people of Israel. No one was immune from the presumption of sin.

After all this, the high priest was ready for the most difficult and most dangerous part of the ceremony—entering the Holy of Holies. The rabbis tell us that while the whole world is holy, for it is God's creation, the holiest place in the world is Israel. And while all Israel is holy, the holiest place in Israel is Jerusalem. And while all of Jerusalem is holy, the holiest spot in all of Jerusalem was the Temple. And while all the Temple was holy, the holiest spot in the Temple was the Holy of Holies. It was only there, at the holiest spot, that the holiest word (the *tetragrammaton*, God's four-letter name), YHWH, could be said by the holiest person (the high priest) on the holiest day.

It was believed that if the high priest was not properly prepared, he could be struck dead on the spot. But if his thoughts were focused, his intentions pure and his performance flawless, he and the people of Israel would be forgiven their sins. When the high priest went into the inner sanctum, the people waited silently, anxiously, outside. Inside the high priest spoke to God, saying, "Dear God, Your people, the House of Israel, has sinned. Forgive them on this day, as it is written in Your Torah, 'This day shall atone for you, to free you of sin, before God.'"

When the high priest finished his prayer and finished reciting the tetragrammaton, he would come out, face the people and say to them, "God will forgive you." And the people would rejoice.

In many High Holiday prayer books you can find the story of the high priest's service. There is no high priest today. There is no Holy Temple. There are no sacrifices. Instead, we speak to God directly, through the prayers on the page and the prayers in our hearts. We have all become like the high priest, standing before God in our personal inner sanctum, praying to God on our own behalf and on behalf of all Israel.

Jonah

One of the highlights of the day's proceedings is the recitation of the afternoon haftarah, the Book of Jonah. Jonah was a prophet who was called upon by God to tell the people of Nineveh that they would be destroyed if they did not change their wicked ways. Jonah was not pleased at having been called to do God's bidding. He tried to run away by boarding a ship. But the ship hit a squall, and Jonah, believing that it was God's doing and that he was endangering the lives of the crew, had himself tossed overboard, whereupon he was swallowed by a fish. After three days and nights, the fish spit Jonah out onto dry land.

Jonah cast forth by the whale ❧

Like Noah's Dove

In "Jonah, Son of Truth," Devorah Steinmetz wrote:

And why was he called Jonah (*yonah*)? Because he was like Noah's dove (*yona*). Noah sent out the dove three times, and Jonah went out three times. The first time Noah sends forth the dove, she returns to the place from which she started out, bearing no message (Genesis 8:8–9). So, too, when God first sends Jonah forth, Jonah returns to the place from which he started out, without having brought a message. The second time Noah sends forth the dove, she returns with a message—she brings an olive leaf, and Noah understands that the flood waters have abated (Genesis 8:10–11). So, too, when God sends Jonah forth again, Jonah delivers a message to the people. The third time Noah sends forth the dove, she does not return to him (Genesis 8:12)—and this is the strongest message of all. For it is not enough for the dove to announce that the world is habitable once more; it is her silent choice to begin life anew in the world which allows Noah to hear God's command to leave the ark and build a new world (Genesis 8:15–19). So, too, Jonah goes out a third time and does not return. Just as the dove's silence is the loudest message for Noah, Jonah's silence is the loudest message for us. It is Jonah's choice to continue, despite his doubts, which urges us to begin again.

Jonah might have been foolish in trying to hide from God, but he wasn't dumb. He understood what had happened and why, and so now he went to Nineveh to warn the people there to change their ways. When the people and the king heard Jonah's prophecy, they repented and changed their ways, and God spared them. But Jonah was angry.

Jews have puzzled over Jonah's behavior for thousands of years. Why did Jonah try to run away from God, who is everywhere and knows everything? Why did Jonah get angry after he helped save the lives of 120,000 people? And why do we read that book on Yom Kippur?

The Book of Jonah teaches us many lessons: that the purpose of Yom Kippur is not punishment but transformation; that we are responsible for one another; that we are the instruments, the hands, of God; and that we cannot hide from ourselves or God.

Ne'ilah, the Closing of the Gates

At the very end of the day, when the sun has slipped below the horizon, at the time when three medium-sized stars can be seen, after reading hundreds of pages, after reciting Al Ḥet and Ashamnu eight times, we add one more service, one more confession, beseeching God to be kind and compassionate: "Open the gates to us, even at this hour of closing: Hear us, accept us, forgive us. Forgo the harsh decree, rid us of evil, heal our sick, seal us in the book of prosperity and worthiness." Only on Yom Kippur do some Jews have five services: *ma'ariv, shaharit, musaf, minhah* and *ne'ilah*. And only on Yom Kippur are the stakes so high.

The praying is done, the confessions complete: We end as we started, in God's hands, only more hopeful and more trusting. We take leave of the day by saying one time, leader then congregation, that which can never be said enough: "*Shma Yisrael*, Hear, O Israel, Adonai is God, Adonai is One." We say it with a mixture of relief and defiance. Despite what the future may hold, we believe.

We continue, saying three times, leader and congregation together: "Blessed be the name of God's glorious majesty forever and ever."

We end with the statement of unquestionable truth, our ultimate confession of faith:

The Compassionate One is God! The Compassionate One is God!
The Compassionate One is God! The Compassionate One is God!
The Compassionate One is God! The Compassionate One is God!
The Compassionate One is God!

And just in case we don't trust our words, just in case our voices have faltered, or our tears have dried up, we blow the shofar: *tekiah gedolah*, the longest, greatest shofar sound of all. One last cry of sorrow, one last cry of hope, one last chance for God to move from the throne of judgment to the throne of mercy. Such a powerful sound, it seems to gain in strength the longer it is held, drawing to itself all the voices of humanity. And for a moment, our voices become one.

With that, court is adjourned until the next year. And everyone wishes friends and loved ones a healthy, happy New Year.

Lashanah haba'ah birushalayim. Next year in Jerusalem!

Building the Sukkah

Five days after Yom Kippur is the holiday of Sukkot, the Festival of the Booths. Sukkot recalls the Israelites' trek through the desert on the way from Egypt to the Holy Land. We celebrate it by having our meals in booths, which are built just for the holiday, with roofs made of branches, thatch or bamboo. According to tradition, we are to begin building our sukkot (the plural of *sukkah*) right after Yom Kippur. Some interpret this law literally and hammer in the first nail even before breaking the fast. Others allow themselves the benefit of food first and only later begin the task of framing their sukkah.

CHAPTER 8

Sukkot, Shemini Atzeret and Simḥat Torah

The Journey and the Joy

15–22/23 TISHRE

Be seated, be seated, exalted guests. Be seated, be seated, holy guests.

Sit in the shade of the Holy One, blessed be the One.

—FROM THE GREETING WELCOMING ANCESTRAL GUESTS INTO THE SUKKAH

W HEN THE ISRAELITES LEFT EGYPT on their trek to freedom, they took with them only enough food and water for a few days. When their provisions ran out, so did their trust in God. And so did their desire for freedom.

"What good is freedom if we are dead?" they said, shouting at Moses and, through him, at God.

"If freedom means starvation, we'd rather be slaves to Pharaoh. At least in Egypt, we had food."

"A people schooled in the ways of slavery, generation after generation, is not able to uproot from their hearts all at once the legacy of slavery," wrote Aḥad Ha'am, an ardent Zionist who lived in the early 20th century, "nor to be fully free even if the chains have been removed from their hands. But the prophet believes in the power of the ideal, certain that this great ideal can root out the remnants of slavery and create in its stead a new heart, filled with the loftiest of dreams."

That is what God had hoped for the people. And perhaps that could yet come to be. But freedom does not look good on an empty stomach. So the Israelites gathered against Moses and God, raised their fists and flung freedom back toward the heavens. God would learn the limits of humankind: The spirit cannot soar when the body aches.

It would take a miracle to keep the Israelites from returning to Egypt, a miracle every bit as great as the ones that had gotten them out. Food now, freedom later. The desert was a place of learning for both God and the Israelites. To ease the Israelites' thirst, God created a well of fresh water—Miriam's well, it would come to be called—that followed them wherever they went. To ease their hunger, God created manna, a frosty-white, doughlike substance that appeared with the morning dew and assumed the flavor of anything the Israelites wanted.

And yet, no matter how God tried, no matter how God threatened or promised, cajoled or provided, the generation of slaves could not move beyond their slavery. They vacillated between timidity and ḥutzpah. Weak-kneed or insolent, cowardly or mutinous, they could not find the way to be free. Their desires became their new masters. They had no patience, too little trust; they were confused about boundaries and averse to risk.

Despite the lofty aspirations God and Moses had for them, this generation of slaves never rose above the status of their birth. They could not be entrusted with the Promised Land for they had not mastered a key lesson of the Exodus story: We need not be bound by the conditions of our birth or the circumstances of the past. Slavery is a condition, not an identity. With all the help and support they received at the hands of both Moses and God, the former slaves did not see that. So the Promised Land waited for their children, who were born in freedom. God kept the Israelites in the desert for 40 years, enough time for the older generation to die out and for the younger generation, adventurous and responsible, to become leaders. And when, at last, the members of the young

Slavery Is a Condition, Not an Identity

We sometimes forget this, even today. We are taken, or overtaken, by our experiences of hurt or loss or victimization. What happened to us becomes who we are. We slip into bondage with the one who mistreated us or the event that turned our world upside down. With help and encouragement and a ritual of transition, we can leave our personal Egypt and begin our journey afresh. Sukkot lends itself to such a ritual. It is a time when we can leave the constricting walls of our homes and enter the security of God and our people.

generation were ready, God led them into the Promised Land, the Land of Israel.

The Holiday of Journeys and Paradoxes

Sukkot is the third in the cycle of the three pilgrimage holidays. (The pilgrimage holidays, Passover, Shavuot and Sukkot, are called *regalim*, from the word for foot or leg [*regel*], for Jews were to make their way to Jerusalem on each of these holidays.) Sukkot is the quintessential holiday of journey. If Pesaḥ is about departures (for it recalls the Exodus from Egypt) and Shavuot is about arrivals (for it celebrates the giving of the Torah at Mount Sinai), Sukkot is about the journey. It is the holiday that best symbolizes where most of us are most of the time: somewhere in between, midway, sometimes moving, sometimes stuck, always heading—we hope—in the right direction. It reminds us that the way we get somewhere, what we do and learn along the way, where we detour and where we pause, whom we meet and whom we travel with, are as essential to the journey as is the arrival.

The word *sukkot* means "shelters," a comforting image as we focus on the vulnerability and the insecurity that accompany travel. It refers to the temporary structures the Jews build and eat in on this holiday. Like the other pilgrimage holidays, Sukkot has two stories attached to it: the historical and the agricultural. The historical story reminds us of the Israelites' travels in the desert over a period of 40 years and how they were protected and fed by the goodness of God's gifts. The agricultural story reminds us of the time when our ancestors were farmers in the Land of Israel. To ease their work during the fall harvest, and to avoid the need to trek the long way home every night, they would build booths to dwell in, far out in the fields.

We decorate the sukkah with fruits and vegetables that remind us of the fall harvest.

Sukkot is a holiday of paradoxes: We erect a building to mark the holiday of journey; it is the last in the pilgrimage holiday cycle but comes first, after Rosh Hashanah; and we leave the sturdy shelter of our homes for the flimsy shelter of the sukkah (singular of *sukkot*) just as the weather is turning colder (in much of the Northern Hemisphere) and rainy (in Israel). Those paradoxes combine to pose the

Where Do We Seek Shelter?

For 2,000 years of exile, Sukkot symbolized the historical condition of the Jewish people: We were homeless, constantly wandering, reaching toward but unable to enter and possess our land. But the resonance of the holiday changed in 1948. Now our wandering is no longer geographic, no longer political, no longer externally imposed. Now the holiday speaks more to our spiritual journeys than to our physical ones. From what are we alienated? What prevents us from going home? What keeps us trapped, wandering in the desert? Addictions, hatred, fear, jealousy—are these the demons that bar our way home? Where is the home we seek?

The Threshold of the Sukkah Can Be Our Threshold of Healing

Gathering our friends and loved ones around us, standing outside the sukkah, we can speak words of change, commitment to transition and reliance on and gratitude for the support of all those who are present. One by one, the friends can enter the sukkah, making it safe, and demonstrating that we do not have to make this crossing alone. When we are ready, we step across the threshold, shedding the unwanted identity and entering a new space in which we can grow.

question, Where is the true shelter in our lives? Is it in the human constructs of bricks and mortar, in the security of walls of wood and locks of steel? Is it found in the consistency of our thinking? in filtering things out? in not letting other things in? in knowing which is which?

Most days of our lives we find a measure of security in our walls and our bricks and our boundaries. "Good fences make good neighbors." And that security—as God learned in the desert—is essential to our well-being. And yet, there are times when our ordinary world meets extraordinary challenges, when our boundaries are penetrated and our fences fail. What then? What will comfort us in the presence of dangers that walls cannot repel: the dread of illness and loss, the pain of shame and uncertainty, the shadow of hopelessness or despair, the fear of failure, the struggles with aging?

To Jerusalem by Foot

The essence of any pilgrimage is the dedication to the journey, which requires out of the ordinary effort and promises out of the ordinary returns.

The first Jew was born through a journey, when Abraham heeded God's call to "go forth out of your land." The nation was born through a journey, too. We renew those journeys every year.

In the time of the Temple, during the pilgrimage holidays, thousands of Jews crowded into the walled city of Jerusalem. Yet, the ancient rabbis tell us, never was anyone turned away due to lack of space, nor was anyone ever heard saying, "There is not enough room for me to spend the night."

Sukkot reminds us that ultimate security is found not within the walls of our home but in the presence of God and one another. Indeed, there is a midrash that says that sukkot are not buildings at all but the glory of God. This holiday helps us understand that sometimes the walls we build to protect us serve instead to divide us, cut us off, lock us in. The walls of our sukkot may make us vulnerable, but they make us available, too, to receive the kindness and the support of one another, to hear when another calls out in need, to poke our heads in to see whether anybody is up for a chat and a cup of coffee. In contrast, our walls of concrete and steel can enslave us in our own solitude and loneliness. Sukkot reminds us that freedom is enjoyed best not when we are hidden away behind our locked doors but rather when we are able to open our homes and our hearts to one another.

How We Celebrate

The sukkah is the central symbol of this holiday of journeys. It is a temporary structure in which we are to dwell for one week. Most people today decorate it with pictures and hangings, place a table and chairs in it, invite guests and eat there. Some rugged souls sleep there. The structure of the sukkah, as determined by the rabbis of the Talmud, must follow certain rules. It can't be higher than 30 feet, for if it were, it would look permanent. It must have at least three walls, or else it would look too flimsy. The roof, called *sechach,* must be made of cut branches or leaves, to remind us of the harvest. The covering can't be too thin or too full. In the daytime, the roof must offer more shade than sun. In the nighttime, the stars should be seen through the branches and leaves.

But there is more to Sukkot than eating or sleeping in a sukkah.

Sukkot is also a time of harvest and thanksgiving, when we show our gratitude to God for sustaining us on our journey through life. Every day during Sukkot, except on Shabbat, we are asked to take four symbols *(arba'ah minim)* of the earth's bounty—the *lulav* (a palm branch) adorned with myrtle and willow, and an *etrog* (a citron)—and shake them in six directions, as if we are showering the earth with the dew of God's kindness. The Torah tells us, "On the first day [of the holiday], you shall take the product of goodly trees [etrog], branches of palm trees [lulav], boughs of leafy trees *[hadasim]* and willows of the brook *[aravot]*, and you shall rejoice before Adonai, your God, seven days" (Leviticus 23:40).

A lulav and an etrog ❧

Zayde's Lesson

Rabbi Harold Schulweis shares the teaching of his grandfather:
Jewish law states that if guests are invited to the sukkah on the first night and rain begins to fall, one should wait until midnight to eat in the sukkah. Perhaps the rain will stop by that time. But if the invited guests are poor, one should not wait for the rain to stop. Being poor, the guests have most likely not eaten anything all day. For them to wait is discomfort enough. Let them eat with you in the dining room and forgo the mitzvah of dwelling in the sukkah. So taught my *zayde* [grandfather].

Second Harvest

Many towns and communities are serviced by organizations that collect food from restaurants, caterers and hotels and take it to soup kitchens and other centers for the hungry. You can use the holiday of Sukkot as a time to get a synagogue, school, Jewish federation, supermarket, bakery or other institution or business to sign a pledge to contribute to such an organization whenever it holds an event at which food is served.

Writings

There are three parts of the Bible: Torah, Prophets and Writings. On every Shabbat, portions of the first two parts are read. On holidays, tradition likes to weave the Writings into the ritual celebration. The books from the Writings that are chosen for that honor are the ones called *megillot* (scrolls): The Song of Songs is read on Passover; Ruth, on Shavuot; Lamentations, on Tisha B'Av, the day commemorating the destruction of the Temple; Esther, on Purim. In some synagogues, on the Shabbat of *ḥol hamo'ed* Sukkot, the Book of Ecclesiastes, Kohelet, is read.

Sukkot, like Passover, is one week long. The Reform and Reconstructionist movements and the Jews of Israel celebrate the first day and last day as full holidays. The Conservative and Orthodox Jews of the Diaspora celebrate the first two days and the last two days (a remnant of the difficulty of proclaiming the New Moon for Jews beyond the reach of the Rosh Ḥodesh signal). The whole day (or two) is devoted to celebration. The pilgrimage holidays are similar to Shabbat in their traditional observance: no work, no business, no school, no shopping, no building. They differ in two significant ways: On these days, it is permitted to carry in the public domain, and it is permitted to cook and transfer fire.

The next five (or six) days are the intermediate days, the *ḥol hamo'ed*. Holiday prayers are said, the lulav and etrog are shaken every morning, and meals are eaten in the sukkah. But we can go to work, shop, watch movies, do anything we would do on a normal day, unless, of course, it is also Shabbat.

Hoshana Rabba, the Great Hoshana

The period of the Yamim Nora'im, the High Holidays, does not completely end until the seventh day of Sukkot, the day called Hoshana Rabba. *Hoshana* means "please save us" and refers to the lengthy version of the prayer we say during the morning services throughout Sukkot. On the other days of the holiday, we recite that prayer, called Hoshanot, while making one circuit around the synagogue. On Hoshana Rabba, we recite that prayer while making seven circuits. It is on that day, the rabbis tell us, that the book of judgment is finally sealed. On that day, we take the willow branches from our lulav (which we do not use on Shemini Atzeret or Simḥat Torah) and beat them on the ground, a final act of riddance and contrition for all that we have done wrong.

Shemini Atzeret and Simḥat Torah

The last day or days of Sukkot are really two additional holidays: Shemini Atzeret and Simḥat Torah. In Israel and in many Reconstructionist and Reform congregations in the Diaspora, Shemini Atzeret and Simḥat Torah are celebrated together on the eighth day. For others, Shemini Atzeret is the eighth day of the holiday, and Simḥat Torah is the ninth.

The Torah tells us that immediately *after* Sukkot, "On the eighth day, you shall hold a solemn assembly [*atzeret*]; you shall not work at your occupations" (Numbers 29:35). That is all we know about the holiday. Some people think it was a formal way to bring closure

The Ritual of the Four Species

We hold the lulav, *hadasim* and *aravot* in the right hand, much as we would hold a banner or a flag. And we hold the etrog—which looks like a large, bumpy lemon and smells even more fragrant—in the left. When we first pick up the lulav and the etrog, we bring the two together (with the *pitam*, the stem, of the etrog pointing downward) and recite this blessing: "Blessed are You, our Eternal God, who has sanctified us through Your mitzvot and commands us to take the lulav." Then we turn the etrog over so that the *pitam* is facing up, and, still holding our hands together, we shake the lulav and the etrog in front, to the right, in back, to the left, up and down. We do this as if to say, "Do you see these, World? They represent the goodness that God has given us, and we are very grateful."

Ushpizin

Along with friends and relatives, we customarily invite *ushpizin*, the patriarchal leaders of old, to join us for a meal in the sukkah: Abraham, Isaac, Jacob, Joseph, Moses, Aaron and David. Today we invite matriarchal leaders, too: Sarah, Rebecca, Rachel and Leah, Miriam, Deborah and Ruth. Many families invite favorite relatives who are no longer alive and who are sorely missed. Some families create an *ushpizin* mural. Names, sayings and remembrances of loved ones whom they wish to invite are artistically represented. Dinners become times of remembering. We can tell the stories of the lives of our loved ones, repeat their favorite sayings, tell their jokes, recite their achievements.

Diaspora

In Jewish parlance, all the lands outside Israel are called the Diaspora. They are also referred to as *galut*, exile. But these two words are not synonyms. Each totes its own baggage. *Exile* carries the associations of emptiness and estrangement, wandering and being forever unsettled. It conveys a sense that to be a Jew outside the Land of Israel is to live a life of loss, apprehension and incompleteness. In contrast, *Diaspora* evokes images of a hub and spokes, a union of those outside the core connected with those inside. *Exile* means "you cannot go home." *Diaspora* means "choosing to live abroad." Many Jews in the Diaspora, certainly those in the United States and other democratic countries, do not think of themselves as exiles. They sing of Israel as their homeland, but they also feel the blessings of living freely as Jews wherever they have chosen to make their home.

Today Israelis have coined yet a third term: *hutz la'aretz*, outside the land. It is free from the negative connotations of *exile*, but it lacks the connectedness of *Diaspora*. It is a term of comparison, not relationship. No doubt the vocabulary will continue to develop as the Jews of the world and Israel settle into a relationship involving vibrant Jewish communities both within and outside Israel.

Law Is the Way to Freedom

At Sinai, the lessons of freedom began. The Israelites learned that the law—always a bludgeon raised against them in Egypt—could be an instrument of justice and security. They created courts to adjudicate disputes and set up a system of elders to represent the tribes before Moses. They learned to exercise their right to bring just claims against one another—without force, violence or fear of retribution.

The Israelites learned one of the paradoxes of life: Law is a necessary prerequisite of freedom. Without the security of knowing that our domain is inviolable, our body our own, our possessions invulnerable to expropriation by the strongest, without a community that will protect us and fight for us and take up our claim, we would spend all our time guarding our doorways, patrolling our possessions, making and remaking alliances just to survive. There would hardly be time for freedom.

I am reminded of the liberation that law provides every time I go into my kitchen or look for a pair of scissors my children have borrowed. I imagine what it would be like if—out of rapture for total freedom—I never organized my kitchen and never taught my children to put things away. I would spend all my time looking for knives and spoons and carrot scrapers instead of writing new chapters or enjoying my children's company. Order releases us from the tyranny of disorder.

Having taken the first steps toward establishing a legal system, the Israelites were ready to receive the law of God. They were ready to become the keepers of their time and their tasks, to assume the obligations and pleasures of being their own masters; to set forth for the Promised Land. They were ready, in other words, to enter into partnership with God.

Sukkot is a holiday of joy and journey for both the young and the young at heart.

A Living Torah

Elie Wiesel tells the story of a group of Jews who gathered in a barracks in Auschwitz to celebrate Simḥat Torah. In need of a Torah, an old man turned to a young boy and asked him, "Do you remember what you learned in school?"

"Yes," replied the child, "I do."

"Do you remember the Shma?" asked the old man.

"I remember much more," replied the child.

"The Shma is enough," the old man said and lifted the boy into his arms. He began dancing with him as if he were the Torah.

"Never before," Wiesel wrote later, "had Jews celebrated Simḥat Torah with such fervor."

The Torah is as old as our ancestors and as fresh as the youngest Jewish child.

to the long, enjoyable holiday, the last harvest celebration of the agricultural year. With Sukkot, the growing season ends in Israel, and the rainy, wintry season begins. The earth lies dormant until the first stirrings of spring. In Temple times, Sukkot was the most festive of all the pilgrimage holidays, with music and dancing and bonfires and jugglers and all sorts of other entertainers. It was a time of lavish parades around the Temple, with Jews, lulav and etrog in hand, singing prayers asking God to protect and save them.

The rabbis taught that on Sukkot, God determines how much rain will fall during the coming year. In the time of the ancient Temple, a water ceremony with torches and song was held on one of the evenings of Sukkot. It would involve the whole city: children from the priestly class, referred to as the blossoms of the priesthood; men and women; old and young; and "men of deeds," who were honored to lead the way. The rabbis said that you have not seen real celebration if you have never seen Simḥat Beit Hasho'evah, the Sukkot celebration in the Temple.

In the morning, a water libation ceremony cleansed the altar. A golden flask was used to draw water from the nearby springs of Shiloah. The water was brought to the Temple, transferred to a silver bowl and poured over the altar. The libation refreshed the altar, bathing it in waters that came from deep within the earth. No doubt this bore a hint of a sympathetic ritual—as water is poured for good over the altar, so may water pour from the skies for good upon the earth (but only after all the pilgrims had safely returned home!). Shemini Atzeret was the closing of that season of joy and extravaganza.

After the Temple was destroyed, Shemini Atzeret became a holiday without a ritual. We are not asked to eat and sleep in the sukkah on Shemini Atzeret. We do not shake the lulav and etrog either. It became a holiday in search of a cause. So its character was taken over by Simḥat Torah. Simḥat Torah is, after all, really the second day of Shemini Atzeret.

Simḥat Torah, Joy of the Torah, is the day on which we finish the annual cycle of readings and immediately start over again. The holiday is not mentioned in the Bible or the Talmud. It came into its own in the years after the Talmud was completed. In Babylonia, the Jews would read the entire Torah every year. In Israel, they would read it every three and a half years. When the Babylonian tradition became dominant, the holiday was born.

On Simḥat Torah, we read the Torah at night, something that is not done in Conservative and Orthodox congregations at any other time of the year. In the midst of the evening service, all the Torah scrolls are taken out of the ark, often to the accompaniment of singing and dancing. Usually we take from the ark only the scrolls that we will read from on that day. But on Simḥat Torah, we take all the scrolls from the ark.

On other days of the year, we make only one ceremonial *hakafah*, one circuit, around the synagogue with the Torah. On Simḥat Torah, we make seven *hakafot* (the plural of *hakafah*). On other days of the year, the *hakafah* is conducted simply, to the accompaniment of a standard liturgical song, and it lasts but a minute or two. On Simḥat Torah, it is more like a parade, a joyous procession, accompanied by a cascade of songs. We clear away the seats and dance. On other days, only a few people walk around the synagogue escorting the Torah. On Simḥat Torah, everyone joins in. On other days, only one person holds the Torah when it is taken out of the ark. On Simḥat Torah, the Torah scrolls are held by everyone who desires to hold them.

To be given a Torah to hold is to be given a license to dance. The first time one holds the Torah is often a moment of elation as well as a rite of adulthood, like being given the keys to the family car. The one with the Torah leads the dancing but must also be careful not to drop or mishandle the scrolls. Supportive and encouraging, the congregation dances—with abandon and love, with joy and energy. Jews dance in the synagogue and in the halls, on the lawns and on the streets. Some congregations dance for hours, with people coming from miles around to join in the revelry.

But, sooner or later the singing and dancing must stop. We set the Torah scrolls back in the ark, save the one we will read. We open to the last *parashah* of Deuteronomy, the last book of the Five Books of Moses. Those verses record the farewell blessing Moses made over the children of Israel on the banks of the Jordan River just before he died. We read all but the last lines, which tell of Moses' death. We save those for the morning. They are too sad to be

Viewing the Torah from End to End

An increasingly popular tradition is the unrolling of the entire Torah scroll on Simḥat Torah. The letters inscribed in the Torah convey the majesty and the mystery of the Torah, embroidered as they are with the crowns that inspired the rabbis. Column upon column, white space and black ink— not a place on the scroll is empty of meaning. Certain sections of the Torah also proclaim their message visually, like the lightly woven columns of song praising God for the miracles of the Exodus or the staccato lines of the Ten Commandments.

Hands are not supposed to touch the parchment, so in some congregations congregants stand shoulder to shoulder in two facing lines. Each person grasps one end of a long pointer or rod while the person facing him or her grasps the other. The scroll is then unrolled, allowing the parchment to rest on the rods. In other congregations, long scarves or kerchiefs are used for a softer but nonetheless sufficient support.

read that night. The Torah is then put away, and we finish the evening service.

In the morning, we again take out all the Torah scrolls and again make seven *hakafot* around the synagogue. (Now it is just as noisy but usually a bit quicker.) After the *hakafot*, the Torah reading begins again. We read the same verses that we read the night before, repeating them again and again so that everyone who so desires is honored with an *aliyah*. After all the grown-ups (that is, anyone over the age of bar or bat mitzvah) have had an *aliyah,* all the children are called up to the *bimah* together. They gather under a tallit for an *aliyah* called *kol hana'arim* (all the children). An adult accompanies them and says the blessings for them.

Only then, after everyone who wants has had an *aliyah,* are the last verses of the Torah read. The person honored with that *aliyah* is given the title *ḥatan Torah* (bridegroom of the Torah) or, in liberal congregations, when the honor goes to a woman, *kallat Torah* (bride of the Torah). Sometimes, a couple receives this honor.

Why *bride* and *bridegroom*? Because these words conjure up images of devotion and love. They remind us of the metaphor of God and the people of Israel as lovers. They inspire visions of Mount Sinai, when God and the Israelites pledged to be true to each other. On Simḥat Torah, we, too, declare that we have something so special that we cannot imagine living our lives without it. In that context, these titles serve as symbols of our renewed vow to God, our Covenantal Partner.

The last lines of the Torah read:

Moses went up from the valley of Moab to Mount Nebo, to the top of Pisgah, which is across from Jericho. And God showed him all the Land [of Israel], from Gilead until Dan....And God said to him, "This is the land that I promised to Abraham, Isaac and Jacob, saying, 'I will give it to your children.' I have shown it to you for you to see, but you will not go there." And Moses, the servant of God, died in the land of Moab, according to the word of God....And there has not arisen since a prophet in Israel who knew the Creator face to face....

In preparation for reading from the Torah, we undress the scroll after the final hakafah.

We feel the sadness of the Israelites as they watched Moses ascend the mountain, this time never to return. We imagine how alone they must have felt and how frightened, losing the only leader they had ever had. But this, too, is the message of Simḥat Torah: that Judaism is greater than any one person or any one moment, that with God and the Torah we are never really alone, and the sadness of today will be woven into our sacred memories and will be joined with the joy of tomorrow.

So we put aside our sadness and begin again. We close the first Torah scroll, call up the *ḥatan* or *kallat B'reshit* (bride or bridegroom of Genesis), open to the first lines of the second Torah scroll and begin reading: "In the beginning, when God began to create the heaven and the earth, the earth was unformed and void, and darkness was upon the face of the earth. And God said, 'Let there be light.' And there was light. And God saw that the light was good."

And so it begins, the stories of Creation, Adam and Eve, Abraham and Sarah, the promise of the Land of Israel, the Exodus, the people, the Torah—all over again.

The Beginning of Torah Study

Throughout the ages, boys were inaugurated into the world of Torah learning with processions and blessings and sweets. "Five years of age," *Pirke Avot* tells us, "is the time to begin the study of Bible." Today many synagogues initiate their children—both boys and girls—into the study of Torah on Sukkot or Simḥat Torah. The children are called onto the *bimah*, in front of the ark, where the Torah scrolls are held. They may be taught the first line of the Shma, gathered under a tallit and blessed with the good wishes of the congregation. That ceremony is frequently referred to as *consecration*.

Sukkot

The following chart shows the variance in the days that are celebrated during Sukkot through Simḥat Torah.

	Jews in Israel; Reform and Reconstructionist Jews Outside Israel	Conservative and Orthodox Jews Outside Israel
FESTIVAL	Day 1	Days 1–2
INTERMEDIATE DAYS	Days 2–6	Days 3–6
HOSHANA RABBA	Day 7	Day 7
SHEMINI ATZERET AND SIMHAT TORAH	Day 8	Days 8–9

CHAPTER 9

Ḥanukkah

The Festival of Lights

25 KISLEV–2 TEVET

These candles that we light are reminders of the miracles and wonders,

the salvation and the battles that You won for our ancestors...

and on all these eight days of Ḥanukkah, these candles are holy;

we are not to read by them or work by them; we are, quite simply, to admire them.

—WORDS RECITED OR SUNG WHEN LIGHTING THE ḤANUKKAH CANDLES

BARELY EIGHT WEEKS SEPARATE SUKKOT FROM ḤANUKKAH, the next holiday of the Jewish year. Yet that period is the longest stretch of time in the Jewish calendar without a holiday. Tishre—bulging with Rosh Hashanah, Yom Kippur, Sukkot, Shemini Atzeret and Simḥat Torah—is followed by the month of Ḥeshvan, sometimes called bitter Ḥeshvan

(Marḥeshvan), for it is not sweetened with the joy of any holiday other than the semiholiday of Rosh Ḥodesh. That period is in a way reminiscent of the Israelites' long, dry journey in the desert: There were no tragedies, but no new celebrations either, just the steady pace of routine existence.

Isn't that the way things work for us, too? Moments of grand celebration fade into our unremarkable daily routines. Some may call it boring; some may consider it drudgery, tedious, flat. But whatever we think, it is the place where we live most of our lives, in the valley of the everyday—getting milk, sharing news, going to work, straightening the house, talking, arguing and laughing whenever we can. Some people seek to rush past those days. They strain to see—or create—the next celebration. But if we listen closely to the rhythm, we can hear the blessings in the humdrum of the everyday. Just as white space frames the letters of the Torah, so intervals of time frame our celebrations.

The task of life is not to trudge through the mire of the everyday, waiting and longing for the redemptive air of the holidays. The

The Blessings of Routine

At this point in my life I find my greatest comfort in the pace and the peace of the daily routine. At a point when my husband took sick, the burden of his illness was evident in the erratic rhythm and broken patterns of the household: His mug of tea was no longer in the sink in the morning, witness to the late hours he usually kept; his wardrobe had to be changed to accommodate his wound and disabilities; he was not present to help the kids with their homework. The broken routine seared the days.

For me, the trash became the symbol of his illness. My husband was the one who always remembered the nights on which the trash had to be put out. He was the one who always bundled it up and took it to the curb. So each time I walked the cans to the corner, I imagined them full of his illness, only no one was coming to cart it away.

And then, months later, when healing had set in, I caught myself quite casually saying to my husband, "Please, take out the trash." At that moment, I felt the shadow of his illness finally slip away. We were almost whole. Still, it took me a year before I let myself make plans again, before I could trust life enough to make future commitments. The future had betrayed me once. How could I ever trust it again? Today, whenever I open my calendar to record an appointment, I feel I am blessed. The tasks of setting meetings, making school lunches, sweeping the floor, folding the laundry, doing the dishes, checking my calendar, coordinating the children's rides—all these comfort me with their quiet blessings of the stability and the constancy of the routine.

task is to bring the inspiration of the air of the holidays into each of our days.

These quiet weeks between Sukkot and Ḥanukkah teach us to do just that.

But soon the quiet, too, must end. After 40 years of wandering in the desert, the Israelites gathered on the banks of the Jordan and together entered the Promised Land. And after 60 days in the quiet, the next holiday on the Jewish calendar also celebrates the victory of reclaiming the land.

Historical Background

In the year 167 BCE, Israel was ruled by a Syrian king named Antiochus Epiphanes (Antiochus IV), a devout Hellenist who believed himself worthy of worship and was eager to unify his nation in one belief. Jealous of the God of Israel, Antiochus banned the practice of Judaism in his realm. He forbade the Jews to circumcise their sons, learn Hebrew, study the Torah, keep their calendar, observe their holidays or offer sacrifices in the Temple. Instead, he commanded them to sacrifice to his gods, the Greek gods. His other subjects did. The Jews should, too.

Young Jewish men were to attend the gymnasium to learn philosophy, mathematics and science. They were to read the finest of Greek plays, study the best of Greek culture and learn to appreciate that physical beauty is among the highest of values. Most important, they were to give up their "mistaken" ways of Judaism.

To ensure that his decree would be obeyed and that all Jews would disavow the tradition of their ancestors, Antiochus desecrated the Temple, the physical, political and spiritual center of the Jewish people. He captured Jerusalem, set up his own sacrifices in the Temple and dedicated them to his own pagan purposes. In place of the holy altar, which had been consecrated by the sacrifices and the prayers of generations of Jews, Antiochus set up a statue of Zeus, the chief god of the Greeks. Pigs were sacrificed there, an act that symbolized the Temple's ultimate pollution. Antiochus believed that he had defeated the Jewish god. With the Temple desecrated, the ruling class converting to the ways of Hellenism, and their political structures overrun, the Jews could no longer continue to

The Book of Maccabees, one of the uncanonized texts of the Apocrypha, tells the story of Hannah and her seven sons. Captured by Antiochus's troops, one by one, they chose death rather than perform acts of idolatry. This 19th-century engraving by Gustave Doré shows Hannah with her youngest son standing defiantly before Antiochus.

be Jews. They would, thought Antiochus, now become Greeks. And many did.

The Allure of Assimilation

In every generation, even without compulsion, there are Jews who are starstruck by the values, customs, style and success of the dominant culture they reside in. For such Jews, the Jewish way of living—with its texts, laws and beliefs—appears parochial, limited, passé. So it was for some Jews in Antiochus's time. They walked through the open door of Hellenism with joy. They willingly adopted worldly ways: the materialism, the physicality, the veneration of beauty, the allure of philosophy and might, the grandeur of the masculine, the art, the dress and the political structure. They took Greek names. The men joined gymnasiums (surrounded by statues of the patron gods of athletics and the kings) and surgically altered their circumcisions. They abandoned Jewish values and Jewish traditions.

Still other Jews, called *zealots*, shut themselves off from the lure of Hellenism. They closed their ears and averted their eyes, rejecting even that which would enrich their understanding of God's world. Cloistering themselves, they rejected all Hellenizing influences and followed none but the most stringent of Jewish practices. When the Greeks attacked on Shabbat, the zealots chose not to defend themselves, for to do so would profane the Sabbath day. So many of them eventually perished.

Most Jews, however, strode the median. They did not flee Judaism out of distaste for their own ways. Nor did they run to Hellenism, persuaded by the attraction of its ways. And they did not choose to die. Rather, in the face of public confrontation, they outwardly embraced the visible symbols of Hellenism—building pagan altars outside their homes—yet they remained faithful to Judaism in their hearts. Perhaps like the Marranos of Spain, who centuries later were forced to convert to Christianity, these Jews practiced Judaism as best they could in private. They were ripe for a leader who would release them from their bondage to this new pharaoh. So, too, were the mighty few who chose to flee their homes and live in the hills rather than offer even the semblance of abandoning their faith.

One day a group of Syrian soldiers came to the town of Modi'in, just northwest of Jerusalem. They built an altar—as was their wont when they entered new towns—to force recalcitrant Jews to demonstrate publicly their loyalty to Zeus and Antiochus. Now there lived in Modi'in a dedicated Jewish family known as the Hasmoneans: Mattathias, the father, and his five sons. They wanted to lift the burden of conversion off the shoulders of their fellow Jews. And they wanted to prevent the Syrians from winning over still others. They wanted to retake the Temple and rededicate it to God.

When the Syrian soldiers gathered the Jews into the middle of the town, a Jew accepted their call to come forward to prostrate himself before the altar they had built. Mattathias stepped forward and killed him. Knowing this was a declaration of war, Mattathias turned to his brethren around him and said, "Let all who choose God follow me."

For three years Mattathias and his sons led the Jews in a battle against the Syrians. In the beginning, the Jewish army was small. The soldiers hid in caves and fought in small bands. They gathered faithful recruits from town to town, and as their number grew, so did their power. Soon they fought in open battle.

Mattathias was old and died during the war. His son Judah Maccabee rose to take his place. Under Judah, the Jewish army led successful guerrilla attacks against the Syrians. After winning many smaller victories, the Maccabees waged the most important battle of all: the fight for Jerusalem. The war had run for several years, but at a critical moment the Syrian military leadership found its attention being drawn elsewhere. So with other armies on the move against Syria, the Maccabees found an opportunity to make a truce with their enemy. And they did.

The Jews controlled Jerusalem once more. They quickly went to the Temple and destroyed the statue of Zeus. They took apart the altar upon which Greek sacrifices had been made. They cleaned out the halls and the courtyards and rededicated the Temple to God and the Jewish people. That is how Ḥanukkah got its name, for Ḥanukkah means "dedication."

Legend has it that when the Jews began to clean the Temple, they found just one small cruse of consecrated olive oil, the only kind that could be burned in the Temple. There was enough oil to burn for only one day, although the restorations and the manufacture of new oil would take at least a week. Still, the Jews lit

Where Was God?

Where was God in the story of Ḥanukkah? For those who believe that God works in this world not only through miracles but also through the daily efforts and achievements of humankind, God's fingerprints may be found on the victorious battle. Perhaps it was God who caused the Syrians to choose a truce. Perhaps it was God who gave the Maccabees the strength to resist after others had lost their will. Perhaps it was God who gave the Maccabees the wisdom and the talent to lead the Jews in war as well as in belief. Perhaps it was God who gave the Jews the faith to fight as David fought against Goliath. Perhaps it was God who gave the Jews the faith to light that one cruse of oil when they knew it would not be enough. Perhaps it was God who made the oil last.

Mattathias and the apostate. Mattathias was enraged by and slew a fellow Jew who desecrated the altar in Modi'in.

that little bit of oil. It burned for eight days and eight nights. Its flame went out only when the new oil was ready. From that time to this day, we say that a great miracle happened there, and sing the words in a song.

Weaving a Miracle

Many of the beliefs and practices that were developing in Hellenistic culture around the time of the Maccabees form the foundation of modern society: democracy, philosophy, science and theater. Today Jews enjoy, study or take part in all these pursuits. So it is and has been with other places where Jews live and have lived. The style of our clothes, the food we eat, the languages we speak and the architecture of our synagogues—all reflect the various cultures that have surrounded us. The challenge for Jews throughout the ages has been how to live in two civilizations: the civilization of Judaism and the civilization of our host or majority culture.

The Hasmoneans understood that it is not all or nothing. Their grandchildren's names reveal it: Hyrcanus, for example, is a Greek name. Perhaps, then, one more miracle of Ḥanukkah is that Jews throughout the ages have intuitively managed to weave into the culture of Judaism certain ways of the world without losing our identity or our purpose or our Covenant with God. And at the same time, we have given the world gifts of beliefs, values and hope.

The Emergence of Ḥanukkah

Like Simḥat Torah, Ḥanukkah is not mentioned in the Bible, having been created after the closing of the biblical canon. It is mentioned briefly in a few lines of the Talmud, although most premodern holidays have an entire Talmudic book devoted to them. History itself threatened to cancel its appearance, for the Temple the Maccabees rededicated was destroyed some 200 years later. It is its own miracle that the Jews preserved the celebration of a realized dream even after the dream had been reduced to ashes.

The political message of Ḥanukkah, a message of military prowess and national sovereignty, of David versus Goliath, of daring and winning, lay quietly in the embers of Jewish tradition for 2,000 years. The rabbis, after the destruction of the Second Temple, and with it the second Jewish commonwealth, played down those aspects of the holiday. Choosing a haftarah text that reframes the message, they portrayed the holiday as evidence of the saving compassion of the Almighty God: "'Not by might nor by power but by My Spirit,' says Adonai Tzva'ot, the Lord of Hosts" (Zechariah 4:6).

A Widow's Bravery

The Book of Judith, part of the Apocrypha, is associated with the holiday of Ḥanukkah. It is the story of a Jewish widow in ancient Israel who saved her city from a devastating siege by entering the enemy camp under the ruse of defecting from her fallen people. She seduced Holofernes, the general of the besieging army, got him drunk and cut off his head. Legend has it that she fed him warm milk mixed with a stronger brew during their meal together; therefore, some Jews serve milk products on Ḥanukkah to remind us of that act of heroism.

But the message of political sovereignty was rekindled by the birth of Zionism, the movement of a small but determined group of people who sought to reclaim the sovereignty, dignity and national identity of the people Israel against the greatest of odds. And they won. The 20th century saw the State of Israel struggle to be born, to free herself from those who had occupied her and sought to deprive her of her liberty. Israel's army grew from a small band of ragtag fighters to a world-class military force. It secured her borders and reunified Jerusalem. Israel reclaimed the Western Wall, the last standing glory of the ancient Temple that the Maccabees had fought to redeem.

Judith and Holofernes ❧

Listen to the words of the prayer we recite on Ḥanukkah:

> In the days of Mattathias, son of Yoḥanan, the Hasmonean high priest, and in the days of his sons, a cruel power arose against Israel, demanding that they abandon Your Torah and ignore Your laws. You, in Your great mercy, stood by them in their time of trouble. You fought their battle, took up their cause, became their champion. You delivered the mighty into the hands of the weak, the many into the hands of the few, the impure into the hands of the pure, the wicked into the hands of the righteous, the wrong ones into the hands that observe Your Torah....Then Your children came back to Your Temple and cleaned and purified Your sanctuary and lit the lights in Your sacred courts and established these eight days of rededication as a time of thanksgiving and praise of Your Holy Name.

This is a prayer of today as much as a prayer of yesterday. Instead of rededicating the Temple, we have rededicated the State. Even as Ḥanukkah kept the dream of return alive, so the return to Israel has kept the story of Ḥanukkah alive.

Yet Hellenism was not completely abhorred. Even the Maccabees showed signs of Hellenistic influence. Unlike the zealots, for example, they chose to fight on Shabbat if attacked, knowing that this one desecration was necessary to allow them to celebrate future Shabbatot (plural of *Shabbat*). It was a bold—some would say blasphemous—decision of accommodation, one that would eventually

Maccabiah

Today, every four years, Jews from around the world compete in sports and games—a Jewish Olympics—under the banner of the World Maccabiah Games sponsored by the State of Israel.

The emblem of the modern State of Israel includes a seven-branch menorah that is styled after the Temple's candelabrum. On either side are olive branches symbolizing the desire for peace, and, at the bottom, is the name Yisrael.

be codified by the rabbis of the Talmudic period. In a similarly brazen move, the Maccabees declared a holiday to mark their victory, an act that was more Hellenistic than Jewish.

As citizens of the world, as travelers within cultures different from our own, as users of modern technology, we are influenced by the ways of our neighbors. It has always been that way with us. Our stories, our foods, our literature, our understanding of Jewish law, have all been influenced by the cultures around us. The question is not whether we should be so influenced but how self-conscious are we about it and how shall we respond. Where should we draw the line of accommodation? Where do our values clash with those of the majority culture, and where do they coincide? How should we respond to fellow Jews who differ from us regarding cultural accommodation? Who is to guide us?

Celebrating Ḥannukah

The Maccabees recognized the historic nature of their victory and the need to codify the celebration. They legislated the dates and the contours of the festivities much as we know them today. Ḥanukkah begins on 25 Kislev, lasts eight days (some think that the number was chosen as a reenactment of the holidays of Sukkot and Shemini Atzeret, which the Maccabees were unable to celebrate during the war) and involves lights. One of the great paradoxes of Ḥanukkah is that for all their desire to preserve and protect Jewish tradition, the Maccabees enacted one of Judaism's most daring innovations: They created, designed and mandated the celebration of the first postbiblical holiday.

That Ḥanukkah's traditions have remained constant throughout the ages is in large measure due to the ancient rabbis who preserved it. Indeed, not all celebrations designated by the Maccabees fared as well. One that did not is Nicanor Day, which marked the victory of the Maccabees over a high priest who had been appointed by the Syrians as part of the peace settlement. That day—perhaps the only Jewish holiday that ever celebrated the defeat of a Jew by other Jews—and others of its kind disappeared from our collective memory.

Although Ḥanukkah does not have a Talmudic *tractate*—a Talmudic book—of its own, the creators of the Talmud noted the holiday by debating the laws of lighting the candles. "What time of day is appropriate for lighting the ḥanukkiyah [Ḥanukkah menorah]?" they asked. "Should you light eight candles the first night and diminish the number every night thereafter, reminiscent of the diminution of the oil, or should you light one candle the first night and increase the number every night thereafter, reminiscent of the growing wonder of the miracle?" The answer is given in the Talmud, *Shabbat* 21a: It is best to light the candles at nightfall, when the last customers are leaving the market. Light one candle the first night, and increase the number every night thereafter, for we opt for the growing sense of wonder and not its diminution.

The purpose of the candlelighting is to proclaim the miracle of the Temple's restoration. Therefore, each Ḥanukkah menorah—which is designed to resemble the seven-branched menorah of the Temple, but has eight branches to symbolize the eight days of Ḥanukkah plus one extra for the *shammash*, the helper—is to be placed in a window for all to see.

How to Light the Ḥanukkah Candles

Put the candles in the menorah, starting from the right, one candle for each day of Ḥanukkah up to the present night. Then, add one more candle in the special place reserved for the *shammash*, the extra candle that is the helper. Since we are not allowed to use the Ḥanukkah candles for anything but celebration, we light the candles using the *shammash*.

Once the *shammash* is lit, the blessings are recited. The candles are then lit, beginning with the newest candle, on the left, and moving toward the candle representing the first day, on the right.

Ḥanukkah candles are like Shabbat candles in that we let them burn out by themselves.

On *erev Shabbat*, the evening we welcome Shabbat, we light the Ḥanukkah candles first, and then the Shabbat candles. At havdalah, when Shabbat is over, we light the havdalah candle first and then the Ḥanukkah candles. These variations are due to the law that prohibits kindling fire on the Sabbath.

In years past, when it was not safe for us to show our pride and celebrate openly, Jews were encouraged to light their candles discreetly, away from the windows. But today we are free, and our broad living room windowsills are perfect places at which to light our candles.

Some families choose to light one menorah, or ḥanukkiyah, together. Others choose to light a ḥanukkiyah for each family member.

Places of Holiness

The job of lighting the seven-branched menorah described in the Torah belonged to the priests of old. But there is no more Temple in which to light other cruses of oil. Instead, today our homes have become the heirs of the Temple, and we have become the priests. "The stones of the ruined Temple were scattered around the world," a midrash tells us. Wherever the stones fell, a place of holiness was built: a synagogue, a school, a home. Our homes are embassies of the Temple that stood so long ago.

On the eighth day of Ḥanukkah we light all eight candles plus the shammash.

An Oil Ḥanukkiyah

Most of us use wax or tallow candles to celebrate the miracle of the oil. And yet an increasing number of Jews are returning to a more authentic ritual: lighting an oil *ḥanukkiyah*. Many Judaica shops sell such candelabra, whose little bowls hold just enough oil to burn for a half hour. Those same stores often stock adapters for candles, so you can choose your medium. And they also sell glass inserts so you can change your candle *ḥanukkiyah* into an oil one. The most user-friendly oil *ḥanukkiyot* (plural of *ḥanukkiyah*) have a place for a wax *shammash*.

Children and adults alike may make their own, which they can use year after year. All sorts of materials can be used: treated wood, clay, bottle caps, assorted glass candle holders individually arrayed. The two things to remember as you craft your *ḥanukkiyah* is that each flame must be visibly distinguishable from the others when it burns and that the holder for the *shammash* should be set apart from the other holders, usually by placing it in a raised position.

Menorah Versus *Ḥanukkiyah*

Technically a menorah is a seven-branched candelabrum that illuminated the Temple. It is the symbol that adorns synagogues and appears on the emblem of the State of Israel. A *ḥanukkiyah* is the eight-branched candelabrum (with one extra branch for the *shammash*), used exclusively for the Ḥanukkah lights.

There are two blessings that we recite as we light the Ḥanukkah candles. The first is over the candles themselves: "Blessed are You, the Source of Life, who has sanctified us through Your mitzvot and commands us to light the Ḥanukkah lights." The second is over the miracle: "Blessed are You, Eternal One, who worked miracles for our ancestors in those days at this very time of year."

This second blessing says *miracles* instead of *miracle*. Tradition has identified two miracles of Ḥanukkah: one military, one supernatural. We can add two more. In the face of the enemy's overwhelming might and an inadequate supply of oil, the Jews dared to fight and they dared to light. Sometimes the miracle is not winning or achieving but daring to try. A sign in a girls' high school says, IT ISN'T OVER WHEN YOU LOSE. IT'S OVER WHEN YOU QUIT.

Rabbi Alfredo Borodowski teaches that the miracle of Ḥanukkah can also be called the miracle of constancy. Were we to have walked into the Temple at any time during the eight days on which the oil was burning, we would not have noticed that a miracle was under way. There was no herald of the miracle, no sign. All would have looked normal to us, the visitors. It would have been only with the knowledge that the oil had burned yesterday and the day before and the day before that, that the miracle would have become evident. So it is with the world around us: Miracles happen in the quiet constancy of their unfolding.

The December Dilemma

The sociologist Egon Mayer estimates that today one million Jewish households count non-Jews as members of their families. It is no wonder, then, that December presents great challenges to many families' holiday celebrations. Differing levels of religious interest and commitment may also cause difficulties in families where both husband and wife are Jewish.

When one of my sons was very young, he told me emphatically that he wanted to be Christian. Calmly reminding myself that he was only three and therefore that this was neither a theological rejection nor a permanent life decision, I asked him why. He answered that he wanted Christmas lights on our house. How much more powerful is the attraction of Christmas in families with mixed religious traditions.

Watching a spouse put up a Christmas stocking for your newborn can open doors to an identity that had been tucked away. Having your children watch their cousins enjoy the presents, magic and warmth of Christmas can lead to some stressful conversations. Adding to the stress is the recognition that holiday celebrations involve not only immediate household members but also close friends and extended family. Trying to do right by everyone else's desires and needs while trying to be true to yourself can be quite taxing.

During this time of year, most Jewish newspapers run articles meant to help families manage the holiday season. Rabbis and friends are also good sources of advice. In the meantime, here are a few suggestions that may help:

1. Begin with You. Before dealing with everyone else, focus on what you want and need. What symbols do you want in your home to express who you are or who you are becoming? If you have children, what symbols and experiences do you want etched into their memories? Your loved ones will make claims on you, as friends and family members have a right to do. You can best be prepared to respond to them with understanding, patience, clarity and generosity when you know what you want.

2. Talk It Over with Your Spouse or Partner. Clearly communicate what you need. Work out ways in which he or she can either be a part of your celebration, or give you the room—literally and figuratively—to celebrate by yourself.

3. Choose One Tradition for the Children. Children enjoy sharing in others' celebrations. They understand going to a friend's birthday party or an aunt's wedding. Their ability to share makes it easy for them to be involved in all kinds of family holiday celebrations. It must be made clear in any celebration, however, whether they are celebrants or spectators, for children need to know who they are. Simply exposing them to the beauty of various traditions and then permitting them to choose when they get older does them a disservice. They never have the benefit of being fully immersed in the fullness of any one tradition. And to expect them sometime later to choose one parent's religion over the other is in reality to ask them to choose one parent over the other.

4. Set a Year-Long (or longer) Schedule of Holiday Celebrations. Where you celebrate each holiday is often more important to a family than how you celebrate it. In discussion with your immediate and extended family decide on your itinerary of holiday celebrations and then send out a written copy to everyone. This is not a panacea, but it can avert recurring arguments and can show that everyone's needs have been considered.

5. Try to Help Everyone Stay Focused on the Religious Integrity of the Rituals and the Symbols. Compromise is great, but not when it violates religious boundaries. No reindeer-shaped Ḥanukkah candles!

As for my son—he was proud of being a candle in his school's Ḥanukkah presentation a few years later. He danced with joy and spun like a dreidel when we sang songs after lighting his *ḥanukkiyah*, the one made from clay and nutshells. He diligently makes up his wish list of Ḥanukkah presents with his siblings. For now, at least, he is pleased that he is a Jew.

The glory of a wedding day may be a sacred, once in a lifetime experience, but reciting the Sheheheyanu blessing on each anniversary invests the miracle of lasting love with sanctity and awe.

What Counts as a Miracle?

Does the miracle reside in the act or in our sense of wonder? When couples still love each other after 30 years together, is that a miracle? Is it a miracle when rivers or lungs cleanse themselves after we stop polluting them? Is it a miracle that we are born hardwired to learn grammar? or that new families of antibiotics are discovered almost as quickly as old ones lose their punch? or that we have the capacity to treat many cancers? or that some inexplicably disappear spontaneously? or that we dare to hope in the face of despair?

There was the time when crisis struck my household. With five children, the youngest of whom was only one and a half years old, we needed help immediately. I placed a phone call to a nanny agency, then to a young woman one state away. The next day she arrived at our house in the middle of a snowstorm, bags and all, ready to work. She stayed six months, just enough time for us to get back on our feet. And then she left. We have stayed in touch, and when she comes to visit, she appears to be flesh and blood. But I secretly believe she is Elijah in disguise, the prophet who was called to heaven in a fiery chariot and who is rumored to return to earth to help those in need.

Where is the realm of miracles? Is it in the human experience or in the human spirit?

On the first night of the holiday, we add the Sheheheyanu, the blessing that is recited at the beginning of every holiday.

The Hanukkah candles are celebrative, decorative. They are not to be used for their light or their warmth. That is one reason we have the *shammash,* the assistant, the candle we use to light the other candles. It prevents us from accidentally lighting one celebrative candle with another, thereby improperly using it. Should we accidentally use the Hanukkah candles to look for the match we dropped or to read the words of the blessings, we are covered by the presence of the light of the *shammash.*

The rabbis asked that we put our Hanukkah menorot (plural of *menorah*) in our windows so that everyone who sees them can be reminded of the miracle, much as families today place replicas of storks on their lawns to announce the birth of a child or hang flags from their houses in honor of Memorial Day. And although the preferred time to light the menorah is nightfall, when it is just getting dark and people are returning home, we can light it later, when all the members of the family can gather or friends have joined us.

It is a tradition among women that no work be done while the Hanukkah lights are burning. Instead, it is a time for rest and pleasure. (Perhaps it is time to make longer-lasting candles.)

In addition to lighting candles, we recite Hallel, the special collection of holiday psalms, every morning of Ḥanukkah and add a prayer to the blessings of the Amidah. The addition to the Amidah recounts the story of Ḥanukkah, "when the cruel Greek kingdom rose against the Jews, to force them to forget God's Torah and abandon God's ways, and how You, God, in Your kindness and mercy, stood with the Jews in their time of distress and fought their fight, delivering the strong into the arms of the weak...." Often Jewish prayer is more than a recitation of praise or petition. It is also a sacred storytelling.

Sharing Dinners

Everyone—young and old, novices and veterans—can light the Ḥanukkah candles. Candlelighting, then, is a perfect time to invite friends and family members who want to celebrate. The refreshments (often the hardest part of any celebration) are easy: *latkes* (potato pancakes), sour cream, applesauce, a green salad with olives if you like, doughnuts and chocolate "coins" for dessert. A bit of wine or grape juice (just for drinking; there is no Kiddush on Ḥanukkah), nuts (for the dreidel game) and dried fruit (to remind us of winter's fare and that the fresh fruits of summer are still months away). Light as many *ḥanukkiyot* as fire laws and windowsills allow and top off the event with songs, gifts and good conversation.

Over the past 100 years, the most popular way for children to celebrate Ḥanukkah has been for them to play with a dreidel (a four-sided top; *sevivon* in Hebrew), to eat nuts as a treat (doubling as chits) and to receive a bit of Ḥanukkah *gelt* (money). Today, while the dreidel may have difficulty claiming victory over fantasy games and computerized gizmos, there are times when the simple thrills of a top, sibling competition and luck can prove irresistible.

On each side of the dreidel is a letter indicating one word of the saying *Nes gadol hayah sham*, meaning "A great miracle happened there." *There* refers to Israel, and a *great miracle* refers to the rededication of the Temple. The players spin the dreidel in turn. The letter that lands facing up indicates what the player is to do—for example, add a chit to the pot or scoop up the contents of the pot.

Some Jews are beginning to make the eighth day of Ḥanukkah a special day of giving. Instead of getting another pair of gloves, they may give a pair to the homeless. Instead of getting another toy, the children may give one to the local homeless or battered-women's

A dreidel showing the Hebrew letter hay on top and gimmel on the side ✑

Here or There?

In Israel they say, "A great miracle happened here."

Part of the fun of playing dreidel is developing a spinning technique. For example, some players begin their spins on a solid surface; others begin midair and let the dreidel drop.

shelter. Instead of getting Ḥanukkah gelt, friends may give tzedakah. Ḥanukkah comes at a time when the weather turns cold and poor people's needs increase. So some Jews help schools and synagogues organize drives to collect coats, boots, gloves and blankets for the needy to use during the wintry weather.

When the last Ḥanukkah candles burn out, the darkness of winter is once again around us. But we have entered a new month; the days will begin to lengthen. Spring will soon be here.

Where It Will Stop No One Knows

While there are several meanings that the Hebrew letters on the dreidel can have, usually the *nun* stands for *nisht*, Yiddish for "nothing," so the one who spun neither gives nor gets anything. *Gimmel* stands for *ganz*, Yiddish for "all," so the one who spun takes everything in the pot. *Hay* stands for *halb*, Yiddish for "half," so the one who spun takes half the pot. *Shin* stands for *shtell*, Yiddish for "put," so the one who spun adds one to the pot.

Fun Day

What to do on December 25? More and more synagogues, day schools, Jewish groups, YM/YWHAs and Jewish Community Centers are organizing community play or social-action programs for the Jewish community on Christmas. Volunteers replace police officers at desk jobs, carry out nonmedical tasks in hospitals, serve food at soup kitchens. Congregants might gather at synagogues to cook hundreds of meals to be frozen and distributed later to a homeless shelter. Schools and JCCs run carnivals or crafts programs for kids, often with a social-action component built in (admission might be an extra pair of gloves, a few cans of food, an old coat, or an old towel to be used to make sleeping bags).

Candle Making

In December, as the Western world is readying itself for its Christmas celebrations, stores and mail-order houses stock all sorts of candle-making kits for adults and children. Since there are so few ritual preparations to get us in the mood for Hanukkah, making candles can fill the gap. Several weeks before the holiday (perhaps on or about Rosh Hodesh Kislev, the beginning of the month in which Hanukkah falls), plan to order or shop for candle-making supplies. You can buy colorful woven beeswax, which simply needs to be rolled into shape; cheery, malleable wax, which can be sculpted into figures; or plain candles that can be warmed in water and twisted, braided or fashioned according to one's fancy. Perhaps there is even a candle or crafts store near you that can help you create a candle-making party. Don't forget to give perfumed candles a try as well. Making Hanukkah an aromatic as well as a visual celebration enhances the moment and the memories.

What Do We Eat?

In America, the traditional Hanukkah food is *latkes,* potato pancakes. People say we eat latkes because of the oil used in the frying, which reminds us of the miracle of the oil. In Israel, the traditional Hanukkah food is doughnuts, called *sufganiot.* They are fried in oil too, and likewise remind us of the miracle of the oil.

Latkes can be made with white potatoes, sweet potatoes, zucchini, other vegetables, or even with cheese.

The Fast of the Tenth of Tevet

"Zedekiah was 21 years old when he became king, and he ruled for 11 years…. He rebelled against the king of Babylon… and on the tenth day of the tenth month, Nebuchadnezzar attacked Jerusalem with his whole army" (Jeremiah 52:4). The city remained under seige for two years, until the walls were breached. Zedekiah was captured, his sons murdered and Jerusalem destroyed. The Fast of the Tenth of Tevet lasts from the first morning light until nightfall.

The slaughter of Zedekiah's sons

CHAPTER 10

Tu B'Shevat

The New Year of the Trees

15 SHEVAT

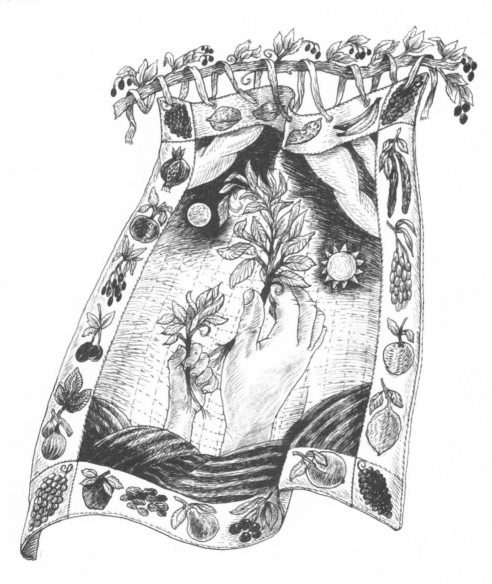

Rabbi Yoḥanan ben Zakkai said,

"If you are holding a seedling in your hand

and you hear that the Messiah is coming,

plant the seedling and then go and greet the Messiah."

—AVOT DE RABBI NATAN

I MAGINE PARADISE WITHOUT TREES. Imagine lullabies, summer camp, the grand sweep of a boulevard, or autumn's canvas—imagine any one of them with no trees. Is it any wonder that God chose to put the first people in a garden of trees? "And God planted a garden in Eden…and God made to grow from the ground all sorts of trees, pleasant to look at and good for eating" (Genesis 2:8). Tending to the trees was Adam and Eve's only divinely ordained task.

Do Not Be Wasteful

Do not destroy mindlessly. *Bal tash'ḥit!* That is a basic principle of Judaism. Cutting down the rain forest needlessly, spewing harmful smoke into the air, failing to recycle, even beautifying our lawns with the excessive use of chemicals—all this wastes and endangers the earth's precious and limited resources.

Shemittah

The Torah tells us that just as we rest every seventh day, the earth must rest every seventh year. This is called the *shemittah* year and is observed in Israel to this day. The land needs time to replenish itself; otherwise, its nutrients will dry up, and its crops will wither. And we need to be reminded that we are stewards, not owners, of the land.

Tu B'Shevat reminds us that conserving the earth's natural resources, such as trees, petroleum and clean air, is a Jewish issue. ❧

Trees give us oxygen and wood, shade and fragrance, fruits and forests, paper and syrup, landscapes and almonds. We could no more live on this earth without trees than we could live without sunshine, air or water. And since the power to plant and destroy trees is in our hands, Judaism gives us a holiday to celebrate them.

Tu B'Shevat is a holiday that calls us out-of-doors. Most days, we dwell in our houses and in other climate-controlled environments, dashing from home to car to office to store, often ignoring—with casual, costly neglect—the state of the world around us. The radio tells us of the weather outside. We live under the heavens all our lives, but most of us can't tell the difference between Sirius and Cygnus. Living in and around the cities, we can hardly see the stars. Yet now and then we feel our loss and seek refuge and peace in the nature we have ignored.

Tu B'Shevat is a holiday of nature, the New Year of the Trees. It reminds us that we are children of the garden of Eden. We remember that we live off the gift of the earth's resources, that some of those resources are renewable and some are not, that we have the power to transform them into blessings as well as curses, and that no one can do it but us. We can chase away night's darkness with the flip of a switch. We can drive from Maine to Arizona to Wyoming on an unbroken network of highways. We can buy our one-serving, two-serving or family-size containers of fast foods, all packaged according to our needs and our lifestyles. These are blessings. But they come with a price.

Tu B'Shevat comes to remind us that in the midst of all this goodness we are stewards, not just consumers, of the earth and its produce. We must not leave a legacy of waste and poison as we satisfy our appetites and our needs. If we do not pay the price now, we will choke the earth and condemn our children.

Orlah and Ma'aser

Truth be told, however, Tu B'Shevat did not start out as a holiday with these ethical messages. It didn't have special celebrations or stories to tell or prayers to say. Originally it was a legal tool for counting the age of a tree, which was important for two reasons: *orlah* and *ma'aser.*

Orlah is the name given to fruit produced during a tree's first three years. According to Jewish law, that fruit may not be eaten or sold. It is set aside, left alone, as a reminder that all food comes from God. The question is, How do we know how old a tree is for the purposes of counting *orlah*? Since a tree may be planted at any time, it would be difficult to remember each tree's age. Jewish law established 15 Shevat as the birthday of all fruit-bearing trees. Come 15 Shevat, every tree is one year older.

Ma'aser, meaning "tenth" in Hebrew, is the name of a particular gift of fruits given to the Temple. Every year the Jews who lived in Israel had to give a tenth (a tithe) of their new fruits to the Levites and the priests who worked in the Temple. It was a way to thank God for the rain and the sun and the fertile earth, as well as a way to support the Levites and the priests, who were not permitted to own land (or trees).

But the question arose: Given that fruit ripens over a period of time, as a part of which year's harvest should the fruit be counted? The rabbis determined that for the sake of tithing, the agricultural year would begin on 15 Shevat, for by that time the winter rains had mostly stopped and the old crop had been harvested. All fruit that ripens on and after 15 Shevat would be counted as part of the coming year's crop; all fruit that ripened before 15 Shevat would be part of the previous year's crop.

After the Temple was destroyed, Jews no longer tithed. No Temple, no gifts. No gifts, no counting. Only *orlah* gave Tu B'Shevat any purpose. The day became another part of the spring rituals, like the morning the linens are aired after the winter rains stop, or the day the plow breaks the soil in the thawing spring ground.

The Transformation of Tu B'Shevat

Four hundred years ago, a small group of Jews immigrated to Palestine from places all around the Mediterranean and settled in the northern town of Safed. These Jews were *kabbalists,* mystics, people who believed that ever since Creation hidden sparks of holiness have been trapped in the material world. Before Creation, they believed, God had filled the universe. To make room for the material world, God contracted, withdrew, moving over to make space

A Prayer for Trees

Trees and their fruit are so important in Judaism that there is even a special prayer we say when we see the first buds of spring: "Blessed are You, Adonai, our God, Sovereign of the universe, who has not withheld anything from the world, who created in it wonderful creatures and good trees for people to enjoy."

A Wedding Canopy

A custom reaching back to the Talmudic period suggests that on Tu B'Shevat we plant a cedar for every boy born the previous year and a cypress for every girl. When a man and woman marry, branches from their trees can be cut and used to weave their *huppah,* their wedding canopy.

for the matter about to be created. Yet a world of matter without godliness would be a barren shell. So God created vessels that could carry the Divine Presence into the material world. At first, all was fine. But as the flow of holiness grew, the pressure of the Divine became too great for the worldly matter, and the vessels burst. The sacred was trapped in all the physical shards of the world. Our task, according to the mystics, is to release those holy sparks and let them reunite with their source.

We can do this, the kabbalists believed, every time we perform a mitzvah, as long as we carry it out with the proper intent. By celebrating Tu B'Shevat in the right way, by attending to the hidden sparks in nature, the kabbalists thought, Jews could release the holiness.

Wanting to use every opportunity, the kabbalists developed a Tu B'Shevat seder, which they modeled on the Passover seder. They drank four cups of wine, each one darker than the one before—white, pink, rosé and red. They ate certain kinds of fruits: those whose outsides cannot be eaten (like nuts), those whose insides cannot be eaten (like cherries); those that can be eaten in their entirety (like raisins).

For many years, the Tu B'Shevat seder was celebrated only by the kabbalists. When they began to die out and disappear, Tu B'Shevat was almost lost again. Then, in the late 1800s, Jews started immigrating to Palestine once more, this time in great numbers. Pioneers, called ḥalutzim, came home to Eretz Yisrael, the Land of Israel. Mostly young people in their teens and twenties, they came from Europe to work the land: A line from one of their songs was, "We have come to the land to build it and be built by it." They knew that just as they were going to reclaim the swamps and the deserts and the abandoned fields and make them bloom, so would the land reclaim them and make them—and their people—bloom.

The pioneers lived in tents and coarse homes. They founded kibbutzim, egalitarian agricultural and industrial collectives. They planted trees, lots of trees. Trees that drained the swamps that bred malaria, trees that protected the new crops from the winds that could have destroyed the harvest, trees that provided shade during the harsh summer days, trees that brought the wastelands of Eretz Yisrael back to life.

Ḥalutzot (women pioneers) in the fields ❧

If Tu B'Shevat had been only a legal device, it might have become a relic of history. But the Jewish people saw a greater value in the day than that of simply being a tree's timekeeper. It became the emblem of the *ḥalutzim*. They celebrated it, and it celebrated them. Even in exile, those Jews who lived far from Jerusalem once again began to celebrate their connection to the Land of Israel on 15 Shevat. They created rituals according to which they ate the foods of Israel that are mentioned in the Bible: wheat, barley, grapes, figs, pomegranates, olives, dates, honey, carobs and almonds. In some places, the carob became the most popular Tu B'Shevat food. Much like a care package sent from home when we are far away, the fruits of Eretz Yisrael on Tu B'Shevat helped the Jews remember that though they were homesick, they were not homeless. A holiday that marks spring's renewal in Israel became a holiday that marks our national renewal.

When celebrating life-cycle events, many people observe the tradition of planting trees in Israel. ❧

How We Celebrate

EXPRESSING THE MESSAGE OF LOVE OF ISRAEL

In 1901, in order to help the *ḥalutzim*, Jewish leadership in the Diaspora created the Jewish National Fund (JNF), an organization dedicated to buying land, planting trees and developing the physical infrastructure of the Land of Israel, Eretz Yisrael. With financial support from JNF and with the pioneering work of the *ḥalutzim*, the Land of Israel once again blossomed.

> ### In Each Generation
>
> Once Ḥoni was walking along the road when he saw a man planting a carob tree. He asked, "How long before it will bear fruit?"
> The man answered, "Seventy years" (*Ta'anit* 23a).
> Ḥoni asked, "And will you be alive in 70 years to eat from its fruit?"
> The man answered, "And what if I am not? Just as I found the world full of carob trees planted by my parents and grandparents, so will I plant for my children."

To strengthen its important work, JNF chose one day of the year, Tu B'Shevat, as the day on which to focus the attention of Jews around the world on Eretz Yisrael. For decades now on Tu B'Shevat, Israeli children have planted thousands of trees all over the country. Israelis young and old, *olim* (newcomers) and *vatikim* (old-timers), visitors and politicians, plant saplings throughout the

I Believe

According to journalist Harry Gersh, "To plant a tree is to say 'I believe.'" We have faith that the sun will rise and the rain will fall. We have faith that neither wars nor malls will destroy our fields. We have faith that we and others after us will care for our saplings.

Growing Your Own Herbs

Many Jews in North America live where snow and frost cover the land on Tu B'Shevat. There are no almond trees that blossom in Ann Arbor or Montreal in January, no warm air that begins to blow. Not to worry. We indoor farmers can still celebrate the holiday: midwinter is the perfect time at which to begin an herb garden. With a trip to your home-garden center or perhaps to a neighborhood supermarket, you can get all you need: paper or pressed-earth cups in which to plant; rich, fertile soil; packets of seeds. Alone in your kitchen or with friends and family members gathered around, you can celebrate the coming of spring with the planting of your favorite herbs: thyme, parsley, basil, chives. Best of all, those herbs will grow to maturity in two to three months, just in time for your Passover seder.

Save the Trees

Even in the midst of war, Judaism teaches us, we must not destroy the trees. "When you lay siege to a city for a long time, you may not cut down the trees, for you can eat from them; you should not destroy them. Is a tree, after all, like a man who can run from you?" (Deuteronomy 20:19) What good is winning, the Torah seems to be asking, if all is destroyed in victory?

countryside, fulfilling the words of the Torah: "When you come into the land, you shall plant all kinds of fruit trees.... For Adonai, your God, will bring you into a good land, a land with streams and springs and fountains issuing from plain and hill, a land of wheat and barley and vines and fig trees and pomegranates, a land of olive trees and honey" (Leviticus 19:23; Deuteronomy 8:7). Towns and kibbutzim hold special celebrations, their inhabitants grateful for the Land of Israel, for the State of Israel.

Today many Jews in America have adopted the idea of planting a tree on Tu B'Shevat: Instead of, or in addition to, planting a tree in Israel, they plant one in their own backyard. Or, if the ground is still hard from the winter freeze, they may start their summer compost or plant a window garden of herbs, which they use at their Passover seder.

Planting Is Healing

Those who are ill or infirm or have suffered losses might find a measure of healing in the act of planting. A friend of mine was devastated by the miscarriage of an unexpected but wanted pregnancy. Time passed, but she could not overcome her profound feelings of loss. A friend of hers suggested that she go to a garden shop, pick out some flowers, dig in the earth and plant them. She dedicated those flowers to the child she never knew, enjoyed them while they bloomed, and was able to accept her loss when they died.

On or around Tu B'Shevat, you can arrange to go to senior citizens' homes or to the home of a friend with AIDS or some other illness and plant bulbs with them to be enjoyed for years to come.

Expressing the Message of Environmentalism

Since the 1970s, Tu B'Shevat has served another purpose as well. It has become a holiday on which Jews celebrate the gift of our world—the earth, the seas and the air—and our responsibility to preserve and care for it. For too many years, people have used the earth's resources carelessly, casually. We have dumped. We have wasted. We have polluted. It is not just a Jewish problem; it is a worldwide problem. But many Jews are turning to Tu B'Shevat as a special day on which to remind ourselves that we, too, must work to preserve the world everyday and that we must teach and remind others that they, too, must take care of the world.

A Tu B'Shevat Seder

Like the earlier kabbalists, some Jews and some schools are celebrating the holiday with a Tu B'Shevat seder, combining the message of love of Israel with respect for the earth. Gathering on the evening of Tu B'Shevat or on a nearby Sunday, the celebrants prepare a seder plate of fruits, and drink four cups of wine or juice, ranging from white (representing the midst of winter) to deep red (representing the full blossoming of spring). Then they tell the story of the trees.

Creating their own Four Questions, they might ask, "On all other days, we eat only one or two kinds of fruits. Why on this day do we eat seven? On all other days, we eat fruits from all over the world. Why on this day do we eat only fruits from Israel?"

Borrowing from the Passover song "Dayenu," some celebrants offer their thanks to God for trees by saying, "If You had only given us trees for shade and not for fruit, *dayenu*—it would have been enough. If You had only given us trees for fruit and not for fresh air, *dayenu*.... If You had only given us trees for fresh air and not for building, *dayenu*...."

A Tu B'Shevat Meal

A modest alternative to the seder is a special holiday meal prepared for your family or friends featuring the seven species, or fruits, that symbolize the verdancy and fertility of the Land of Israel. Such a meal could begin with "Kiddush" recited over wine or grape juice from Israel, continue with round ḥallah, barley soup, fresh salad with olives and olive oil, a vegetarian main course, a pomegranate, figs, dates and carob-topped almond cake for dessert.

The multiple lessons of Tu B'Shevat continue to speak to us: Israel is our homeland. As we build her, so she builds us. We must treat the earth with respect; it is on loan to us from God and from our children. If we are good to the land, the land will be good to us.

Family and Community Seders

A synagogue, Hebrew school, Board of Jewish Education, Jewish National Fund office or Jewish Community Center will have copies of Tu B'Shevat seders. One of these organizations may even be sponsoring community seders. Contact the organization right after Ḥanukkah to beat the Tu B'Shevat rush.

A Taste of Home

Do you have a child away at college? a parent who has gone south for the winter? a cousin or a friend shivering up north? Tu B'Shevat is a perfect time to send them treats from home. Just as Tu B'Shevat became a holiday connecting far-flung Jews to one another and their homeland through the symbolism of Israel's produce, so, too, can it become a holiday of connection for widely dispersed contemporary families.

A variety of fruits, including watermelon, grapefruit, oranges, pears, apples, pomegranates, grapes, dates and figs, are grown in modern Israel both for internal consumption and for export.

Connecting the Holidays

On the day after Sukkot, plant etrog seeds in shallow containers full of moist, rich soil. By the time Tu B'Shevat rolls around, the seeds should be germinating. Transfer them to little pots, and wish them a happy birthday. Come Passover, they might be strong enough to be planted outside.

CHAPTER 11

Purim

The Holiday of Masks and Miracles

14 ADAR

(15 Adar in Jerusalem and other cities
that were walled in ancient times)

And the month was turned from sorrow to gladness, from mourning to joy.

—THE SCROLL OF ESTHER 9:22

MANY SCHOLARS BELIEVE the story of Purim is a fantasy. They think that the characters recorded in the Book of Esther never existed (save a king named Aḥashverosh) and the events never happened. I do not find such beliefs blasphemous, nor a blow to the credibility of Judaism. On the contrary, I think such a reading enhances the book's appeal. For why, we are compelled to ask, would such a tale be created? What was its purpose, and who was its audience? What were the needs that gave rise to a tale of such audacious adventure, and what were the historical realities that fed the mind that crafted it?

Beyond the genesis of the book, what does it mean that this tale, of all the thousands of tales that were told over time, was canonized by the Jewish people and is cherished to this very day?

Endowed with the authority that 2,000 years of sacredness confers, the story of Esther serves, more than most other books in the Bible, as an ancestral looking glass. It allows us an encounter with the vanity, humor, pride, needs, dignity, fantasies and hopes of the Jewish people, long ago and today. If it does not present history, it still reveals our ancestors' spirit. And for that reason alone, it commands our allegiance and our admiration.

On its face, Purim is a holiday that marks oppression and redemption, a time when, once again, government-sponsored thugs sought to kill the Jews with the aid of enlisted civilian executioners. And once again the oppressor was thwarted, and the Jews prevailed. The Scroll of Esther, which we read every Purim, is a story of wit and entertainment, loved every bit as much for its amusement, barbs and naughtiness as for its instruction. And the holiday's appeal is not harmed by its ritual requirement of revelry and drinking.

But at root, it is a serious story with lofty ideas about the roles of bravery, sacrifice, luck and hope, a story about our ability to overcome fate, a story about believing in ourselves even though we were never taught how. And it is a story about our romantic desires to be rulers—just and benevolent rulers—and to be desired for our beauty as well as for our wisdom, to save those we love, to command fealty, to root out evil, to throw ourselves into danger and emerge victorious, to be hailed a hero.

Mordecai and Esther—the heroes of the tale—are painted with just enough strokes to give them form but with too few to provide clear definition. They become the faces of all the Jewish people metamorphosed into the male and the female who represent us all. Megillat Esther, the Scroll of Esther, is a story that invites us to dress up in it. It is a story of make-believe of the highest order, for it makes us believe that we can be grand, that we can be noble and that we can make a difference.

The Scroll of Esther is a coming-of-age story; it is the story of a young Jewish woman who is transformed from bauble to strategist and ruler; it is the story of her struggle with her identity as a Jew

A megillah is much smaller than a Torah scroll and has only one roller.

and as a woman; it is the story of a woman whose actions helped her people become victors rather than victims. It is a story about a Jewish woman who passes as a Persian, is chosen to be queen, and has to come out of the closet to save her people.

In this light, Purim is a holiday of theological growth that is designed to wean the Jews from reliance on the commanding God of the Exodus. Purim teaches us that God will no longer intervene for us and save us, at least not obviously and supernaturally. It is a story that, through humor and hope, teaches Jews how God will function in the modern Diaspora community, for the story of Purim takes place in the Diaspora. It says that God will be hidden but not distant, silent but not inactive. God will work through us in our daily lives. And any one of us, every one of us, can become the instrument of God, for good and not for evil, for life and not for death.

Purim is a holiday of many faces. In the time of the Inquisition, when Jews were banished or killed or forced to convert to Christianity, the Scroll of Esther offered comfort to the Marranos, the *anusim,* those who chose to convert publicly but retain their Jewish traditions and faith privately. They took comfort in Esther, who had to hide her identity, as did they, yet was not defiled as a Jew. Even as her hiddenness became an instrument of salvation, so, they hoped, theirs would be.

In Israel, Purim—like Ḥanukkah—celebrates the belief that the Jewish people can defend themselves through the art of war and can defeat their enemy in battle; that as a small nation whose borders are constantly threatened by issues of security, Israel has not succumbed to fear and Jews can walk the streets with joyous abandon.

In America, Purim is a holiday that suits our psychotherapeutic culture. Masks—the accessory of choice on Purim—are a favorite contemporary metaphor. They can both conceal and create. They hide what we choose to hide and show what we want to reveal. Alcohol—a prop for Purim—can be a mask we don (or down) to reveal what we wish to deny later. Costumes permit us to assume styles that might otherwise clash with the persona we normally project. Properly selecting and acknowledging our daily masks is a hard-won skill of the well-adjusted. On Purim, we are allowed to push the envelope even further.

A Book of Faith

Though it never mentions God, Megillat Esther is a book steeped in faith, faith that good will win out over evil, that we can and must take a lead in shaping our destiny, that we will not be abandoned to despots and greed mongers.

On Purim, fantasy rules as we don our holiday costumes.

Most recently, Purim has assumed two new meanings. According to the first new meaning, the holiday has become an opportunity to examine and appreciate women's exercise of power. Both Esther and Vashti (the banished queen whom Esther replaced) have come to serve as feminist models, each defiant in her own way, each proud and able to bear the challenges and the consequences of choice and leadership. Each pursued a different method of confrontation: Vashti refused seduction as an avenue to power; Esther availed herself of it. In this postmodern second- and third-generation feminist era, the lines of the right ways and wrong ways of leadership are being redrawn. Both men and women are struggling with the image of the woman of power.

According to the second new meaning, the book has become an opportunity to revisit the concept of command. Throughout the generations in all of Jewish literature, God is known as the One who commands, and we, God's people, are the commanded ones. Yet the human spirit, no matter how great and awesome the commander, demands freedom. As early as the Bible itself, we read that the Israelites responded to God's commandments by saying, "We will do, and we will listen" (Exodus 24:7). Why was it necessary at the moment of Revelation to acknowledge the Jews' acceptance of God's word? Because forced obedience is not the fulfillment of God's will. Throughout the books of the Bible, images of God and Israel as lovers abound, the two choosing and seeking and hiding from each other. God and Israel are covenanted partners, each with promises made to the other. Both choose and allow themselves to be chosen.

One midrash on the experience of Sinai says that God held the mountain over the people and said, "Accept My commandments or this will be your grave." If an agreement were to be entered into under such conditions, it would not be binding, for covenants sealed through coercion are not valid. So how is it, according to that midrash, that we remain bound in covenant with God? It is because of what the Jews said in Persia at the time they celebrated their first Purim: "They established it, and they accepted it upon themselves..." (Esther 9:27). While this text refers only to the holiday of Purim, the midrash reads "it" as a proxy for all of Torah. Here, in the Diaspora country of Persia, the Jewish people voluntarily accepted upon themselves for all time the terms of this sacred covenant. For the generation of Jews living in the post-emancipation era, in which individual rights and autonomous behavior are the reigning values, the story of Purim offers a compelling message: We are covenanted to God because we have so chosen, and we cast our lot with the Jewish people because we so desire.

The Story of Purim

The plot begins after seven days of drinking and feasting, when Aḥashverosh, king of Persia, invites his queen, Vashti, to parade her beauty in front of his drunken companions. She refuses and is punished with banishment, an appropriate if severe measure, say the king's advisers, else he and every other man in the kingdom would suffer the derision of their wives and would lose control of their households. Aḥashverosh, lonely now, searches the land for a new queen. After months of "interviewing," he chooses a beautiful young woman named Esther. (Her real name is Hadassah, which means "myrtle" in Hebrew. But this is a book of hidden identities so only *we* know her real name, and only we know that she is Jewish. "Esther" itself recalls the Hebrew word meaning "hidden.")

Meanwhile, Esther's uncle Mordecai has enraged Haman, the king's chief adviser, for Mordecai would not bow before him. Haman receives permission from the king to decree that on 13 Adar the people of Persia should rise up against the Jews and kill them. His argument is one that will echo throughout the ages: "There is in your land a people spread out and living among all the nations of your kingdom, whose religion is different from all the others. They are dangerous and do not obey the rule of the king" (Esther 3:8).

When the royal decree is made public, Mordecai tells Esther that she can no longer hide the fact that she is a Jew. She must petition the king for the safety of the Jews. Esther replies that she cannot appear before the king unless he calls for her; otherwise, she can be put to death. Mordecai tells Esther that no matter what the risk, she must go to the king—uninvited, if necessary. So Esther fasts for three days and calls upon all the Jews to fast with her. Then she presents herself before the king.

This Rembrandt print portrays a sequence from the Scroll of Esther—Mordecai, on the king's horse, being led by Haman through the streets of Shushan.

Lots

Purim means "lots," numbers that are picked at random, as in a lottery. The holiday gets its name from the way Haman chose the day on which the Jews were to die. The name implies that the Jews' destiny was left to chance. But this is a holiday when things are not the way they appear.

Hamakom

One of God's many names is Hamakom, meaning "the place." While God is not explicitly mentioned in the Megillah, some read in Mordecai's message a veiled reference to God: "'Do not think you will escape this decree in the house of the king. For if you withhold your help at this time, relief and deliverance will come from another Place, but you and your father's house will perish'" (Esther 4:13–14).

The Fast of Esther

"And Esther sent word to Mordecai: 'Go and assemble the Jews of Shushan and fast on my behalf. Do not eat or drink for three days. I and my maidens will fast too. Then I shall go to the king, though it is against the law. And if I perish, I perish'" (Esther 4: 15–16). In remembrance of Esther's bravery and the solidarity of the Jewish people, we fast for one day (from daylight to darkness) on 13 Adar.

Haman, meanwhile, impatient for 13 Adar to arrive, determines to tend to Mordecai himself and so builds a gallows—50 cubits high—upon which to hang him.

The king is not angered by Esther's sudden appearance in his court. In fact, he is delighted to see her and offers to grant her most extravagant wish. Esther does not tell the king about Haman's plan right away. Instead, she invites the king and Haman to a dinner, and after the dinner she invites them to a second dinner. It is only at the second dinner that Esther reveals herself as a Jew and accuses Haman of wanting to kill her and all her people.

The king is furious and orders his men to hang Haman immediately, on the very gallows that he has built for Mordecai. That is the end of Haman. But even the king cannot annul a royal decree. (Sometimes when hatred is unleashed, it is impossible to rein it in.) So he does the next best thing: He issues a second decree, permitting the Jews to defend themselves against those who choose to rise up against them.

The Persians react with shock and fear. Many become Jews, "for the fear of the Jews had fallen upon them…" (Esther 8:17). Others support them: "Many princes and governors and those who did the king's business helped the Jews" (Esther 9:3). Still others cannot resist the royally sanctioned opportunity to fight the Jews. But the Jews successfully defend themselves on 13 Adar and celebrate their victory on 14 Adar. That is the day that has become Purim. The Jews of the walled city of Shushan fought on the 13th and 14th of the month and celebrated on the 15th. That is why today Jews in Jerusalem and other cities that were once walled celebrate Purim on 15 Adar.

How We Celebrate

We celebrate Purim at home and at the synagogue, and we take our cue from the Megillah, the Scroll of Esther: "The month [of Adar] was turned from sorrow to gladness and from mourning to joy. The Jews celebrated days of feasting and merry-making, of sending packages from neighbor to neighbor and giving gifts to the poor" (Esther 9:19).

A noisemaker used during the reading of the Megillah

Jews don't celebrate alone. On Purim as on other holidays, we share our bounty with others. Many Jews assemble elaborate baskets of fruits, pastries and candy to give away, baskets with at least two kinds of food given to at least one friend. But usually we give much more: to our neighbors, to our friends and to people at work. In addition, we give tzedakah (*matanot la'evyonim*, gifts to the poor) to help make Purim a happier day for everyone.

We go to the synagogue on Purim to hear the reading of the Megillah. We hear it read in the evening and in the morning. But we don't just listen. We cheer with it and yell at it. Some Megillah readers use different voices to act out the roles of the characters. Most synagogues use noisemakers—called *graggers* or *ra'ashanim*—to drown out Haman's name whenever it is read. Some even have prompters who help the congregants catch the name should they miss it and to quiet them down when they don't, so that the reading can continue.

*Graggers—noisemakers—
at the ready, these children are
enjoying the Purim festivities.*

On Purim, as on Ḥanukkah, there are no work restrictions. But toward the end of the day, families and friends gather for a festive meal. They may write funny poems or stories or even a funny Kiddush. Almost nothing is too irreverent on this day.

Purim Se'udah

A *se'udah* is a special meal. On Purim, toward evening, families and friends get together for food, laughs and fun. It is a time for sharing the family newsletter or giving a family roast, or just hanging out together in joy.

And of course we eat *hamantashen*, three-cornered pastries filled with jelly or prunes or poppy seeds (sometimes called *muhn*) or even chocolate. They can be bought in some bakeries, but it is great fun to make them. Jewish newspapers always publish hamantashen recipes before Purim. Jewish cookbooks, even Jewish cookbooks for kids, have hamantashen recipes. Chances are you can find some on the Internet, too. You can choose to make your dough more like cake or more like a cookie. No one knows how hamantashen became the traditional food for Purim. They are also called Haman's pockets and *oznei Haman*, Haman's ears.

Purim Shpiel

Many schools put on Purim plays that retell the story of Purim. In former times, whole communities would gather and make fun of their teachers and leaders, all in love and the spirit of sacred comedy, of course.

Most synagogues also hold carnivals and costume parades on Purim or on a Sunday close by. Sometimes even the rabbis dress up.

Unfortunately, the story of Purim has happened not once but many times, not only in Persia but in many places. It became a tradition in many of the towns where Jews' lives were threatened and then saved, to mark the occasion with a special Purim just for that place. Someone from the town would write a megillah that told the particulars of their story. And year after year the people of the town would gather on the anniversary of the event and celebrate their victory.

And thus it was, in 1996, in Teaneck, New Jersey, at Congregation Beth Sholom, that the special megillah, *Purim-Stalin*, was read for the first time. Written by Bella and Alex Rashin, immigrants from the former Soviet Union, in partial celebration of their 25th wedding anniversary, it tells of the murderous legacy of Joseph Stalin and how the evil decree calling for the wholesale destruction of the Jews of Russia was miraculously undone precisely on Purim.

Despite the laughter and the joy of the Purim celebration, we hope and pray that there will be no new Purims for the Jewish people.

Completing Liberation

Rabbi Bea Wyler teaches that the Book of Esther tells of the complete liberation of the Jews—and the incomplete liberation of women. This is perhaps most evident in chapter 9, in which Esther silently vies for power with Mordecai through dueling letters sent to the populace, proclaiming the ways in which to mark the holiday. At first, Esther seems to have the upper hand. "And the pronouncement of Esther established this tradition of Purim, and so it was written in the book" (9:32). With that, the story appears to end. Only just as we are about to close the book, we see another three verses, which speak of the authority of Ahashverosh and Mordecai and say not a word about Esther: "For Mordecai the Jew ranked next to the king and was highly regarded by the Jews....He sought the good of his people and interceded for the welfare of all his kindred" (Esther 10:3). Rabbi Wyler suggests that we dedicate the Fast of Esther, which occurs the day before Purim, to this incomplete liberation of women.

Purim holds many opportunities for parent and child activities, including making masks and costumes, baking hamantashen and crafting baskets in which to put mishloaḥ-manot, gifts of cakes and other sweets.

Making Mishloaḥ-Manot

Decorated bags with little gift cards attached make perfect *mishloaḥ-manot* containers; so do paper bags decorated with stickers and ribbons. After you have determined what bags or baskets you are going to use, the next question is, What food to put in them? Most *mishloaḥ-manot* contain some form of hamantashen. Nuts, dried fruits (Have any left over from Tu B'Shevat?), apples, oranges, raisins and candy round out the menu. Don't forget to attach a card to let the recipient know whom the *mishloaḥ-manot* are from!

College students, friends and family members far away love to receive Purim care packages. For those closer to home, some synagogues and schools organize *mishloaḥ-manot* drives. Such drives help busy people send packages they might not otherwise have time for, limit waste (what do you do with so much food?) and raise money for the institution. A list of members is distributed, and a flat, reasonable fee for sending each package is specified. Participants select the names of those whom they want to receive a package in their name. Their orders are then coordinated by an organizing committee. One package is sent to each recipient, with a list of names of all the people who joined in sending it. The packages are then either picked up at one central location (if organized by a school) or distributed on Purim day by volunteers (if organized by a synagogue).

CHAPTER 12

Passover

The Festival of Freedom

15–21/22 NISAN

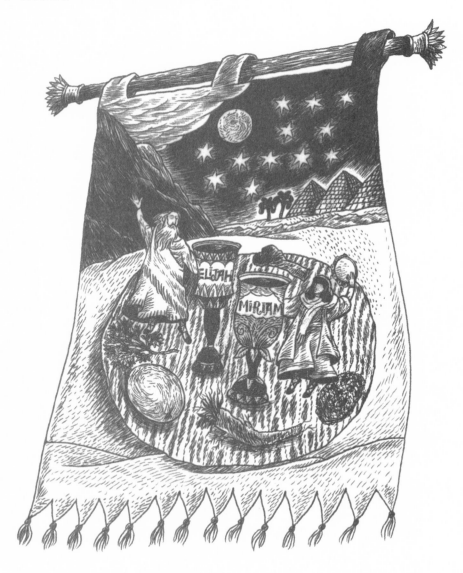

"My father was a wandering Aramaean. He went down to Mitzrayim with just a few people and stayed. There he became a great nation, mighty and numerous. But the Egyptians dealt harshly with us and oppressed us, and they imposed hard labor on us. We cried out to God, the God of our ancestors. God heard our cries and saw our affliction, our misery and our oppression. So God took us out of Egypt with a strong hand and an outstretched arm, with awesome power, with signs and with wonders."

—DEUTERONOMY 26:5–8

PASSOVER IS THE STORY OF FREEDOM, defiance, hope and renewal. It is the retelling of how a rabble of slaves was infused with a sacred purpose and grew to enter into a covenant with God. It is the story that has taught the world that birth is not destiny, oppression is not defeat, "victim" is not an identity and partnership with God is open to us all.

The plot is well-known. The Israelites were strangers in a strange land, enslaved to Pharaoh because they were different. Generations earlier, the Israelites—70 men and the uncounted women and children of the family of Jacob—settled in Egypt during a time of great famine. Joseph, the son of Jacob and Rachel, had devised a plan to

Why Were the Israelites Enslaved?

The Bible tells us, "There arose a new king in Egypt who did not know Joseph [and all he had done for Pharaoh and Egypt]" (Exodus 1:8). And the new king went to his people full of fear and said to them, "There is a great and numerous people in our midst. Perhaps they will want to turn on us one day. Quick, let us enslave them before they can harm us." Fear of the other, the one who is different, the one who comes from somewhere else, leads us to the plague of darkness. In darkness, we see not with our eyes but with our fear, with our imaginations, and on a communal level that too often leads nations to the tenth plague.

Pharaoh's daughter finds Moses among the reeds. ❧

The Ten Plagues

This is the sequence of the ten plagues: blood, frogs, vermin, beasts, cattle plague, boils, hail, locusts, darkness, death of the firstborn sons.

spare Egypt the hardship of famine and was rewarded by receiving permission to settle his father and brothers and their families in the land of Goshen with the blessing of the pharaoh. Time passed. Pharaoh died and the memory of the reign of Joseph was forgotten by the new pharaoh. The Israelites were now seen not as welcome guests but as dangerous interlopers, a fifth column in the making that had to be subdued.

For 430 years, we lived in Egypt, the Torah tells us. For 210, we were enslaved, forced to build the cities of Pithom and Raamses. We were beaten and abused, but we never forgot God's promise to Abraham, to settle us as a great people in a land of our own.

In the midst of our oppression, we called to God, and we were answered in the form of the liberating defiance of a band of remarkable women: Shifra and Puah, the midwives who disobeyed Pharaoh's order to slaughter all newborn Hebrew sons; Yocheved, the mother of Moses; Miriam, his sister; and the daughter of Pharaoh—all of whom conspired to save Moses' life. Each acted out of a personal sense of justice and bravery, and their combined actions changed the course of history. They taught us, as would Harriet Tubman and Rosa Parks, that small, well-placed acts of resistance sustain the human spirit and bring down the mighty. They keep alive the passion for freedom and, ultimately, with persistence, lead the way to the Promised Land.

With the stage set, Moses began training—albeit unknowingly—for his sacred mission. In the house of Pharaoh, he learned of the gifts, the dignity, the abilities, the limits, the seductiveness and the temptation of earthly power. Later, in exile from Egypt after slaying an Egyptian, he felt the sadness of homesickness, learned the wisdom of other nations and honed his skills of survival. In the wilderness, he mastered the lessons of compassion, patience, awareness and action. When ready, Moses was called by God to lead his people out of Egypt.

Ten plagues later we were free, as all people are meant to be: free to eat when we wanted, to sleep when we wanted, to name our children and sing our songs, and to come and go as we wanted; free from oppression and the ruler's injustice; free from pursuing the dreams of another instead of our own; free to show the world that even when slavery is thrust upon one people by another, it need not become either the enslaved people's identity or their destiny.

Yet freedom comes at a price. It is, as our ancestors discovered, a harsh taskmaster. For freedom demands choices, responsibility and adherence to values in a shifting, seductive world. It constantly tugs at us, asking whether we will decide yes or no, do this or do that. It makes no difference whether the choice is meaningless (do I buy the green toothbrush or the blue one?) or fraught with importance and risk (do I tell what I know?). We must endlessly decide. And each choice is momentous. It precludes the alternative, and its consequences determine our next set of choices, for we must stand where we last landed.

The Challenge of Freedom

Sometimes we ache for the possibility of freedom without the burden of choice. I know families that have a weekly dinner regimen: Monday—spaghetti, Tuesday—hamburgers, and so forth. I know people who won't shop in department stores or eat in restaurants with oversize menus. Most of us tend to sit in the same seat at weekly staff meetings, at the dinner table, in the synagogue. Judaism has a name for such constancy of place: *makom kavua,* a designated seat reserved for so-and-so by dint of that person's habit of sitting there, which we are bidden to respect even in the absence of the person whose seat it is.

Freedom of choice moves us to create rituals and routines, responses to the need for order in the face of chaos. Their performance reflects and reinforces the values we are trying out or have chosen. They give us identity, a center, a spiritual home. Routine limits our exposure to the incessant clamor of choice, enabling us to leash the chaos that swirls around us and to maintain an attitude of control. It is what allows us to open our front doors every morning, dressed and ready to go, with a destination in mind. But if haphazardly, inappropriately or inadvertently chosen, routine can also strangle the vitality of our humanity.

A misguided response to the desire to tame the chaos around us was evident in the biblical episode of the golden calf. Freedom created a vacuum of values for the former slaves, a desperate search for

Nightly rituals, such as reading in bed and spending time with pets, can bring back the calm we have lost during a hectic day.

meaning and purpose that needed to be filled. How to fill it? The Israelites' solution was to erect a sacred calf, the symbol of power revered by the oppressors they had just fled. Despite themselves, they adopted the very values of those who had enslaved them.

Not a surprise, for without vigilance our own desires and dreams will be sculpted by the winds around us. They will slowly and subtly metamorphose into the image of the culture that surrounds us. We must forever ask, Are our appetites, yearnings and goals truly worthy? From where do they come? Have someone else's desires slyly supplanted our own? What—or whose—purpose do they serve? How can we be certain that we do not fill the substance of our lives with golden calves? Whom can we trust? What can guide us? What is a worthy motivator for our life's actions?

The Exodus offers an answer: Seek a way to hear God's voice, and live a life in response to it.

That is not easy. And it cannot be done vicariously. That is why the Haggadah tells us to imagine that each of us was a member of the generation of the Exodus. Each of us needs to remember the thrill of freedom before it became a burden to be tamed, and each of us needs to remember the desires and the dangers involved in seeking to tame it.

Retracing the Road to Freedom

Once a year we return, to the degree that we can, to the event that started it all. We don't so much celebrate Passover or mark Passover or remember Passover as we experience it, relive it, retell it.

That is where the seder comes in, the ritual meal at which we tell the story of the Exodus. It is, somewhat paradoxically, a celebration of freedom guided by a set order. For that is what *seder* means, "order." We may hold it where we want to, gather at the time we set, pace the telling as fits our needs, sit in the fashion we desire, use the language that we are most familiar with. But we are to touch 15 landmarks. We are our own ritual experts this evening, but we are gathered in a cause that transcends our personal desires. We are in the pursuit of the true voice. We seek it in the company of one another, claiming as witnesses and as guides those who came before

The True Meaning of Freedom

Rabbi Abraham Joshua Heschel taught that the true meaning of freedom "is the liberation from the tyranny of the self-centered ego." Slavery is not always externally imposed. Sometimes we can be our own worst Pharaoh. Passover encourages us to liberate ourselves from our destructive restraints and fears.

Seder Means "Order"

The meal is called a *seder* because over the thousands of years, a specific order of the ritual meal developed. That order helps Jews remember everything they need to do. For many families, it is a joyous tradition to sing the "order" as an introduction to and table of contents for the seder.

us. So we use a book called the Haggadah, the collective memory of the generations.

The Haggadah is more than a book, really. It is a script suggesting what we may say, showing us how we may sit, recommending what we might eat. It serves as a series of cues to the various parts of the seder. When we feel uncertain, we anchor ourselves in the text, and the story unfolds through the age-old words. But the Haggadah also bids us to free ourselves from the limits of the written word: "Whoever expands upon the telling of the story is to be praised."

Many traditional Haggadot include passages from the Torah to help retell the story of the Exodus.

Haggadah, the Telling

Next to portions of the Bible, the traditional Haggadah is the oldest Jewish liturgical text in continual use. After 2,000 years, a lot of the text is read much the way it was recited ages ago. Today the seder is one of the most popular of Jewish rituals. Almost every Jew attends a seder at least once in their life. Over the centuries, literally thousands of editions of Haggadot have been printed, including extravagant and extraordinary illuminated editions. Perhaps because the seder is based in the home, perhaps because the text is so flexible, perhaps because it invites embellishment, many families create their own Haggadot.

If you are organizing a seder, you might invite each guest to bring readings on a related theme (overcoming one's external and internal demons, beginning a journey, creating a family). Then, set some time aside during the seder to share them. Or you might invite your guests to bring their favorite Haggadot so that you can compare commentaries and texts. The evening is dedicated to questions more than to answers, to sharing more than to owning. As with most things in life, the more you prepare, the more you enjoy.

So it is today that families and friends often supplement the tradition with their novel ways of telling the story and their own Haggadot (plural of *Haggadah*). Based on the trials of our ancestors, these Haggadot expand on the lessons and the readings and the hope found in the original tale. The plagues might be embellished with a roll call of contemporary environmental calamities; the Israelites' struggle for freedom might presage modern social inequities. Some communities sponsor feminist seders a week or two before Passover, attracting many women as well as some men, young and old, seder veterans and newcomers to the ritual. Those seders blend song and story to recapture the memories and values of Jewish women of the past and offer a celebration of Jewish women of the future. Songs and readings from those seders are then sometimes added to home seders.

A modern exodus story was played out in 1985. The Jewish communities of Israel and North America saved the Jews of Ethiopia from oppression and famine through a dramatic airlift that brought them to Israel. The mission was called "Operation Moses."

Telling and retelling the story in our own way frees our imaginations to enter into the mystery and the marvels of the Exodus from Egypt. To simply read the Haggadah is to tell the story from the outside, to focus on getting it right. The story is then something we hold in our hands, when it needs to be something we hold in our hearts. To speak the story in our own words, however, is to enter into the tale and have the tale enter us. We become the Israelites; we feel the Egypt in our lives. We recall what it is like to feel trapped, oppressed, forgotten. The Haggadah tells us that is what is supposed to happen: "Each of us should imagine that we personally went out from the Land of Egypt."

And in many ways, the story is our own. Egypt in Hebrew is Mitzrayim, meaning "narrow place." Each of us is constricted by our own fears of change. We know that the pull of freedom is threatened by the tug of laziness or the lure of the familiar. Each of us can use the help of valiant men and women who call us to be free. We can pass through the narrow canal of the parted waters and emerge new on the other side if we have the help and the encouragement of others. Passover is the beginning of such encouragement.

But for the Jews, freedom is just the beginning. It is the prerequisite, not the goal. The goal leads through the ethical to the spiritual: to serve God willingly instead of Pharaoh forcibly, to be part of the sacred instead of the mundane, to be joined to the ultimate instead of to the finite. When Moses first appeared before Pharaoh to ask for the freedom of the Israelites, he said, "Thus said Adonai: 'Let My people go so that they may worship Me in the desert'" (Exodus 5:1). Freedom with purpose. Journey with destination.

Celebrating the Holiday

HOW OUR ANCESTORS CELEBRATED

The Torah tells us how the Jews of old celebrated the holiday. Long ago, when the Temple still stood, the Jews were commanded to go to Jerusalem on the holiday of Passover. At the Temple, they were to sacrifice a lamb to remind them of the lamb's blood that the Israelites put on their doors in Egypt, a sign that God should pass over their houses and not kill their firstborn. They roasted the lamb, prepared their matzot (plural of *matzah*) and

Two Kinds of Slavery

The Haggadah speaks of two kinds of slavery. "We were slaves in Egypt," it says of the Israelites, and "we were idol worshipers." What is the difference? To be enslaved is to surrender our bodies. To worship idols is to surrender our wholeness.

bitter herbs, sat down to eat together as a family and to retell the story of Passover.

Passover, *Pesah* in Hebrew, has always been celebrated in a family setting. Even in biblical times, if a family could not afford a whole lamb or could not eat a whole lamb, they would join with another family to eat the meal and tell the story.

After the Temple was destroyed, how could the holiday be observed? The ancient rabbis decreed that each family should observe Passover at home. The major symbol of Passover shifted from the lamb sacrifice to the *matzah,* the flat, unleavened bread that reminds us of the haste with which the Israelites prepared to leave Egypt. That is one reason why the holiday is also called The Festival of Matzot, Hag Hamatzot. The shift in symbolism was promoted by the rabbis, who wanted to play down the reminder of the loss of the Temple and, at the same time, protect the Temple's ritual domain.

HOW WE CELEBRATE

The preparation for Passover begins weeks before the first seder. Traditionally, every room in which food could have been eaten, including bedrooms and playrooms, are thoroughly cleaned. Sofas are moved, cushions are pulled out, shelves are dusted. Then, in the days just before Passover, the kitchen is transformed, scoured and scrubbed, with the regular dishes and utensils packed up and put away and Pesah dishes and utensils brought out from storage.

Why do we clean so thoroughly? The Bible tells us that we are not supposed to eat anything during Passover that contains *hametz,* leavening. The rabbis tell us that we are not to possess anything, not a bit, containing *hametz*: no liquor or breads, nothing that is made from leavened grain. So we clean the entire house to remove all the *hametz*—cereal and crackers, leftover bites of doughnuts and bagels, pizzas and pretzels. Whether packaged or not, those foods must go.

One way to clean is to throw things out. But often that is wasteful. Another way is to eat all the *hametz* before the holiday. But that can be onerous, if not fattening. So right after Purim some families begin drawing down their *hametz* stock and carefully monitoring

What's in a Name?

Names for Passover include Hag Ha'aviv, Holiday of Springtime (symbolized by the greens on the seder plate); Z'man Heruteinu, Season of Our Liberation; and Hag Hamatzot, Holiday of Matzot.

Leavened Food

Hametz, leavened food, is any grain product that contains yeast or was moistened for more than 18 minutes before baking. Most baked products, cereals, breads, even liquor, are *hametz.* To be certain that all their Passover products are free of *hametz,* many Jews buy only those foods that are marked "Kosher for Passover." (Even matzah must be labeled "Kosher for Passover," since matzah made during the year does not always conform to the regulations for Pesah.)

Collecting canned and packaged ḥametz to give to the needy helps teach our children the lessons of Passover. ❧

their purchases. Others throw pasta parties for their friends, inviting them for evenings or Sunday afternoons of talking, playing and eating. But perhaps the best way to clean out the stock of ḥametz is to give it away. Some people make food packages to give to the needy, either through a Jewish Federation or a neighborhood food pantry. Some synagogues and Hebrew schools arrange food collections and donate the goods to a hunger drive.

That is a variation of an old tradition, *ma'ot ḥittin*, meaning "money for wheat." Begun in Talmudic times, it was a tzedakah campaign conducted on the eve of Pesaḥ and designed to provide the very poor with enough flour to make matzah, enough wine for the four cups and enough food for them to enjoy a seder as everyone else would. For Passover is not just a story about freedom but an experience of freedom. And how can one experience freedom if one is enslaved by hunger?

Matzah

So, you may ask, if baked grain products are ḥametz, how can we eat matzah? Isn't matzah a baked grain product too? The answer is in the timing. Kosher for Passover matzah is made when the time elapsed between adding water to the flour and thoroughly baking the dough is less than 18 minutes. Any more, and the dough begins to ferment, or rise, and it is considered ḥametz. You don't need to be a rabbi or a sage to bake matzah. But you do need to be fast, and you need to clean everything thoroughly between batches. Even the tiniest morsel of dough left over from a previous batch becomes ḥametz and on Passover can turn everything it touches into ḥametz. Given such stringencies, most people prefer to buy their matzah.

The Haggadah teaches this lesson, too. We begin every seder with the following invitation: "Let all who are hungry come and eat; let all who are in need come and share our Passover meal." It extends the mitzvah of tzedakah from gifts to physical presence, from giving of our things to giving of ourselves.

According to tradition, Jews are to study the laws of Passover beginning the day after Purim. The reason is clear: No other holiday has so many laws. It takes time to learn and prepare as we should. Here are four of the laws we must know:

• No ḥametz may be owned or eaten by a Jew on Passover.

• Matzah must be eaten on the first day of Passover.

- No utensils that have come into contact with *ḥametz* may be used on Passover. Therefore, all *ḥametzdik* utensils must be removed and replaced with Passover utensils.

- The ritual foods to be presented and eaten at the seder must be carefully prepared.

Such preparations engage our whole bodies and seep into our emotions. Just as blowing the shofar during the month of Elul prepares us for the High Holidays or counting the days of the *omer* prepares us for Shavuot or building a sukkah prepares us for Sukkot, so study and cleaning prepare us for Passover. Some people think—and only partly as a joke—that the work that leads up to Passover is meant not just to prepare us for the holiday but also to symbolize the hard labor the Jews suffered in Egypt.

The night before Passover final preparations are made. The house is now as clean as it will be; the Passover food has been bought, and the utensils have been hauled out of storage. The *ḥametz* is waiting for morning to be eaten or burned. Still, you can never be too careful when it comes to *ḥametz*, so one last check, called *bedikat ḥametz*, is made. A member of the household hides a small piece of *ḥametz* (one that does not make crumbs—for example, a piece of dry cereal) in each room of the house. (Some people put it on a napkin to assist the hunt and protect the cleanliness.) Then in a darkened house, armed with candles, a feather, a wooden spoon and a paper bag, the search crew begins its mission: to find the last remnants of *ḥametz* and gather them in the bag so that they can be burned the next morning.

Each time a piece of *ḥametz* is found, it is ceremoniously swept onto the wooden spoon and from there placed in the paper bag. The successful hunter adds another notch to his or her belt. Sometimes in our house it is necessary for the swiftest to hold back and let the others feel the thrill of the capture. When all the *ḥametz* is found, the bag is put aside in a safe place until morning. By approximately ten o'clock the next morning (check your synagogue bulletin or Jewish newspaper for the exact time), after the last of the edible *ḥametz* is eaten or thrown out, the bag is burned in a fireplace or a safe spot outside. Unopened packages containing *ḥametz* either can

Shabbat Hagadol

The Shabbat before Passover is given the special name of The Great Shabbat, Shabbat Hagadol. It takes its name from its haftarah, Malachi 3:4–24. Malachi is the last of the books of the Prophets. It was chosen for that Shabbat because it speaks of what we remember on Pesaḥ: Moses and the giving of the laws, Elijah's coming, and family members loving or reconciling with one another.

The Selling of Ḥametz

Because it is impossible (and sometimes costly) to eat up or give away all the *ḥametz* in your house or business before Passover, many Jews sell their *ḥametz* to a non-Jew, who will then be asked to sell it back after Passover. The sale is usually coordinated by a rabbi. You can call your synagogue one or two weeks before Passover to get on the list. Other Jews prefer to pack up their *ḥametz* and store it away, out of sight for the duration of the holiday.

The Nullification of Ḥametz

According to some mystical traditions, *ḥametz* symbolizes the blemishes and the demons in our darker selves, our swollen egos, our puffy pride. Although we are bidden to rid ourselves of those undesired scraps of self, we cannot always grasp them, lurking as they do in dark places. How, then, can we hope to destroy them? We can learn from the ritual of declaring *ḥametz nullified and ownerless.* Perhaps we can best our demons simply by declaring them null, empty, powerless. If we cannot banish them, perhaps we can deny them power.

be given away to the needy or stored away and sold, usually by a rabbi, to a non-Jew for the rest of the holiday. In this way, whatever *ḥametz* remains in your house no longer belongs to you.

You might think that is quite enough. But *ḥametz* is cunning: It can hide almost anywhere. Maybe there are cookie crumbs in the pockets of your child's baseball jacket. Or maybe you or an apartment mate left a snack in a rarely used handbag in the back of the closet. And who knows whether you ever found all the popcorn that slipped under and between the cushions of the sofa. So the rabbis suggest that we take one more precaution. They created a special declaration for us to recite that legally cancels all the *ḥametz* that we inadvertently leave behind: "All *ḥametz* that is in my house, whether I have seen it or not, whether I have removed it or not, is hereby nullified and as ownerless as the dust of the earth." Now, with that last act, the house is declared clean.

The Ceremony of the Firstborn

If you are the firstborn son, the day before Passover has special significance for you. The tenth plague that God visited upon the Egyptians was the death of firstborn males. God told the Israelites that if they wanted to save their own children, they must smear the blood of a lamb on the doorposts of their homes. Seeing the blood, God would "pass over" their houses.

In memory of the loss suffered by the Egyptians and as thanks to God for sparing our children, the firstborn sons of every Jewish family are called upon to fast on the day before Passover. The day is called Ta'anit B'chorim, Fast of the Firstborn. Because a joyous holiday is only hours away, however, and because fasting is onerous for some, many firstborn sons, instead of fasting, participate in a special celebration called a *siyum*, a ceremony of completion.

Many synagogues therefore organize groups of congregants who study a book of the Talmud throughout the year, pacing themselves so that they finish it on 14 Nisan, the day before Passover. Reaching the end of a traditional Jewish book of learning is a grand achievement, one worthy of acknowledgment. All who join in are free to celebrate with food and drink at the *siyum*.

The Seder Plate

With the ḥametz removed and the *siyum* complete, all that is left is to prepare for the seder. Family members often come from out of town—sister goes to brother; mother comes to child. The latter event represents one of the unnamed Jewish rites of passage: A child takes on the responsibility of the family seder. But wherever you go, the work will be the same. The meal must be prepared; the table must be set; the matzah and seder plate, salt water, wine and Haggadot must be put out. Pillows, the symbol of reclining and freedom, must be placed at the leader's chair and perhaps at the other chairs around the table.

Seder plate ❧

Two Seders or One?

As on the two other pilgrimage holidays, on Passover the number of days that are celebrated varies by denomination and location. Reconstructionist and Reform Jews, and Jews who live in Israel celebrate the holiday for seven days, with a seder on the first night (although many choose to have a second seder, sometimes a communal one in a synagogue, on the second night). Conservative and Orthodox Jews living in the Diaspora celebrate for eight days, with seders on both the first and second nights.

On the seder plate are five ritual foods:

ZEROA

The roasted shank bone symbolizes the Passover (lamb) sacrifice that the Israelites brought to the Temple and ate at their evening meal. Today, since we no longer make sacrifices as we did at the Temple, we do not use roasted lamb, but substitute for it any available piece of roast meat. (Traditionally, it was the less desirable cuts of meat that were used. In my family, we used the *gergel*, the neck of the chicken.) For vegetarians, the rabbis allow a roasted beet or other elongated root vegetable.

BEITZAH

The roasted egg symbolizes the sacrifice that was offered at every pilgrimage holiday. My family's tradition is to hardboil the egg, then hold a burning match just under it to darken the shell. The smoke from the match makes the egg look roasted. An artistic hand can make stunning swirls.

Parsley is often served as the karpas. ❧

ḤAROSET

The mixture of fruits and nuts, chopped and mashed, reminds us of the mortar with which our ancestors built the storehouses of Pithom and Raamses. Families from Russia and eastern Europe tend to use chopped apples, walnuts, wine and cinnamon. My grandfather's secret ingredient was prunes. The rabbis in Babylonia used ingredients that reminded them of Israel and of God's love as symbolized by the fruits of the gardens described in the Song of Songs: pomegranates, figs, dates, apples and nuts in a red-wine base.

KARPAS

Greens such as lettuce or celery or a boiled or baked potato (a tradition left over from the time when greens were hard to get) remind us of the freshness of spring.

MAROR

Bitter herbs, usually horseradish, raw or processed, remind us of the bitterness of our ancestors' lives. Some seder plates also include *ḥazeret,* an additional bitter herb, often Romaine lettuce, which is used for the Hillel sandwich.

Some seder plates have a place for salt water, to remind us of our ancestors' tears.

The Seder

The table is set. The wine is poured. The food is warming. The family gathers. The seder begins. As we do on most holidays, we open with the Kiddush. With that prayer, we thank God for giving us the holidays as a gesture of love and remembrance.

After the Kiddush, the greens, *karpas,* are eaten as an appetizer, but not in the usual way. The Haggadah instructs us to wash our hands before we eat and to do so in the manner of the rabbis of old: by pouring water from a vessel (any cup will do) twice over each hand, this time without a blessing. (Later in the seder we wash our hands again, that time with a blessing.) We dip the greens, which remind us of the promise of spring, into salt water, which reminds us of the tears of the Jews.

Then comes the part that children watch most intently: *yaḥatz,* the taking and breaking into two of the middle matzah. (We use three matzot at the seder.) The smaller piece is returned to the plate. The larger piece is set aside for the afikoman and hidden. *Afikoman,* a word that some scholars think means "dessert," is the last thing we eat at the seder. The meal cannot be completed without it. So it is the time-honored tradition of adults to hide the afikoman, to keep it out of the reach of the children.

Ah, but the children are smart and search and search to find the afikoman, knowing that if they find it, they can ransom it for a handsome prize, for no other matzah can serve in its stead. Sometimes the parents are prepared and have stashed away gifts for all the children, big and small. Sometimes the children negotiate with their parents for a hefty reward to be delivered after the holiday.

After the breaking of the matzah and the setting aside of the afikoman, the story of the seder begins. "Why is this night different from all other nights?" Children all over the world, in Hebrew and in dozens of other languages, sing the Four Questions to the delight of the adults.

The seder service invites everyone — adults and children, hosts and guests, pros and novices — to participate fully and joyously.

On all other nights, we eat either *ḥametz* or matzah. Why on this night do we eat only matzah? On all other nights, we do not dip even once. Why on this night do we dip twice? On all other nights, we eat all kinds of vegetables. Why on this night do we eat only bitter herbs? On all other nights, we eat either sitting up or reclining. Why on this night do we recline?

Asking these questions is another time-honored tradition. Indeed, posing questions is so basic to the holiday that the Talmud insists even learned people must ask each other questions. But do not be overwhelmed, any question you ask about the evening would be fine. "Sometimes Grandma Margie comes for dinner. Sometimes Grandma Jackie comes. Why on this night do they both come?" "Why did we have to get all dressed up tonight?" "Why are we sitting on pillows on the floor?" "What is all that strange stuff in the middle of the table?" Even "When do we eat?"—all are good seder questions, for they all provide an opportunity to explain the ritual and the timing of the evening.

Whatever the questions, they should lead to the same end, the *maggid,* the telling. That is the longest section of the seder, next to

Four Is a Popular Number at the Seder

There are four cups of wine, each cup representing one verb that recalls God's miracle of freeing the Jews from Egypt: "I will *take* you out" (Exodus 6:6), "I will *free* you" (*ibid*), "I will *save* you" (*ibid*), "I will *bring* you to Me" (Exodus 6:7). The seder opens and closes with a cup of wine, and the meal itself opens and closes with a cup of wine. The Haggadah speaks of four children: the wise, the wicked, the simple and the one who does not know how to ask. And it poses four questions.

Drops of Wine

At the seder, we remember with a heavy heart the Egyptians who suffered and died. A cup full of wine is a symbol of a heart full of joy. So at the seder, when we recite the ten plagues, we pour out a bit of our wine, thus reducing our joy.

the meal. It is in that section that we retell the story of how the Israelites went down to Egypt, looking for food during the time of famine, how they were made slaves, how they remained proud, and how God saved them "with a mighty hand and an outstretched arm." There is no end to the stories and the lessons and the comments that flow from the Exodus. The Haggadah itself tells us that some of the most learned rabbis of the second century retold the story of the Exodus all night long.

As the discussion progresses, stomachs may start to growl. To allow plenty of time for the *maggid,* some hosts put out expansive displays of *karpas:* carrots, broccoli, cauliflower, artichokes, plus raisins, nuts and all sorts of dried fruits. My family's tradition was to offer hard-boiled eggs dipped in salt water during the time the *karpas* was served. At many Reform seders, the blessing over the matzah is recited early in the seder, as may have been the original tradition. This way matzah can be nibbled throughout the seder.

The *maggid* culminates in the celebration of freedom. Even as Moses, Miriam and the Israelites sang at the shores of the Sea of Reeds, so we sing our anthem of freedom and joy, Hallel:

> Halleluyah, praise the Source of Life, sing praises to God, servants of the Creator....When Israel was freed from Egypt, when the House of Jacob went out from a strange people, the sea fled at the sight, the mountains skipped like rams, the hills like young sheep....

> I praise You, God, for having answered me....The stone that the builders rejected has become the cornerstone. This is the doing of the Eternal One; it is marvelous in our sight. This is the day the Compassionate One made; let us rejoice in it.

At the conclusion of that song, we drink the second cup of wine. The meal awaits. Rabbi Gamliel said that the seder is not complete without mentioning three things: *pesaḥ* (the passover sacrifice), matzah and *maror.* So we begin the meal by speaking of those foods and by eating matzah, *maror* and *ḥaroset.*

Most of the seder takes place before the meal. But two important parts are saved for after the meal. One is the cup of Elijah. Passover is a holiday of hope and purpose. No matter who is holding us down or what is holding us back, Passover teaches us that we can be freed from those chains. And with that freedom, we can change the world.

Elijah the prophet symbolizes that hope. It is thought that Elijah will one day come and answer all arguments we cannot now resolve, that Elijah appears now and then disguised as a stranger to help us when we are in trouble, and that Elijah will come to announce the Messiah. At the seder, we welcome Elijah by filling a large cup with wine and opening the door for him, to welcome him and to demonstrate our faith and our hope. During the Middle Ages—in fact, up until the early 20th century—Passover was often a time of danger and blood libels. Jews would be accused of killing Christian children to use their blood in our seders. To open our doors at such a time of fear demonstrated confidence, pride and defiance, as if we were saying, "We have nothing to hide and nothing to fear." Today we open the door as a gesture of hospitality and openness and as a symbol that even the most jaded of us still dare to hope.

The Cup of Miriam

When the Jews left Egypt and safely crossed through the Sea of Reeds, Moses and Miriam led the people in song: "I will sing to God, majestic in triumph; rider and horse were thrown into the sea. God is my strength and my might; God will be my salvation...." Today, in celebration of the remarkable women throughout Jewish history, those who are known and those unnamed, many seder tables are decked with a cup of Miriam, brimming with water, prominently placed next to the cup of Elijah. The water represents the well that miraculously followed the Israelites through the desert until the day of Miriam's death.

Filling Elijah's Cup

Some families choose to fill Elijah's cup before the seder begins so that it can serve as a visual symbol of hope and redemption even at the beginning of the tale of oppression. Other families choose to fill Elijah's cup only after the meal dishes have been cleared away. (That way the cup won't spill during the hubbub of dinner.) Whenever you fill it, you can either pour wine directly into it from the bottle or pass the cup around, allowing all the participants to pour a bit of their wine into the cup of Elijah. That latter practice symbolizes the belief that Elijah needs our help in bringing the age of redemption and that each of us can do our share, no matter our age, our talents or our disabilities.

The other postdinner element is song. First we sing additional praises of God, the conclusion of the psalms called Hallel. As a rule, we recite Hallel only during the day. But the joy of Passover is deep. And the miracles happened at night ("Then Pharaoh summoned Moses and Aaron at night, saying, 'Arise and leave from among my people; go and worship your God'" [Exodus 12:31]). So, only on Passover do we say Hallel at night.

A Miriam's cup made of copper, by Linda Leviton ❧

By the end of the seder, we are tired, full and comforted by the knowledge that once again redemption has come. So we end the seder with songs of levity, songs whose performance requires skill, like "Who Knows One?" and the House-That-Jack-Built-style "Ḥad Gadya."

On the second night of Passover, an additional ritual is performed. No sooner is Passover upon us than we begin the seven-week countdown to the holiday of Shavuot, the celebration of the giving of the Torah. That sacred period is called *s'firat ha'omer*, meaning "counting of the *omer*." (*Omer* refers to the measure of grain that was brought to the Temple during those weeks.) Sometimes the countdown period is called simply *sefirah* or *omer*. Every night, the new day is counted as a reminder that we are yet one day closer to the ultimate purpose of our freedom: joining in the Covenant with God.

The middle days of *Pesaḥ, ḥol hamo'ed,* are a time when we can work, go to school, shop. What we cannot do is eat or buy *ḥametz*. We celebrate the last day or last two days of Passover (depending on our affiliation) by refraining from work and all related tasks, and we continue to avoid *ḥametz*. As the last light of the holiday fades and three medium-sized stars appear, the prohibition against *ḥametz* is lifted. The Passover dishes are carefully put away, their week of glory spent. The rabbi buys back our *ḥametz* and returns its ownership to us. The familiar order of the kitchen returns. We feel as though we have been away. It was fun, but it's good to be home—and free.

Maurice Mayer, a 19th century goldsmith, made this omer counter.

The Pilgrimage Holidays

Despite Rosh Hashanah, Nisan is called the first of months, making Passover the first of the three pilgrimage holidays, *shalosh regalim*. The Bible tells us that Jews would travel three times a year to Jerusalem, to the Temple, to offer a holiday sacrifice to God. Those three times were Passover, Shavuot and Sukkot. During these holidays Jews could become spiritually reinvigorated by the convergence of thousands and thousands of their fellow worshipers at one spot, the portal through which God's presence poured into the world. During the pilgrimage holidays, Jerusalem was a city awake 24 hours a day with Jews buying animals to sacrifice, redeeming money that had been hallowed and could be spent only in that city, and purchasing gifts to take home to friends and family members who had not come along. It was alive and inspiring, a great place to be a Jew.

Each pilgrimage holiday has two stories that are told about it, one historical and the other agri-cultural; Passover celebrates the Exodus and the beginning of the spring harvest; Shavuot celebrates the giving of the Torah on Mount Sinai and the end of the barley harvest; Sukkot reminds us of the 40 years that the Jews wandered in the desert and marks the end of the summer harvest.

A Time of Mixed Emotions

The period of the *omer* is a happy time, a time of joyous expectation. But it is also a time of sadness, even a time of mourning. Tradition tells us that in Israel in the early part of the second century, in the weeks between Passover and Shavuot, thousands of Rabbi Akiva's students died from a plague. Perhaps it was a plague of illness, perhaps a plague of Roman soldiers. Either way, the losses were great. To mourn these precious lives, many Jews today refrain from going to concerts, shaving their beards, cutting their hair or getting married during the weeks of the *omer*.

Still, there are five days during the *omer* that are days of joy, days on which weddings may take place and celebrations may be held. Two are Rosh Hodesh Iyar and Rosh Hodesh Sivan, the first days of the months of Iyar and Sivan. The third is the classic day of refuge from the season's period of sadness, Lag Ba'omer, the 33rd day of the *omer*, for on that one day, tradition tells us, the plague that killed so many Jews miraculously and mysteri-ously vanished. The other two days, added since 1948 and 1967, respectively, are Israel's Independence Day (Yom Ha'atz-ma'ut) and the celebration of the reunification of Jerusalem (Yom Yerushalayim).

Lots of weddings, concerts and community gatherings are planned for those days. In Israel especially, bonfires are built on Lag Ba'omer, and field days and picnics for the schoolchildren are held.

The Telling of Tales

For 3,000 years, the story of the Exodus has brought a message of hope and deliverance to oppressed people all over the world. That's the way it is with stories. Once they are told, no one can own them. They belong to the listener, to everyone. So even though Passover pointedly speaks of the national liberation of Jews, others hear its message of freedom and take heart. The slaves of America sang of the Exodus. Liberation theology speaks of the Exodus. Whether someone is a political prisoner, a prisoner of addiction or a prison-er of his or her own fears, the story of the Exodus tells every lis-tener, "Do not give up; there is yet hope. At the darkest of hours, in the dead of the night, with faith and fortitude, freedom can come."

Counting the Omer

Every night between Passover and Shavuot, during *ma'ariv*, the evening prayers, we count the days of the *omer* by reciting this blessing: "Blessed are You, Compassionate One, our God, Sovereign of the universe who commands us to count the *omer*." Then the congregation counts, "Today is the [such-and-such] day of the *omer*." For example, on the 32nd day of the *omer*, we would say, "Today is the 32nd day of the *omer* corre-sponding to 4 weeks and 4 days of the *omer*."

CHAPTER 13

Yom Hashoah

Holocaust Remembrance Day

27 NISAN

I believe in the sun when it is not shining.

I believe in love when I do not feel it.

I believe in God even in the silence.

—WORDS WRITTEN ON A WALL IN A CELLAR
USED BY JEWS AS A HIDING PLACE SOMEWHERE
IN COLOGNE, GERMANY, DURING WORLD WAR II

B ETWEEN 1939 AND 1945, Adolf Hitler led his followers in the pursuit of two monstrous goals: the conquest of Europe and the murder of every Jew and other "undesirable"

in the area under German control. At first, it appeared that he might succeed. Nation after

nation caved in or joined forces with him. And he relentlessly perfected his tactics of mass

destruction. Bullets proved too tedious and too costly; asphyxiation
in the backs of trucks, too slow; burial, too burdensome. Mass
roundups, death marches, work and starvation, gas chambers,
crematoria—these became the methods of choice.

Even when the Allies had evidence—irrefutable evidence—that Hitler was murdering Jews on a scale unprecedented and unimaginable, good people and good governments allowed themselves to deny it. As Rabbi Neil Gillman teaches, we don't so much believe what we see as we see what we believe. To be believed, reality must first find a place in our hearts and our minds, a niche in which to secure itself. If we cannot imagine it, if we cannot create a receptive place for it, the truth that enters our minds clasps the walls for a moment, dangles, but ultimately slips off.

When the reality grows too great to deny and our seeing turns to believing, we may still choose to protect ourselves by reframing the truth. Whether through fear, laziness, latent prejudices or selfishness, we imagine that in this way we can limit our exposure, our upset, our guilt, our vulnerability, our responsibility. We somehow manage to assimilate those horrors, tame them, explain them, excuse them, even justify them so that they do not succeed in upsetting our world or placing on us a claim to action. We manage to live quietly next door to those horrors, or worse, join them and become part of them.

How did those living downwind of the camps go to work every day, send their children to school, celebrate birthdays, make love in the stench? How did the Nazi military and civilian death corps justify what they were doing? How did the Allies not feel the imperative to bomb the crematoria and the railroad tracks leading to the camps? How did Hitler find willing executioners not only in Germany but also in Poland, Italy, France and Greece—almost everywhere he went? How can there be "scholars" today who deny the truths of the Holocaust?

Remembering the Holocaust

The questions keep looming out from the darkness of the Holocaust. Where do we draw the line between what we allow ourselves to see and what we turn a blind eye to? Where is the line between inaction and culpability? How much risk shall we expose ourselves and our families to on behalf of others? Are we strong enough to withstand the onslaught of hatred that we witness? Would we have acted differently if we had been there? In reference to the

Holocaust, Rabbi Abraham Joshua Heschel said that we are not all guilty but we are all responsible. What claims does that statement place upon us?

Though ultimately Hitler failed at both his goals, he inflicted a wound so horrid that it has scarred the face of humanity for all time.

In the early part of the 20th century, the legacy of the Enlightenment, coupled with theories of human evolution based on Darwin's concept of natural selection, led people to believe that humanity's development—physical, mental, cultural and ethical—was on an inexorable path upward. We were getting better. Our arts had flourished, our technology was advancing, and so, clearly, were our souls.

World War II proved us wrong.

Hitler not only murdered millions of Jews and other minorities. He also murdered the myth of the natural, irrevocable improvement of the human spirit. We can no longer count on time and natural selection to make us better. Indeed, time, along with technological advances, could allow us to destroy entire peoples, whole nations, maybe even the world. The human spirit too easily succumbed to hatred and temptation. Because of Hitler, the world saw how ugly and how dissolute we can become. And we trembled.

The legacy of World War II is caution and vigilance. Great effort is required to fashion from ourselves the masterpieces of goodness that lie within. We must all be sculptors chipping away at the jagged parts of our souls to reveal the beauty underneath. A world of human goodness will not happen naturally.

For the Jews, Hitler's legacy was that and more: the slaughter of six million Jews, one and a half million of them children—more than all the Jews who live in the United States today, more than all the Jews who live in Israel, two thirds of all the Jews in Europe in the 1940s, one third of all the Jews alive at the time. Such a staggering loss demands a way and a time for mourning and for remembrance. To remember the goodness of our loved ones' lives, to pick ourselves up, to find a way to trust the world again, to place the moment in our sacred calendar—these are the tasks that are embodied by Yom Hashoah.

This drawing is from the diary of Liesel Feisenthal. Her work portrays life, hour by hour, in the concentration camp of Gur in France. Each page is only two inches square. Liesel was about 15 years old when she made her diary. She died while being transported to Auschwitz.

How Many Is Six Million?

One hour is not enough time to read the names of all the Jews who died in the Holocaust. Neither is one day, nor one week, nor one month. It takes almost one year to mention—however briefly— the names of all the Jews killed in the Holocaust. But remember we must, one by one, name by name. And perhaps that is the best way. For it is so hard to grasp the meaning of six million deaths, though we are moved to tears by the suffering of one child. Lists of names of the martyrs of the Holocaust can be obtained from your local B'nai B'rith offices or by contacting B'nai B'rith headquarters, 1640 Rhode Island Avenue, N.W., Washington, D.C. 20036-3278.

Kristallnacht, the Night of Broken Glass

Some people consider the night of November 9, 1938, to be the start of the Holocaust. On that night, thousands of Germans—encouraged and organized by the government—destroyed more than 200 synagogues, burned tens of thousands of Jewish books in town squares, ransacked 815 stores and homes owned by Jews and arrested thousands of Jewish men for no other reason than that they were Jews. Today many communities hold special events to commemorate Kristallnacht and to remind us how important it is to protect freedom and democracy around the world.

Remembering the Lives

We remember the Jews who were killed in the Holocaust: parents, aunts, uncles, grandparents, cousins and friends; scholars, tailors, peddlers, scientists, dancers, cooks and poets. We build monuments in our midst in part to remember their deaths. But even more, we build monuments so that we will not forget their lives.

Today the legacy of the Holocaust is in the process of transformation. Memorials are giving way to museums, and mourning is giving way to a celebration of the lives that were snuffed out. Already in Los Angeles, Washington, D.C., and New York City, major Holocaust museums have opened and are teaching visitors about the richness of the victims' lives as well as about their tragic deaths. Oral histories are being recorded with a sense of urgency while the last generation of witnesses is still with us.

Schools throughout the United States teach about the Holocaust, reminding all Americans of the importance of tolerance, understanding and living with one another in peace. Holocaust education is not just about what happened to the Jews. It is about how easy it is to let evil live next door, how easy it is for us to close our eyes, our ears and our noses. And it is about how, after a while, once we get used to it, we might even be duped into lending the devil a cup of sugar. The lessons of the Holocaust are for everyone. They teach us that evil must be challenged the moment it speaks, that it should be allowed no compromise because compromise only makes it want more, that knowledge and technology are only as benevolent as the hands that wield them, that good people contribute to evil causes when they sit and do nothing.

At the dedication of the U.S. Holocaust Memorial Museum in Washington, D.C., Elie Wiesel said, "Indifference to evil is evil." And so it is, for evil left unchecked will flourish. Once the Nazi killing began, Hitler targeted other minorities, including Gypsies, Communists and homosexuals. Anyone who was different was at risk.

"First they came for the Jews and I was silent," teaches Pastor Martin Niemöller, who lived in Germany during World War II, "for I was not a Jew. Then they came for the Communists, and I was silent, for I was not a Communist. Then they came for the trade unionists, and I was silent, for I was not a trade unionist. Then they came for me. But there was no one left to speak for me." After welcoming the Nazis as they rose to power, Pastor Niemöller recognized the dangers of their ways and spoke against them. As a result, he spent the war years imprisoned in Nazi concentration camps.

Mordecai Anielewicz led the Warsaw Ghetto Uprising. He died three weeks later at the age of 23.

The Warsaw Ghetto Uprising

Yom Hashoah is sometimes referred to as *Yom Hashoah Vehagevurah,* Day of the Holocaust and Heroism, for amidst the overwhelming tragedy there were extraordinary acts of bravery.

Starved, humiliated, tortured though the Jews were, there were many acts of Jewish courage and resistance during the Holocaust. Some were heroic acts carried out, in the impulse of a terrifying moment, by an individual mother, father, grandparent, child, or neighbor, and some were sophisticated strategies implemented by the community. The largest and most famous—the Warsaw Ghetto Uprising—took place in Poland on the eve of Passover, April 19, 1943. It was the very day targeted by the Germans to deport the ghetto's inhabitants to concentration camps.

The Jews of the Warsaw Ghetto understood that their battalion of starving civilians armed with only a few hundred guns and homemade bombs was no match for a modern army rich in trained soldiers, machine guns, and tanks. Yet they fought with will and courage. It took the Nazi troops 27 days to take the ghetto, longer than it took them to overcome all of Poland. If the uprising failed to liberate the Jews of Warsaw from their oppressors, it failed with heroic glory.

—*The New American Haggadah,* Gila Gevirtz, editor

Righteous Gentiles

There is yet another legacy of the Holocaust, a legacy of quiet yet boundless heroism. It is the legacy of the Righteous Gentiles.

In two countries, good people, led by their heads of state in acts of civil disobedience, succeeded in thwarting Hitler. In order to identify who was a Jew and who was not, Hitler ordered all the Jews in all countries he controlled to wear yellow Stars of David on their clothing. He relied on non-Jews to identify all those who did not comply. That worked in many countries, but not in Holland or Denmark. When the order for Jews to wear the star was issued in Holland, 300,000 Jewish stars were sewn and worn by the country's non-Jews. Each star proclaimed, "Jews and non-Jews stand united in their struggle." It is reported that in Denmark, the law

Yad Vashem is the Holocaust Memorial located in Jerusalem. It includes a tree-lined path called the Avenue of the Righteous, a memorial to the non-Jews who risked their lives to save Jews.

Two Righteous Gentiles

Among the many heroes of the war, two have achieved great fame. One is Raoul Wallenberg, a Swedish diplomat who saved thousands of Jews by giving them food, clothing, medicine and false passports for safe passage in and out of Europe. He is believed to have died in a Soviet prison, a prisoner of war, without knowing that the world praises and honors him. Another is Oskar Schindler, who saved more than 800 Jews by convincing the Germans that he needed them to work in his munitions factory. Quietly, without fanfare, without fame, thousands of other gentiles endangered their lives so that Jews could live.

Righteous People Today

On the holiday of Hanukkah in 1993 in the small city of Billings, Montana, one of the few Jewish families there put a menorah in their living room window and lit the candles. Soon thereafter a rock came hurtling through the glass: The house had been attacked by vandals. The good people of Billings rose as one to defend and support the Jewish family. A day or two later the local newspaper printed a large picture of a menorah and with the help of local churches encouraged all families in Billings to tape that picture to their living room windows. Thousands did. That night, one or two churches and some non-Jewish homes had rocks thrown at them, too. But the menorahs stayed up, and the vandalism stopped.

was never even ordered because King Christian X had warned that if there were such a law, he would wear a yellow star himself.

Today, as survivors of the Holocaust tell their stories, we hear more and more about the hidden children, Jewish children who were saved by Righteous Gentiles. They were either hidden in secret places, as Anne Frank was, or they were "adopted" by Christian families or convents who pretended that they were their own children. Tens of thousands of Jewish children were saved that way, as those who harbored them risked death.

In the face of evil, everyday goodness becomes a sacred act of resistance.

How We Observe Yom Hashoah

The 27th of Nisan, five days after the last day of Passover, is the day that the State of Israel has declared Yom Hashoah, the day dedicated to the memory of the Jews who were killed in the Holocaust. The holiday is too young to have developed one standard ceremony or prayer acceptable to all. Still, some customs are gaining popularity.

On the evening of Yom Hashoah, many families light a yellow *yahrtzeit* candle in their homes to keep alive the memories of all the Jews who died in the Holocaust. (A *yahrtzeit* candle marking a personal loss is most often white.) Others light six. On college campuses, in synagogues and schools, in statehouses around the country, people gather to read aloud the names—one by one—of those who perished, the towns they came from, their age when they died.

The Unimaginable Horror

Shoah, translated as "holocaust," refers to something that is entirely burned up, as were many of the Jews of Europe. They were killed in many ways—starvation, sickness, the cold, shootings, hangings and gassings. But what stands out most in the memory of the Jewish people are the concentration camps where Jews did forced labor, the "showers" where they were gassed and the ovens in which they were burned.

Communities and schools often sponsor memorial and educational programs that include the lighting of a six-branched menorah, one branch for each million. Survivors, children of survivors, liberators of the camps, Righteous Gentiles and hidden children are sometimes asked to tell their stories and are given the honor of lighting the menorah.

Members of some communities gather together and sit on the floor, as on Tisha B'Av, and read stories of the Holocaust by contemporary writers. Others read memoirs by victims of the Holocaust or diaries of those who lived through the horror.

A book of recipes, written from memory as an act of defiance by the starving women of Theresienstadt and salvaged from the fires of the war, gives us a way to celebrate their lives in terms that they themselves chose. Many of the recipes are rich, sweet cakes and desserts. A recipe chosen from that book, *In Memory's Kitchen,* can turn into a ceremony of remembrance. Friends or members of a synagogue or family can gather in the kitchen to prepare it. While it is baking, they may study Torah together, in memory of the victims and in celebration of their lives, or they may read from the diaries or the memoirs of the survivors or their children.

When the baking is done, the participants can sit at a table and with modest ceremony eat of the food that kept the hopes and the dignity of the Jews of Theresienstadt alive. The meal can be simple or elaborate, but it should be one for which the diners are seated, one at which the pace is leisurely, with plenty of food set on the table. For the memory of food in the camps is a memory of the prisoners, bowls in hand, lining up only to be told how much they could have and how long they could sit. At the meal, stories of the lives of the Jews who perished, stories of the Righteous Gentiles or stories of the survivors and their children should be told. A new Haggadah of memory, sadness, defiance and celebration will unfold for the next generation.

Yom Hashoah began as a day of communal mourning. In the face of the unthinkable, in the wake of the ungraspable, Jews found comfort in being with one another. To see Jews gathered in freedom is itself to declare victory over Hitler. As time passes, however, Jews will be increasingly eager to bring this commemoration into the home—the center of Judaism—and to remember the lives as well as the deaths. The yellow candle, the baking, the readings, the meal taken together, form the foundation of an enduring Holocaust

In Memory Of

A *yahrtzeit* is the anniversary of someone's death. In Judaism, we remember our loved ones on that anniversary. Usually families light white *yahrtzeit* candles for their loved ones. The candles are designed to burn for 25 hours, so that every moment of the day will be filled with the light of the person's memory. On Yom Hashoah, to distinguish between a personal loss and a national loss and to remind us of the yellow star the Jews were forced to wear under Hitler, a yellow candle is lit.

Yahrtzeit candle ❧

remembrance ritual. For when a tradition comes home, it can never be forgotten.

Psalms and Poetry

Appropriate readings can help mark the day. Some people read psalms of hope. Others read poetry. Here is a poem by Pavel Friedmann. The poem was written in Theresienstadt in Czechoslovakia when Pavel was 21. He died two years later in Auschwitz, an "extermination center."

The Butterfly

The last, the very last,
So richly, brightly, dazzlingly yellow.
Perhaps if the sun's tears would sing
against a white stone...

Such, such a yellow
Is carried lightly 'way up high.
It went away I'm sure because it wished to
kiss the world goodbye.

For seven weeks I've lived in here,
Penned up inside this ghetto
But I have found my people here.
The dandelions call to me
And the white chestnut candles in the court.
Only I never saw another butterfly.

That butterfly was the last one.
Butterflies don't live in here,
in the ghetto.
—I Never Saw Another Butterfly

Laws Against the Jews

The Nazis slowly built their war against the Jews. Little by little they took the Jews' rights away—not all at once, not in such a way that would cause alarm or warn the Jews or their neighbors—or the world—of the fullness of the tragedy ahead; not with enough severity to cause the Jews to flee. After all, Jews had always had trouble in the Diaspora, and they had always survived. For many Jews, the early German restrictions must have seemed like just one more ugly but survivable chapter in their 2,000-year history of living in the Diaspora. Little did we know.

Acknowledging the Righteous Gentiles

Today, on behalf of Jews around the world, the State of Israel is trying to locate the uncommon heroes whom we call Righteous Gentiles. If they are able to travel, they are brought to Israel and honored at Yad Vashem, the memorial center of the Holocaust Martyrs' and Heroes' Remembrance Authority, in Jerusalem. A garden of remembrance has been dedicated to them and their heroism.

Some Righteous Gentiles are very poor or sick and themselves need help. Through the assistance of the Jewish Foundation for the Righteous, they are given funds so that they may live out the rest of their days in dignity, knowing that they earned the profound gratitude of the Jewish people and that they serve as models of sacred defiance for the whole world.

Hannah Senesh

Some Jews managed to escape the Nazi roundups. Many who did fled to America, England, Palestine, even China and Australia. Hannah Senesh was one such person. Born in Budapest, Hungary, Hannah left to settle in Israel in 1939. In 1942, however, she decided she could not sit quietly by while her people were being murdered. She joined a group of Jewish parachutists dedicated to helping the Allies fight the Germans. In March 1944, she was caught in Hungary trying to free prisoners of war. On November 7, 1944, at age 23, she was executed.

Hannah Senesh (1921–1944)

Hannah Senesh was not just a freedom fighter. She was also a poet who spoke knowingly of hope and faith in the presence of despair. One of her most famous poems, which has become a popular Hebrew song, speaks of that eternal hope: "My God, my God, may these things never end: the sand and the sea, the rush of the waves, the lightning of the sky, the prayers of humankind."

In a prophetic poem, Hannah Senesh speaks of the selfless sacrifice that some had to suffer in those desperate years:

Blessed is the match
consumed in kindling flame.
Blessed is the flame that burns
in the secret vastness
of the heart.
Blessed is the heart
with strength to stop
its beating for honor's sake.
Blessed is the match
consumed in kindling flame.

—Hannah Senesh,
Saradice, Yugoslavia, May 2, 1944

The Holidays Are the Storehouse of Jewish Memory

Reaching across thousands of years, they form the diary of the Jewish people, etched by our lives in the journal of time. Each page preserves the sights, the sounds, the struggles, the joy, the pain, the hope, the stories and the feelings our ancestors experienced. Around each story, a holiday and a memory grew.

The journal never closes, not for those who will read it and not for those who will add to it. For as long as the Jewish people live, we will continue to have experiences that will lead us to give birth to new holidays. In the 20th century, we Jews suffered one of our most grievous tragedies and celebrated some of our greatest joys. As a people, we sought to sanctify those moments. So over the course of the past 50 years, four new holidays have been established and have been placed on the Jewish calendar by a decree of the Knesset, the parliament of the State of Israel, and by the ratification of Jews around the world.

The first of those observances, both in annual appearance and in historical occurrence, commemorates the Holocaust. The three others revolve around the State of Israel: her birth and independence (1948), the reunification of the city of Jerusalem (1967) and the loss of thousands of Jewish lives in the defense of a Jewish homeland. It is interesting that all those holidays fall in the sacred period of s'firat ha'omer, the 49 days that are counted between Passover and Shavuot.

CHAPTER 14

Yom Hazikaron, Yom Ha'atzma'ut and Yom Yerushalayim

Songs of Israel

4, 5 AND 28 IYAR

We never lost our hope, the hope of 2,000 years,

to be a free people in our own land, the land of Zion, and Jerusalem.

—FROM "HATIKVAH," THE UNOFFICIAL ANTHEM OF THE STATE OF ISRAEL

From Zion shall come the Torah, the word of God from Jerusalem.

—ISAIAH 2:3

JUST AS EVERY PERSON NEEDS A HOME, so the Jews need Israel. Israel is the earthly center of the Jewish people. It is the land that inspired our psalmists and poets, the land by which we set our spiritual clocks. Its physical landscape inspires our inner landscape: "I lift mine eyes to the mountains; from where will come my salvation?" (Psalm 121:1). Israel is our fulcrum. We cannot move the world and bring it nearer to perfection if we do not have a firm place to stand. Israel is that place. We lived in Israel during times of sovereignty, and Israel lived in us during times of exile.

A newspaper article from the Dreyfus case ❧

The Dreyfus Trial

In the fall of 1894, it was discovered that a classified French document had been sent to the military attaché in the German embassy in Paris. With little evidence and a great deal of anti-Semitism, the sole Jew on the general staff of the French army was accused of treason, tried *in camera* (in secret) and convicted. He was sentenced to life in prison. Although Alfred Dreyfus was exonerated many years later and reinstated in the army, the trial was a scandal and the object of international protests. Theodor Herzl, a secular Jew, covered the trial for the Vienna *Neue Freie Presse*. That experience radically awakened him to his own Jewishness and led him to embark on his odyssey: the creation of a Jewish homeland.

Israel is the home of our youth, where we are forever God's beloved people, beautiful and strong. It is the home of our wise men and women, the ones who spin our dreams. It is the home to which our thoughts constantly return. Every Passover and Yom Kippur we say "next year in Jerusalem." Every time we recite the blessings after a meal, we speak of our return to Israel. We thank God for endowing us with "the pleasing, good and spacious land." We ask God to be gracious to Jerusalem, for the welfare of Jerusalem determines the welfare of the Jewish people.

We shatter a glass at a wedding ceremony to recall the pain of the ancient destruction of Jerusalem. In the early rabbinic period, brides would wear a *Yerushalayim shel zahav*, a golden crown in the shape of Jerusalem, to symbolize that the City of Gold is higher than our greatest joy. When a Jew is buried, a bit of soil from the Land of Israel is often placed beside the body in the coffin.

Three times a day for 2,000 years, we have faced Jerusalem and prayed to be returned to our homeland:

> Sound the great shofar…and gather our exiles from the four corners of the earth….Return to Jerusalem, Your city, O God; let Your presence dwell there as You have promised. Rebuild her speedily in our day. Blessed are You, Builder of Jerusalem…. May our eyes witness Your merciful return to Zion. Blessed are You, O God, who restores Your presence to Zion.

It is no surprise that a secular Jew witnessing the trial of Alfred Dreyfus in France in 1894 was moved to initiate the effort that would lead to the establishment of the modern State of Israel.

The Establishment of the State of Israel

No birth takes place without a struggle; no birth takes place without a dream. As it is with people, so it is with nations. Early in the 20th century, Jews of the Holy Land were pitted against the British, who governed Palestine after gaining control of it from the Turks earlier in the century. In the 1920s, at the beginning of their stewardship, the British sought to accommodate the Jews who lived there. There was freedom of movement and little to no animosity between the two. Indeed, in 1917, even before Britain won its international mandate to oversee Palestine as part of the post-World War I League of Nations' peace agreement, it declared its support of "Jewish Zionist aspirations" in a formal document, the Balfour Declaration, named after the British foreign secretary who signed it.

But soon thereafter tensions arose. In the 1930s and 1940s, many Jews seeking to escape the oppression of Germany and the horrors of the Holocaust tried to settle in Palestine. But the British, fearing trouble with the Arab residents and the surrounding Arab nations, did not want them. Blockades were established; boats laden with war-weary and sea-weary Jews were turned away.

World Jewry could not bear to watch Jews being denied entry to their homeland. With or without Jewish sovereignty, conquered or not, occupied or not, Eretz Yisrael was the Jewish homeland, as it had been for 3,000 years. Diaspora Jewry fought the British blockade by helping to smuggle Jews and weapons into Palestine.

In 1947, the British decided to withdraw from Palestine and allow the United Nations, only two years old, to resolve the problem. In an effort to keep the peace, the UN voted on November 29, 1947, to divide the territory, giving half to the Arabs and half to the Jews. Jerusalem was to be controlled by an international group; the Jews of Palestine agreed to this arrangement. The Arab nations did not.

The Vote

On November 29, 1947, Jews around the world gathered in front of their radios, pencils and paper in hand. The United Nations' vote on the partition of Palestine into an Arab entity and a Jewish entity, a recommendation made by its own Commission on Palestine, was to be broadcast. The roll call began, and thousands of pencils kept score in sync with the secretary of the General Assembly. "Afghanistan, no; Argentina, abstain; Australia, yes." Then Belgium, Belorussia, Bolivia, Brazil, Canada—all yes: the first run of affirmative votes. And so it went, country by country, 56 times. "Syria, no; Turkey, no; Ukraine, yes; Union of South Africa, yes; USSR, yes; United Kingdom, abstain; United States, yes." When the voting was done, 33 nations had ratified the motion for partition; 13 were opposed and 10 abstained. The pencils were still. The first borders of the modern state had been drawn. Today there would be dancing in living rooms, kitchens, hallways, courtyards, schoolyards, orchards, valleys and streets. Tomorrow, war.

On May 14, 1948, the 5th of Iyar on the Jewish calendar, the day before the last British officer left its soil, Israel declared its independence. That night the neighboring Arab nations attacked. It was

The Birth of Hebrew as a Modern Language

Eliezer Ben-Yehudah (1858–1922) is thought of as the father of modern Hebrew. An early Zionist who was raised in Lithuania, Ben-Yehudah knew that a people returning to its homeland from dozens of cultures needs a common language. Hebrew had long been a language of study and of religious, legal and literary correspondence. It had ceased to be a spoken language, however, and thus lacked the vocabulary to facilitate both the sophisticated and the casual discourse of modern life. Ben-Yehudah sought to change that. Upon landing with his family in Jaffa in 1881, he set up the first Hebrew-speaking household since biblical times. In his tireless campaign to revive the spoken language, Ben-Yehudah created the first modern Hebrew dictionary, which was completed by his wife Ḥemdah after his death.

David Ben-Gurion reads the Declaration of Independence of the newly created State of Israel on May 14, 1948. A portrait of Theodor Herzl hangs on the wall.

Golda Meir, a former school teacher from Milwaukee, Wisconsin, became Israel's fourth prime minister in 1969.⁓➧

Many synagogues and Jewish community centers hold fairs on Yom Ha'atzma'ut. They offer a taste of Israel—selling products that are made and grown there, playing Israeli music and teaching Israeli dances.⁓➧

The Dates of the Holidays

Sometimes the modern celebrations or remembrances attached to the new holidays collide with the laws and the spirit of Shabbat. Therefore, if one of Israel's national holidays (Yom Hashoah, Yom Ha'atzma'ut, Yom Hazikaron or Yom Yerushalayim) falls on Shabbat or *erev* Shabbat, it is celebrated one or two days earlier.

a difficult and costly war. Every Jew who could hold a gun or a rock, drive a vehicle or deliver a message, became a soldier. Every piece of land that the partition agreement gave the Jews needed to be defended. The Jews were outnumbered, and many died. But they defeated the Arab nations.

We were a people who had been to hell and back. We had no place left to go. So before the eyes of the world, the State of Israel was born—with half a capital but land we could call our own. A great miracle happened there.

How We Celebrate Yom Ha'atzma'ut

To many, that victory was as miraculous as the splitting of the Sea of Reeds, the Maccabees' victory over the Syrians and the Jews' victory over the Persians. Six hundred thousand Jews lived in Israel in 1948, the same number of households that gathered at Mount Sinai after the Exodus from Egypt. Within a decade, the Jewish population doubled. By the end of the 20th century, Israel was home to five million Jews, 700,000 of them refugees from the former Soviet Union. What shall we call that if not a miracle? And so Independence Day, Yom Ha'atzma'ut, on 5 Iyar, was added to the calendar of Jewish holidays, the first new holiday in 2,000 years.

Because it is still new, we are refining the ways to celebrate it. Some people add a prayer and psalms to the morning services. Some add a prayer to the evening services as well. Many say Hallel, the psalms of praise and victory recited on the pilgrimage holidays, Rosh Hodesh and Hanukkah. Others create whole services devoted to the occasion. Almost every Jewish school and community sponsors a public gathering marked with song, speeches and dancing.

In time, the development of the celebration may follow a different course in Israel, where Jews represent the majority culture. For in Israel, the very air is filled with the mood of celebration. Schools, businesses, government offices, places of recreation—all Jewish citizens proclaim the joy of the day. You feel the day by breathing the air and walking in the streets. Silly String is spewed everywhere. Every head is fair game for the noisemaking plastic hammers. There are picnics, fireworks, and dancing in the public squares. The celebration comes to you.

In the Diaspora, you must go to the celebration, which means that you must develop rituals for the home and the synagogue and you must arrange communal celebrations. You might eat a meal rich with Israeli beverages and foods: wine and oranges and nuts and chocolates. Or you might have a meal of classic Israeli foods: falafel, pita, ḥummus, teḥina and a salad of cucumbers, tomatoes and onions chopped fine. You might give tzedakah to an Israeli cause, plant a tree through the Jewish National Fund, visit a Web site that publishes Israeli songs and history, support a program that sponsors trips to Israel for teenagers.

Family members and friends can gather to make *mizraḥim*, works of art that depict scenes of Jerusalem and are hung on the eastern wall of a home or office as a reminder of the way to Zion. And in our living rooms, we can gather to read aloud Israel's Declaration of Independence, the sacred retelling of the founding of the state.

Between Heaven and Earth

Yisrael shel matah, the earthly State of Israel of the first 50 years, is not the same as *Yisrael shel ma'alah,* the heavenly Israel envisioned over the past 2,000 years. The State, unlike the vision, is subject to the grit and the grime of reality: the struggles of power among the nation's estates, the questionable ethics of some political leaders, the use and misuse of military might, the rhetoric of social equality measured against the actual practice of national policy, the problematic alliance between government and religion, and the unique challenge in the coexistence of a Jewish nation and a full democracy.

But the earthen feet of the young nation—even its missteps, cockiness and excesses—should not repel us away from its heart and its soul. The land has been ours for more than 3,000 years; the nation, for barely more than 50. Any missteps should not cause us to turn our backs on Israel, or to take up arms, Jew against Jew. Tradition teaches that such internal hatred was the cause of the final destruction of the Temple and the loss of our national sovereignty. We cannot afford to lose Israel again. As the state continues to evolve during its second 50 years, we must continue to help it achieve peace with its neighbors, peace within its borders, prosperity that it can share with all its citizens and the community of nations.

A Prayer for the Soldiers of Israel

May the One who blessed Abraham, Isaac and Jacob, Sarah, Rebecca, Rachel and Leah, bless all the fighters of Israel, all who stand guard to defend our land and these holy cities, from the border of Lebanon to the Egyptian desert, from the Mediterranean Sea to the sands in the far distance. May God thwart the designs of those who rise against us.

God, protect and shelter our soldiers from all grief and harm, from all wounds and injury. Grant them blessing and victory in all they do. Crown them with the wreath of deliverance and the garland of victory. And let Your words be fulfilled through them: For the Eternal One walks with you, to fight alongside you, against your enemies, to bring you victory.

One way to celebrate Yom Ha'atzma'ut is to take a trip to Israel, enjoy its historical, cultural and religious sights and scuba dive in the blue waters of Eilat.

This armored tank was left on the road to Jerusalem as a memorial to the soldiers who died bringing supplies to the city during Israel's War of Independence.

Yom Hazikaron: Memorial Day

The birth of any nation comes at a price, and Israel's birth was no different. So every year on Yom Hazikaron, 4 Iyar, the day before Yom Ha'atzma'ut, the people of Israel and Jews around the world remember the pain and the price of the creation of the state. We remember the pioneers, the hardships they endured and how they built up the land from sand dunes and marshes to make it hospitable to those who followed. We remember the soldiers, the men and women of the Haganah, the pre-1948 defense force, and how they defended the land, sometimes with nothing more than faith and stubbornness.

But the War of Independence was not the only war the State of Israel had to fight. Every few years another war threatened her existence: the War of Attrition (1950s), the Six-Day War (1967), the Yom Kippur War (1973), the *intifada* (1987–1993). So today on Yom Hazikaron, we remember not only those who fell in 1948 but also all the soldiers and the citizens of Israel who fought and died for their homeland.

On that day in Israel, the national flag is flown at half-mast, and people visit the cemeteries where their grandparents, parents, children, siblings, cousins, aunts, uncles, nieces, nephews, neighbors and friends are buried. Hardly a family exists in that small country that has not lost a loved one to bombs or bullets. For two minutes on the morning of 4 Iyar, throughout the entire land a siren is sounded. Wherever people are—on a highway, on a bus, at home, in a store, walking—they stop and stand in silence. In that one moment, every Jew throughout Israel remembers the pain of the birth of Israel.

The newness of the holiday and their distance from the Land of Israel deny the Jews of the Diaspora a universally accepted ritual or liturgy. In some communities, Jews recite special prayers (including Psalms 9 and 144) and light memorial candles. In others, they gather to recount their stories of Israel's struggles, sing songs of deliverance and read the narratives and diaries of those who live there.

Yom Yerushalayim: Jerusalem Day

"If I forget you, O Jerusalem, may my right hand wither. May my tongue cleave to the roof of my mouth if I do not remember you, if I do not raise you above my highest joy" (Psalm 137:5–6). Ever since King David, Jerusalem has been the worldly center of the Jewish people. Its spectacular views capture your heart. No airport serves Jerusalem, so everyone approaches her the same way, by climbing her majestic hills. Silent yet relentless, the hills pull you upward, ever upward toward the mountain of Jerusalem. In Hebrew, you don't travel to Jerusalem, you *go up* to Jerusalem. Body and soul rise through the journey.

The City of Peace

According to an ancient legend, the place where the Holy Temple was built was once owned by two brothers. One brother had a wife and many children, while the other had no wife and no children. Both brothers lived well, comfortable with their lot, on the land they inherited from their father.

They hoed and tilled and planted together. And together they reaped, dividing the harvest up equally. One night, the brother who was blessed with family said to himself: *If I should become ill, I have my wife and children to look after me. But if my brother is needy, who will look after him? Surely he needs the grain more than I.* And so, in the dead of night, he sneaked out to where the piles of grain stood and took from his pile and added to his brother's.

Meanwhile, his brother began to wonder as well. *I am all alone, but my brother has a whole family to feed and clothe and care for. I can do quite well with less, so why should my portion be the same as his?* And so, in the dead of night, he sneaked out to where the piles of grain stood and took from his pile and added to his brother's.

Come morning, each brother was amazed. His pile was not reduced, and his brother's pile was not enlarged. But they said nothing.

Night after night they continued to do this, and each morning their piles were the same. Finally, one night, this one had been delayed in leaving his home, and that one had gone early. This one had in his arms a mountain of grain and that one had in his arms a mountain of grain. And they met. At once they understood what had been happening, and they embraced. And it is on the site of that embrace that the Temple was built.

—Based on the tale as found in *Mimekor Yisrael: Classical Jewish Folktales*, collected by Micha Joseph bin Gorion, translated by I. M. Lask

Yom Yerushalayim, Jerusalem Day, is the latest holiday to be added to the Jewish calendar. In 1948, when the Arabs rejected the

Going Up

The Hebrew word *aliyah* means "going up," a physical rising from one plane to another. But it also evokes the awareness of growing holiness. When we are "called up" to read from the Torah, we do not just ascend to the place where the Torah rests; we also ascend in holiness. When we go to France or England, we travel there. When we go to Israel, we say we "go up" to the land. When we move to Israel, we say we "make *aliyah*." Never is that going up more evident than when we go to Jerusalem, rising ever higher on the broad, rolling Hills of Judaea.

The Western Wall ❧

United Nations' partition agreement, the vision of a united Jerusalem governed by international rule died. Instead, the outcome of the War of Independence decided the city's fate. When the fighting stopped, Israel had control over the western part of the city, the modern part, but not the eastern part, the part containing the Old City, the Western Wall, the place of our sacred memories. That part was under Jordan's control. Jews were forbidden to go there.

Jerusalem, the City of David, the City of Peace, the eternal capital of the Jewish people, was divided for 19 years. In 1967, the Arabs once again provoked a war against Israel, hoping not just to conquer Israel but also to destroy her. So began the Six-Day War. In a victory that astonished the world, Israel established herself as a formidable power; buoyed the spirit, image and pride of Jews everywhere; and recaptured the Old City. The Western Wall was once again in Jewish hands. Jerusalem was united. The image of the Jews as victims being led like lambs to slaughter was finally put to rest. In its place stood a warrior, a victor, a soldier who fought with the ethic of *tohar haneshek,* purity of the weapon. Battles were for winning, not for vengeance. Civilians were to be protected; prisoners, kept secure. Jews around the world stood taller after the Six-Day War.

Yom Yerushalayim is celebrated on the anniversary of Jerusalem's reunification, 28 Iyar. As on Yom Ha'atzma'ut, Hallel is recited in many synagogues, and in Israel many people go to the Western Wall to praise God for returning our city to us, whole.

Jerusalem is more than a city to Jews. She is the symbol of our national unity, the seat of our sovereignty, the earthly model of the heavenly City of Peace, the place where Jews feel closest to God and one another. "All the world is holy," the Midrash tells us, "but the Land of Israel is the holiest of all. All Israel is holy, but the city of Jerusalem is the holiest of all." Jerusalem once was the meeting place of God and the Jews. Today it is the meeting place of the Jewish people. For wherever we pray, whether alone or in a minyan, whether with statutory prayers or prayers from the heart, wherever we stand, we turn toward Jerusalem, our home, and thus toward one another.

An Ethical Will

The following is an excerpt from an ethical will written by Dvora Waysman:

As I write this I am on my Jerusalem balcony, looking through a tracery of pine trees at the view along Rehov Rupin. I can see the Knesset, the Israel Museum, and the Shrine of the Book—that houses the Dead Sea Scrolls.

I am at an age where I should write a will, but the disposition of my material possessions would take just a few lines. They do not amount to much. Had we stayed in Australia, where you—my four children—were born, they would be much more. I hope you won't blame me for this.

For now you are Israelis, and I have different things to leave you. I hope you will understand that they are more valuable than money in the bank, stocks and bonds, and plots of land, for no one can ever take them away from you.

I am leaving you the fragrance of a Jerusalem morning, the unforgettable perfume of thyme, sage and rosemary that wafts down from the Judaean hills. The heartbreaking sunsets that give way to Jerusalem at night, splashes of gold on black velvet darkness. The feel of Jerusalem stone, ancient and mellow, in the buildings that surround you. The piquant taste of humus, tehina, felafel—foods we never knew about before we came here to live.

I am leaving you an extended family—the whole house of Israel. They are your people. They will celebrate with you in joy, grieve with you in your sorrow. You will argue with them,

criticize them, and sometimes reject them (that's the way it is with families!). But underneath you will be proud of them and love them. More important, when you need them—they will be there!

I am leaving you pride. Hold your head high. This is your country, your birthright. Try to do your share to enhance its image. It may call for sacrifice, but it will be worth it. Your children, their children, and all who come after, will thank you for it.

I am leaving you memories. Some are sad—the early struggles to adapt to a new culture, a new language....But remember, too, the triumphs—the feeling of achievement when you were accepted, when "they" became "us." That is worth more than silver trophies and gold medals. You did it alone—you "made" it.

And so, my children, I have only one last bequest. I leave you my love and my blessing. I hope you will never again need to say: "Next year in Jerusalem." You are already here—how rich you are!

The Western Wall

The Temple was a massive complex inside the walls of the city of Jerusalem. It was made up of a series of supporting walls, open courts and inner chambers that possessed increasing degrees of holiness the closer they stood to the innermost Holy of Holies. Of all the Temple's structures, only the Western Wall withstood the attack on Jerusalem in 70 CE. The enormous stones at the base of the wall, averaging 3¼ feet high and 10 feet long, with some as long as 12 feet, are believed to have formed the base of the wall

of the First Temple, built by King Solomon almost 3,000 years ago. The wall was not part of the Temple proper but was part of the retaining walls surrounding the Temple. With the collapse of the Bar Kochba rebellion in 135 CE, the last hope to recapture Jerusalem after its fall to the Romans in 70 CE collapsed as well.

Ever since, Jews around the world have turned during prayer toward the Western Wall. As an outer wall standing alone, the Western Wall represented our exile. It was an orphan as we were orphans. Whenever we could, we visited it, letting our tears and our deepest yearnings wash over it. We stuffed our prayers and our hopes into its crevices, and we imagined that it shared our sorrow. And we learned from it: As it was strong, so we could be strong. It stood as a witness to the grandeur of our people, a reminder that the holiness of Jerusalem and the Jewish people could never be destroyed. Throughout the ages, we have loved that wall.

Today archaeological excavations have added another site: the majestic southern approach to the Temple Mount. The grand and spacious Southern Wall is beginning to reclaim its place in the hearts of world Jewry. It has already begun to attract bar and bat mitzvah celebrations, much like the Western Wall. And given that the Southern Wall is still free from the controversies surrounding the religious administration of the Western Wall and its plaza and that it is still free from the prohibitions that keep women and liberal Jews from gathering in groups to pray at the Western Wall, its popularity will most likely grow.

CHAPTER 15

Shavuot

The Giving of the Torah

6/7 SIVAN

When God gave us the Torah, no bird twittered, no fowl flew, no ox lowed, the

ophanim did not flutter a wing, the seraphim did not say, "Holy, Holy, Holy,"

the sea did not roar, no creature made a sound, the whole earth was hushed

into breathless silence. The voice went forth, "I am Adonai, your God."

When God spoke on Mount Sinai, the whole world became silent so that

all the creatures might know that there is none beside God.

—Exodus Rabbah 29:9

THERE ARE A VARIETY OF JEWS in the world. There are Diaspora Jews and Israeli Jews; Reform, Conservative, Reconstructionist, Orthodox and secular Jews; Jews who believe in God and Jews who do not. There are Jews from the East and Jews from the West; those who pray alone, those who pray in a minyan, and those who do not pray at all.

There are homosexual Jews and heterosexual Jews. There are coupled, married, divorced, never married and widowed Jews; Jews from traditional families and Jews from nontraditional families; Jews from Jewish families and Jews from non-Jewish families. There are

Four Levels of Meaning

The rabbis teach that the words of the Torah can be read on four levels, known by the acronym *PaRDeS*, meaning "orchard." The first level, *peshat*, is the literal or contextual meaning of the text, what the words mean on the surface. The second level, *remez*, is the allegorical or philosophical meaning. The third, *derash*, is the homiletic or ethical meaning. And the fourth, *sod*, is the hidden or mystical meaning. A Jew can spend a lifetime reading the same texts over and over and still not plumb their deepest meaning.

On Passover we imagine that we personally went out from the Land of Egypt. And on Shavuot we imagine that we personally received the gift of Torah from God. ❧

generous Jews and selfish Jews; Jews who eat deli and Jews who eat Chinese. With so many different kinds of Jews, what is it that keeps us together? What is it that makes us all Jews?

The answer is Torah.

What Is the Torah?

The Torah is the Five Books of Moses, known in English as Genesis, Exodus, Leviticus, Numbers and Deuteronomy, and in Hebrew as B'reshit, Sh'mot, Vayikrah, B'midbar and D'varim (the first important word of each book). In the Torah are the stories and the sayings and the laws and the lessons that are the spirit of the Jewish people. Some of the world's most important lessons come from the Torah: Honor your father and your mother; do not murder; love one another as you love yourself. The world learned the meaning of the Sabbath from the Torah. The world learned monotheism from the Torah. The inscription on the Liberty Bell comes from the Torah: "Proclaim liberty throughout all the land unto all the inhabitants thereof" (Leviticus 25:10). The Torah is an inexhaustible storehouse of wisdom. A rabbi named Ben Bag Bag said it best almost 2,000 years ago: "Turn it and turn it, for everything is in it" (*Pirke Avot* 5:24).

The Torah belongs to all of us. It is our history and our destiny. It is our source of values, wisdom and purpose, our common vocabulary, our narrative, our memory. Amid the internecine strife that has plagued Jews across the millennia, it is the Torah that has bound us together. It is what all Jewish life is based on. The Torah is the soul of the Jewish people. As long as we are Jews, the Torah is ours and we each have a share in it.

Exactly how the Torah was created, where and when it was committed to writing, is something we can only speculate about. Were the words dictated by God to Moses on Mount Sinai? If so, how many of those words? all of them? the Ten Commandments? all but the last verses, which speak of Moses' death? Is Torah a response to God's encounter with history, inspired but not dictated by God? Is it a midrash on Revelation, as Rabbi Abraham Joshua Heschel put it? Is the Torah a compilation of sacred tales of a remarkable people, full of wisdom and truth, but not divine?

In truth, the origins of the Torah remain a mystery. Although it would be satisfying to know, the authority of the Torah need not be diminished by the mystery, for its authority goes beyond the origins of the text. It is grounded in the millions of Jews over hundreds of generations who claimed it, cherished it, nurtured it, obeyed it, embellished it and built out of it a tradition that enriches the world and illumines our lives. That history both confers and confirms its holiness. Where the Torah came from is not as critical as what it means to us, how it has built our people and helped us map our world and our destination. "Would that they forsake Me," says God, "but let them keep My Torah" (*Lamentations Rabbah,* Proem II).

The Giving of the Gift

The Torah itself tells us its own story of origin. It tells us that much of it was given by God to the Jews through the hands of Moses 3,500 years ago at the mountain of Sinai. And Moses speaks several times of "the book" that is being written to record the history that is unfolding in the wilderness (Exodus 17:14, 24:7, 32:32–33; Numbers 21:14; Deuteronomy 17:18, 31:26). The story of the giving of the Torah begins when God freed the Israelites from Egypt and brought them in safety through the Sea of Reeds. God led them to a remote mountain, sometimes called Horeb, most often called Sinai. It was there that God promised to come down to the mountain and speak with the Israelites. For three days, the people prepared themselves as they had been instructed. They cleaned their clothes, refrained from sexual activity and waited to meet their God.

The giving of the law on Mount Sinai ❧

Where Is Mount Sinai?

Truth be told, we do not know the location of Mount Sinai. There are some attractive candidates, so attractive that travel companies now book pilgrimages there, complete with early morning climbs to greet the sunrise on the mountaintop. But each of those places is, at best, a guess. And while our curiosity is insatiable, there is merit in our ignorance. Not knowing denies any one group the right to claim ownership of the place of Revelation.

Finally, in the words of Exodus 19:16, "the morning [of the third day] dawned, and with it came thunder and lightning, and a thick cloud hung on the mountain; the voice of a shofar sounded, strong, and all the people in the camp quaked....The mountain was filled with smoke because God was descending upon it." And God spoke the words of the Ten Commandments, saying, "I am your God, who brought you out of the land of Egypt....You shall have no other gods before Me" (Exodus 20:2).

What exactly happened that day is not clear. The biblical record of events is itself fuzzy. (Read the original story, beginning with

Tending the Torah Scroll

The Torah is the most sacred object of the Jewish people. We don't leave the Torah scroll lying around when it is not being used. Nor do we leave it open and exposed when no one is reading from it. We roll the scroll by turning the rods (atzei ḥayyim) to which the parchment is attached. We use a pointer, called a yad, to help us keep our place when we read. We tie the scroll when it is closed so that it will not unravel, and then we dress it in beautiful covers so that it is both attractive and protected. We build a revered place for it in the synagogue, called the Aron Kodesh, the Holy Ark. It stays there, protected, whenever we are not using it. We stand whenever the ark is opened or the Torah is raised, and we do not turn our backs to it when it is before us.

The printed Bible, bound in book form, enjoys comparable respect. We do not place it on the floor or stack other books on top of it. We do not store it upside down or use it to prop open windows. It is the tradition of some Jews to kiss the Bible after studying from it or after accidentally dropping it. Some Jews kiss the mezuzah on the doorposts they pass, for it, too, contains words of Torah.

Exodus 18, and see whether you can keep track of who is where at every moment.) In a way, that is understandable, for the rabbis tell us that the Revelation of the Torah was like a wedding, when emotions often overwhelm memory.

History Versus Memory

Or perhaps the Torah, in codifying the imprecision, is striving to tell us that the pursuit of an accurate historical account is quite beside the point. Let the people weave their own sacred account from the remnants that have been preserved. That is how religious memory works. Yosef Hayim Yerushalmi, Professor of Jewish History, Culture and Society at Columbia University, argues that memory should not be confused with history. History seeks data and explanations; memory seeks meaning. History walks in earthen shoes; memory is spun from the soul. We create history; memory creates us. Could not the redactor, the purported editor of the Torah, have synthesized and homogenized this biblical story? Could not the redactor have removed the fuzziness and the contradictions? Why preserve discrepancy? After all, not only the events surrounding the Revelation but also the content of the Revelation itself is confusing. In Exodus, for example, the wording of the fourth commandment is, "Remember the Sabbath day to keep it holy…for in six days, God created the heaven and the earth." In the retelling of the Revelation in Deuteronomy, the fourth commandment becomes "Keep the Sabbath day…and remember that you were once a slave in Egypt, but God brought you out by a mighty hand and an outstretched arm." Perhaps the discrepancy is preserved to say there are multiple explanations of God's will and God's word. Perhaps it is preserved to teach us that just as the mountain was wrapped in fog and smoke for the Israelites, so it must always remain for us.

Understandably, though, some people find the uncertainty unsettling. They choose to force the issue of clarity. Over the centuries, they have spun different theories of the origins of the Torah. Some think God spoke every word of the commandments and wrote every word of the Torah as we now have it. Others think God spoke and wrote only the Ten Commandments (based on Exodus 24:12: "Adonai said to Moses, 'Come up to Me, and I will give you the law and the commandments that I have written, that you may teach them'"). Still others believe that God spoke only the first two commandments, for they alone appear in the first person. Some suggest that God spoke only the first letter of the first word of the first commandment, the *aleph*, because humans cannot bear to hear the unmediated voice of God (Moses having been God's chosen exception).

A Shavuot cup, made in late 18th-century England 🐟

Honoring Your Father and Your Mother

The picture in the newspaper was stunning. A son had returned to his East Asian homeland and to his mother, whom he had not seen in 35 years. He, his wife and their children met her outside a building. As she stood erect, teary-eyed and clearly moved, her family members bowed down in their western suits and fine clothes, foreheads to the ground, to greet her and honor her.

When I was a child, my brothers and sister and I would run to greet my father when he came home. It was a joy to receive him at the end of the day, but it was also expected of us, for we were taught that such honor was due him. We could not sit in his chair, either at the dinner table or in the den, whether he was present or not.

How do we honor our parents today? How can we reclaim that tradition? In this age of psychological sophistication, it is often tempting to attribute to our parents a multitude of flaws—if not accuse them of a multitude of sins—that served to mold our lives and our character. The Torah does not make the law requiring us to honor our parents conditional, however. It does not say, "If your parents are worthy, then honor them." Rather, just as parents are called upon to offer their children unconditional love, so children are called upon to offer their parents unconditional honor. All households, all children, must create opportunities and traditions to honor their parents.

Yet there are some parents who behave in ways that are beyond the pale. They may abuse their children or neglect or abandon them. In doing so, they strain their children's ability to fulfill the commandment to honor them. They strain their children's ability even to forgive them. Just as the Torah recognizes the existence of rebellious children, so it recognizes the existence of unworthy parents. In such cases, honor is circumscribed and even reconciliation may not be possible.

Your Ten Commandments

The Ten Commandments are the foundation of our relationship with God and the fundamental rules of any ethical society. Day to day we are each faced with many important challenges to living ethical and dignified lives. What are the ten everyday commandments that you need to guide your home, social or work life? Control your temper; call Mom; cut down on the fats—you get the idea. Place the list in your desk drawer, on a night table, or on your refrigerator for easy reference. Check up on yourself regularly to see how you are doing.

No matter what really happened back then, we do know one thing: Somewhere, sometime, something occurred that was so awe-inspiring that a people was born, their belief system founded on the principle that they are holy, connected to one another and to the Source—whatever that may be—that conferred meaning on them and on life everywhere. And in response to that discovery, the Jews pledged themselves, individually and collectively, to join their will to God's and to seek to increase holiness in this world.

"We Will Do, and We Will Listen"

In this case, listening means understanding. But as a declaration of commitment—an oral signature, so to speak—isn't the phrase backward? My father, a lawyer, taught me never to sign anything without reading it first. How could the Israelites have ratified the most important contract ever offered them, committing them to Lord knows what, without first knowing fully what it said?

As in all religious experiences, understanding comes mostly through doing. Just as we cannot know whether we like a food until we taste it, so we cannot know a religious experience until we live it. Just as we cannot appreciate an emotion until we feel it, so we cannot appreciate the power of ritual until we experience it. Working with a mentor or as an intern or receiving on-the-job training are experiences based on that wisdom. Until you live the moment, there can be no real understanding of it. And until we begin to understand it, we cannot ask the right questions or appreciate the answers. So we must commit ourselves to the learning and the doing and the living before we can claim to understand.

We All Stood at Sinai

Every Jew today is a witness to that promise made on our behalf by our ancestors thousands of years ago. To be more precise, the promise was made not so much by our ancestors on our behalf as by us. The tradition tells us that every Jew—of any time and any place—stood together with the Children of Israel at Sinai. Each of us was a witness to the birth of the Jews as a nation; each of us was a witness to the Revelation; each of us responded with that curious statement, "We will do, and we will listen." In the language of the Midrash, the Torah was written with 600,000 letters corresponding to the 600,000 Jewish souls who stood at Sinai, a vast number meant to include every Jewish soul ever. If even one letter of the Torah is missing, Jewish law has it, the Torah is incomplete. How much more so if one Jewish soul is lost.

Why did the experience of Sinai, the giving of the law, the consummation of the Covenant, follow immediately upon the Exodus, three months into the trek to freedom?

When the Jews were slaves in Egypt, they had one law, the law of their taskmasters. The law was neither just nor fair. It had only one purpose: to serve the will of Pharaoh. Neither the details nor the model of Egyptian law could serve the Israelites' needs now. Nor could the Israelites rely on their experience before slavery. Before Egypt, the Israelites had been a family, 70 households in all. They had not been a people. They had never set up a society or wielded national military or economic power or established their own system of law or negotiated as a people.

Now, however, the Jews were on their own. Internal cohesion would no longer be enforced by external terror. If the Jews were going to be a holy nation, they needed to build a new identity. They could not adopt the Egyptians' identity of oppressors. They needed a different sense of self, a different purpose for their community, a different system of government. They had to be able to tell their own stories in their own language, name their own ancestors, choose their own God, craft their own view of history. All that would be encoded in their laws, for a culture's laws encode its sacred story, through the structure of its calendar, through its holidays and rituals and through the source of its justice and its values.

So God liberated the Jews physically by removing them from Egypt and spiritually by giving them the Torah. And the Jews were free to emerge as a new people.

Torah Flows Through the Generations

Moses received the Torah at Sinai. He transmitted it to Joshua, Joshua to the elders, the elders to the prophets, the prophets to the members of the Great Assembly....Shimon the Pious was one of the last members of the assembly. This was his favorite teaching: The world rests on three things, "Torah, doing the work of God, and deeds of lovingkindness." Antigonus of Socho received the tradition from Shimon the Pious.

And on the tradition goes. That is how *Pirke Avot*, the *Ethics of Our Fathers*, begins. The words and the lessons of Torah flow through the generations, from father and mother to son and daughter, from teacher to student and student to friend. The list is not closed; the task of transmission is never complete. Each of us is a link in the tradition.

Even after thousands of years, the Torah continues to be the foundation of Judaism. Through the symbol of Sinai, God and the Jewish people are joined. Tradition tells us, "Israel, Torah and God are one." Through stories and lessons, laws and songs, the Torah reminds us of who we are and Whose we are. Torah builds a way of being and a way of belonging. It is a symbol of our promise to love God and of God's promise to love us and it is the contract that codifies those promises. It is a promise of each Jew to be a faithful member of the Jewish people. As Heschel reminds us, we do not approach God as an "I" to a "Thou" but as "we" to "You."

No wonder, then, that there is a holiday that celebrates the giving of the Torah. That holiday is called Shavuot.

How We Celebrate

As one of the three pilgrimage holidays, Shavuot has both an agricultural and a historical explanation. Agriculturally, Shavuot marks the end of the spring harvest. Grateful for their good fortune, the people of Israel would come to Jerusalem with much fanfare and celebration, bringing their harvest offerings to the Temple. Although tradition stipulated that only fruits from the seven species specifically associated with Israel needed to be

Torah Is Where the Jews Are

The Torah might have been given on a mountaintop, but it belongs in the everyday life of the people. It was not meant to be the exclusive domain of the priests or the king. It was not meant to be only for dress-up or special events. The Torah, its words and its message, were to be the possession and the legacy of every Jew.

A Love Story

Some communities symbolize Shavuot as the wedding anniversary of God and the Jewish people. They imagine God as the groom, the Jewish people as the bride and the Torah as the wedding document. Some synagogues even reenact the wedding, complete with *huppah*, or wedding canopy, and a specially worded *ketubah*, or Jewish wedding contract.

When We Celebrate

All Jews celebrate Shavuot on 6 Sivan. Conservative and Orthodox Jews outside the Land of Israel also celebrate it on 7 Sivan.

The first fruits of the season are called bikkurim in Hebrew. One way we celebrate the harvest and the giving of the Torah is by donating food to the hungry.

brought, the Jewish people chose to embellish this commandment and often brought other crops as well.

The Time of the Giving of the Torah

Some people wonder why the name Z'man Matan Torateinu refers only to the *giving* of the Torah and not to the *receiving* of the Torah. The traditional answer is that the Torah was given only once, years ago on Mount Sinai, whereas it is received every day. Every day each Jew receives the Torah in his or her own way and must approach it within the terms of his or her unique capacity. With every Jew, the Torah must be accepted anew.

Of the three pilgrimage holidays, Shavuot has the fewest rituals associated with it. There are no mandatory foods, no special places to sit, no things to shake or to blow. We tend to eat dairy on Shavuot — cheesecake is popular. We have our holiday Torah readings. We chant the Book of Ruth in the synagogue. We hold confirmation celebrations. But it is a quiet, unassuming holiday, the least celebrated and the least understood of the three pilgrimage holidays. Yet it represents the most remarkable moment in the story of the Jewish people, the moment when God stepped out from behind the curtains of heaven and chose to enter into a covenant with the Jewish people. What ritual could begin to reenact that?

Understanding Chosenness

The Bible speaks of the Jews as a special people, a treasured people. The rabbis speak of the Jews as chosen. Chosenness is a concept some are uncomfortable with. If God is the God of all Creation, they challenge, then in what way are the Jews chosen? In the middle of the 20th century, Rabbi Mordecai Kaplan, the founder of the Reconstructionist movement, rejected the idea of chosenness, and Reconstructionist prayer books have removed all references to this idea. And yet the traditional texts continue to say we are chosen. The prayer all but the Reconstructionists recite before every Torah reading asserts: "For You have chosen us from among all the nations." How can we understand this?

Some liken chosenness to a child and a parent, or to a bead on a necklace. Many children are beloved by their parents; many beads may be combined to make a necklace. Each is precious, each uniquely fills its place and performs its roles, but none is alone in its quality of uniqueness. So it is with the Jewish people. We do have a unique relationship with God. We fill a place that no other people can fill. Yet we are not alone in our uniqueness. God is the only God, but we need not be God's only chosen people.

In the medieval period, mystics celebrated the holiday with a ritual called *tikkun leil Shavuot*. They would study the mysteries of

Torah all night to prepare for the opening of the heavens at midnight. They believed that just then they could hear the echo of Revelation, still audible in the universe to those who knew how to listen — just like the echo of the big bang.

Today many synagogues and families re-create their own *tikkunim* (plural of *tikkun*), inviting friends to join them for study and food. Often, guests are invited to bring a text and a nosh, and everyone takes a turn teaching and learning. The study lasts as long as the energy and the food hold out. Some groups study until it is light enough to begin the morning prayers.

Shavuot marks the coming of age of a people, a people who were ready to pursue their own destiny guided by the hand of God. At Sinai, the Jews met God and were given their constitution. Where to then? Onward to the Promised Land. But given the stubbornness of the Israelites, the trip took a little longer than expected.

Milk and Shavuot

Why is it traditional to eat milk products on Shavuot? No one really knows. Perhaps, some suggest, the Israelites abstained from eating meat as part of the purity rituals undertaken to prepare themselves for Revelation, and so we do, too. Or perhaps, as Rabbi Andre Ungar suggests, we do so to show that just as milk is life-giving after the birth of a baby, so the Torah is life-giving after the birth of a nation.

Confirmation

Today many synagogues choose Shavuot as the time for young Jews to renew their commitment to God and the Jewish people. In many synagogues, confirmation is a graduation ceremony from Hebrew high school or a commencement after several years of post-bar and bat mitzvah study. In others it is a graduation to a higher level of learning. Boys and girls wearing white give a presentation from the *bimah*, telling of their commitment to learning and living Torah. Through readings from the Torah and a ritual procession, they relive for us the experience of the giving of the Torah.

Reclaiming the Theme of Shavuot

For two thousand years, Shavuot has been celebrated as the holiday of the Giving of the Torah. So seamlessly do Shavuot and Matan Torah fit together, that the marriage seems to have been ordained in the Bible.

But it wasn't. Though the Torah clearly speaks of Shavuot (see Exodus 34:2 and Leviticus 23:9–22, among other places), nowhere does it link Shavuot with Mount Sinai. Indeed, the wedding of the two apparently is a rabbinic invention. And justifiably so. For until then, the most God-filled moment in the history of our people had no holiday to mark it, no sacred date in our calendar to celebrate and relive it. That was a lapse that needed to be remedied. And since the Torah itself tells us that Revelation occurred in the third month after the Exodus, and that Shavuot falls in the third month after Passover, the connection—once made—seems God-given.

And yet the fit, perfect though it be, remains a recasting of the original image of the holiday. Deuteronomy 26 offers a detailed description of the day's celebration: "When you enter the land that Adonai your God is giving to you as a heritage, and you possess it and settle in it, you shall take some of every first fruit of the soil that you harvest from the land that Adonai your God is giving you, put it in a basket and go to the place where Adonai your God will establish the divine name. You shall go to the priest in charge and say, 'I acknowledge this day [with this fruit as my witness] that I have entered the land that Adonai swore to our ancestors to assign us.'"

Such was the ritual that was performed during the hundreds of years that the Temple stood. Shavuot was a holiday devoted to the *land*. It was a celebration about entering the land, possessing it and being nourished by it. It was a holiday on which the bringing of the bounty of the fields to Jerusalem served as a witness to the tripartite covenant of God, the Jews and the land of Israel. And the message was made all the more powerful by the ritual recitation that the celebrant spoke: "I have entered the land." In fact, the Jewish people entered the land hundreds of years before. Yet each year, one by one, the Jews spoke of themselves as if they were the generation who entered the land.

And so Shavuot was celebrated, for almost a thousand years, until 70 CE when the Temple was destroyed and the land was lost. The Jews, in exile, could no longer recite their sacred liturgy. Its words mocked their reality. Shavuot, a holiday of Temple and land, was now orphaned, like its people.

The need to reclaim Shavuot was bundled into the early rabbis' daunting challenge to re-create, with authenticity and holiness, a Temple-centered Judaism in a world without a Temple. No doubt the rabbis saw a remarkably elegant, even sacred pairing when they looked at Shavuot and Mount Sinai: a holiday without a ritual and a moment without a holiday. Forever after, Shavuot became associated with the Giving of the Torah.

Meanwhile, the original message of Shavuot was not lost, just dispersed, like the people who once reveled in its pilgrim pageantry. Declarations of our dedication to the land, our faith in God's promises, and our trust that we would one day return home, were woven into our daily prayers, recited after every meal, in every service, at every wedding.

But today, how shall we respond? For in 1948, the miracle came true. Our long exile ended. We returned to Israel. Now, for the first time since the dawn of the rabbinic era, we are able to rise and recite, with joy and with tears, "We acknowledge this day that we have entered the land that Adonai swore to our ancestors to assign us." And yet, we don't. Not here, at least; not on Shavuot. The question is, shall we?

Returning to the land of Israel has spawned spiritual as well as political implications. The gift of landedness that the State of Israel has bequeathed to all Jews affects each of us, body and soul. It has defended and elevated the social and political status of Jews in countries throughout the world. It has expanded our sacred calendar and our prayers. The question remains, however: Will it cause us to recast our age-old traditions? Will we rethink, as some have begun to do, how we should mourn the loss of the Temple, now that Jerusalem is once again our capital? Shall we return the celebration of the land to the holiday of Shavuot, along with its storied celebration of the Giving of the Torah? If so, how shall we integrate the two?

And the questions continue: How shall we then integrate Shavuot with the celebration of Yom Ha'atzma'ut, Israel's modern Independence Day? Will such a renewed definition of Shavuot create a greater rift between *Israeli* culture and *Jewish* culture? Will it strengthen or weaken the ties between Diaspora Jewry and the State of Israel?

All these questions point to the fact that Jewish history has powerful sacred implications. And throughout our history, Jews have worked to craft powerful sacred responses. Just as the rabbis of old had to reconfigure Judaism to respond to a world *without* a Temple, so we must now work, together, to respond to the blessing of a Judaism *with* a state.

Marriage Vows

Sinai has been depicted as the wedding of God and the people of Israe!. Shavuot is the celebration and the renewal of those wedding vows. Given that asso-ciation and ambience, some couples choose Shavuot as the time to renew their vows. You might want to arrange such a celebration for your parents, friends or yourselves. The center-piece of those ceremonies is often a custom-made *ketubah*. Modeled on the original document, that Jewish marriage certificate may speak of the gifts each partner has given the other, the ways in which each has enriched the other's life, what each has learned from the other, and the love that continues to grow between them. The words can be illuminated by a calligrapher or a graphic artist and hung in the couple's home.

Ruth gleaning sheaves of grain in the Land of Israel❧

Reading Ruth

On each pilgrimage holiday, a different *megillah*, or scroll, is read from the section of the Bible known as Writings. On Shavuot, we read the Scroll of Ruth. Ruth was a Moabite who married an Israelite. Suffering the dual tragedies of childlessness and widowhood, Ruth was determined to stay with her mother-in-law, Naomi, and go back with her to the Land of Israel. In joining Naomi, Ruth chose to give up her Moabite ways. Although Naomi urged her to return to her family, Ruth remained faithful, declaring, "Wherever you will go, I will go. Wherever you lodge, there I will lodge. Your people shall be my people and your God, my God. Wherever you die, I will die, and there I will be buried." For her devotion, tradition claims her as a direct ancestor of King David.

Decorating One's Home

It is a tradition in some synagogues to drape the sanctuary with greenery during Shavuot, as a reminder of the bounties of fruits and grains that the pilgrims brought to Jerusalem in the time of the Temple. Some families practice that tradition in their homes. Boughs of lilacs and roses and sprays of baby's breath, carnations, ferns and herbs, as well as vegetables of all kinds (perhaps planted during *hol hamo'ed Pesah*, the intermediate days of Passover and ripening just at this time!), can fill the family room, den, dining room and living room for the holiday of Shavuot. You may even want to accent the house with fragrant oils—rosewater or peach or orange—to conjure up smells from the orchards and the fields.

CHAPTER 16

Tisha 'B'Av

A Time of Mourning

9 AV

How lonely sits the city that once was filled with people. She has become a widow.

She cries alone at night, and tears scar her cheeks. None of her beloved are left to

comfort her....The lips of the nursing child are parched with thirst; children ask

for bread, but there is none to give them....Our possessions have been claimed

by strangers, our homes by foreigners....We are orphaned, without fathers.

—FROM THE BOOK OF LAMENTATIONS

I WAS BORN AFTER THE FOUNDING of the modern State of Israel but less than a decade after the Holocaust. My parents instilled in me the supplicant's and the wanderer's sense

of insecurity. My father would purchase pieces of jewelry made up of separate stones, jewelry

that could be taken apart and used to buy safe passage for all the members of my large family.

When I was young, my friends would run through imaginary drills
and declare what they would save from their homes in case of fire.
My musings had to do with escape: What would I take that could
be easily carried, and what would I carry that could be used to bribe

the border guards? Where would my family gather if we were separated? I remember the lesson of the girl who was rounded up by the Nazis in the summertime. Her grandfather told her to wear her boots. "In the summertime?" she protested. But she did as she was told. The boots saved her life during the long winters of hell. I know the habit of many Jews to have a valid passport at all times. The insecurity of exile does not fade easily, even in the presence of the reestablishment of our homeland.

The Centrality of the Temple

For a thousand years, the Temple was our protection, our refuge. Until its final destruction in 70 CE, the Temple in Jerusalem was the heart and soul of the Jewish people. It was in the Temple that the Jewish people gathered, bringing their gifts of grain, fruits, animals and wine to thank God for the land's bounty. At the Temple they sought comfort in their mourning and healing for their sick, celebrated the birth of a child and even went to search for an object they had lost. It was from the Temple that the leaders of Israel ruled; where Jews sought the presence of God and one another's company.

This is a model of how the Second Temple appeared in 70 CE, just before it was destroyed. ❧

Seeking What You Lost

An early rabbinic text on mourning teaches us, "All Jews who come to the Temple enter from the right and exit from the left, except for four [kinds] who enter from the left and exit from the right: the mourner, the outcast, the one whose loved one is ill, and the one who has lost something" (*Semaḥot* 6:11). The Temple was a place where comfort was always offered, where one could bring one's loneliness, fear and pain, hoping they would be eased.

The Temple was the kitchen table of Judaism, where compassion and justice and wisdom were dispensed. Synagogues, study houses and the family home had not yet emerged as centers of sacred activity. The Temple was the place where heaven and earth met, the earthly portal through which the Divine Presence flowed. It was a symbol of God's love for and devotion to the Jewish people. As long as the Temple stood, so the Jews thought, God stood with them. To lose the Temple was to lose more than the Jews' physical, political and economic center. It was to lose the affection and favor of God. It was, in short, to be rejected by God.

In the year 586 BCE, the Babylonian king Nebuchadnezzar, long a rival of the Jewish nation, destroyed the Temple. He looted its treasures and forced the people into exile to Babylonia. Where once golden buildings had stood, only rubble remained. All was lost. There was no food, no water, no work, no government, no leaders, no hope.

What could that mean about the Covenant? Was it broken or was it still intact? The enemies of Israel thought the former; the prophets of the First Temple and the rabbis of the Second Temple thought the latter. And that made all the difference.

The prophets of the exile believed that the destruction was punishment, not abandonment. They spoke from Babylonia of the people's loss but kept them focused on their hope. "'Take comfort, take comfort, My people,' says God," writes Isaiah. "'Tell Jerusalem to take heart, proclaim unto her that her time of service is accomplished, her guilt paid off'" (Isaiah 40:1).

Mourning over the ruins of Jerusalem ❧

The prophet Jeremiah offers the promise of return: "Refrain from crying, Rachel, stop your eyes from weeping, for your work shall be rewarded; your children shall return from the enemy's land" (Jeremiah 31:16).

And so it was. About 50 years later, King Cyrus of Persia defeated Babylonia and encouraged the Jews to return to Jerusalem and rebuild their Temple.

"When God returned our exiles to Zion, it was like a dream. Our mouths were filled with laughter; our tongues sang with joy....Those who sow in tears will reap in grateful song" (Psalm 126). The Second Temple served as the religious and spiritual center of the Jewish people for another 500 years. It stood even longer than the First Temple. The Jewish nation was reborn.

It was a time of great political realignment. Israel was the land bridge between Europe, Asia and Africa and therefore occupied a strategic and highly prized position. As armies would travel through, many tried to occupy and conquer Jerusalem. Yet Jerusalem survived as Israel's capital until it encountered Rome. In the year 70 CE, after a long battle, a hard siege and internal division, Jerusalem and the Temple were destroyed. Now, however, the Temple would not be rebuilt. There would be no more home for the priests

To this day, we recall the
loss of the Temple and the
destruction of Jerusalem of
old when we break a glass at
the end of a wedding ceremony. Some Jewish families
and artists leave a portion
of their home or their work
unfinished (a corner unpainted
or a molding cut short),
zecher l'ḥurban, as a reminder
of the destruction. And
perhaps it reminds us as
well that despite our best
efforts, perfection is a goal
we can pursue but never
achieve. And that is OK. The
best, so they say, is often the
enemy of the good.

and the Levites, no more sacrifices, no more psalms offered in song, no central place to go to be comforted at a time of illness or loss, no sacred hearth at which to celebrate new life. The 1,000-year-old tradition of cultic, priestly, centralized Judaism would be no more.

And yet, as the walls of the Temple were collapsing, a remarkable drama was being played out that would secure the future of Judaism for the next 2,000 years. A rabbi named Yoḥanan ben Zakkai, tradition tells us, believing defeat imminent, had himself placed in a coffin and smuggled out of Jerusalem. It was a ruse that was intended to get him past both the Jewish zealots on the inside, who guarded the gates against defectors, and the Roman soldiers on the outside, who guarded the gates against escapees. Once outside, Yoḥanan ben Zakkai sought permission from the Roman leadership to set up a school in the port city of Yavneh.

The Ascendancy of Rabbinic Judaism

The rabbis who survived the siege of Jerusalem began gathering in Yavneh. That first academy secured the establishment of rabbinic Judaism, the Judaism of the Mishnah and the Talmud that we know today. The old order was gone; a new order had to be built. Paradoxically, the rabbis began building the new world by preserving and appropriating the memories of the old.

> Once Rabbi Yoḥanan ben Zakkai was leaving the remains of the burned-out city of Jerusalem. Rabbi Yehoshua, walking behind him, looked at the ruins of the Temple and said, *"Oy lanu!* What shall we do? This place that atoned for the sins of the people Israel is no more." Rabbi Yohanan responded, "My son, do not worry. We have another source of atonement in its stead. That is, *gemilut ḥasadim,* deeds of lovingkindness, as it is written, 'For *ḥesed,* kindness, is what I want,' says God, 'and not sacrifices'" (Hosea 6:6) (*Avot de Rabbi Natan,* 11a).

The shofar that had been blown only in the Temple was now blown in Yavneh; the songs of praise were recited in Yavneh; the house of study became the successor of the Temple. Wherever a stone of the Temple fell, the Midrash tells us, there was built a place of study.

Those rabbis created the Talmud, the premier compendium of rabbinic law and lore, conversation by conversation. It began as a compilation of oral laws and eventually blossomed into the voluminous library of Jewish knowledge. Our Temple was no longer made of stones and metal but of black ink on paper, parchment and vellum. God dwelt within the pages of the Talmud just as surely as God had dwelt in the precinct of the Temple. Our Temple was no longer subject to the bows and arrows of our enemies. It was not even subject to fires. For now it was bound between the covers of a book, a big book with many volumes, housed in homes and synagogues across Europe and North Africa, a book that contains cross-generational conversations, a book that is woven into the collective memory of the Jewish people.

A nighttime view of the Kotel, or Western Wall—the part of the Second Temple's retaining wall that was nearest to the Holy of Holies.

Bereft of a worldly Jerusalem, the rabbis created the heavenly Jerusalem, the eternal counterpart of the earthly Jerusalem. This time our city could never be destroyed. We face Jerusalem whenever we pray; we place Jerusalem at the top of our wedding documents; we sing of Zion at every festive meal. At the end of every seder, at the end of the long day of Yom Kippur, we declare with certitude, "Next year in Jerusalem." If we cannot live in Jerusalem, Jerusalem will live in us.

And although we Jews might have been exiled from the land, we were not exiled from God. For as Rabbi Shimon bar Yoḥai taught, "Come and see how precious are the Jews in the eyes of the Holy One. For wherever the Jews go in the world, the Shechinah [God's earthly presence] goes with them" (*Megillah* 29a).

For 2,000 years, the holiday of exile has captured and rekindled the secret of hope when the logical response was despair. It has shown us how to hold on to a vision even when we have lost sight of our goal. It promises us that if we never give up, we, too, will reach the promised land. "Look, Rachel, look," the modern Zionist song says, "your children have returned to their land."

How We Observe the Day

Tisha B'Av, the 9th of Av, is a day of mourning. For a full 25 hours, from sundown to nightfall, we fast. It is not a fast of atonement; it is a fast of grieving.

On the night of Tisha B'Av, the lights of the synagogue are dimmed. Only the eternal light on the ark shines clearly, a reminder

Fairest of Them All

Ten measures of loveliness were given to the world: Nine are in Jerusalem and one in the rest of the world. Ten measures of wisdom were given to the world: Nine in Jerusalem and one in the rest of the world. Ten measures of Torah were given to the world: Nine in Jerusalem and one in the rest of the world (*Kiddushin* 49b).

Never on Shabbat

Tisha B'Av cannot be observed on Shabbat, for the joy of Shabbat overrides the sadness of the destruction of the Temple. Therefore, when Tisha B'Av falls on Shabbat, it is postponed one day and observed on Sunday, 10 Av.

According to Tradition, Tisha B'Av Was Beset by Tragedy

The following tragedies occured on the 9th of Av:

- Sixty-five years after the destruction of the Second Temple, in 135 CE, the fortress of Betar, the last stronghold of Bar Kochba's revolt against the Romans, fell. The Jews no longer believed that they would rebuild the Temple in their day.

- The Jews were expelled from Spain in 1492 (the same year in which Columbus set out on the voyage on which he would "discover" America).

- The first serious skirmish between Arabs and Jews in the 20th century broke out in Tel Aviv in 1929.

of the Temple's past glory and God's eternal presence. Congregants sit on the floor or in low chairs, one of the signs of mourning. Candles serve as the light. The Book of Lamentations, Eichah, is chanted plaintively, mournfully, like an ancient ballad telling the tale of love and loss. *Kinot,* poems of mourning and remembering, are sometimes sung as well. Often the ark and, occasionally, the walls are draped in black. For the 25 hours of this holiday, Jews are bidden not to wear leather or listen to music or bathe. Those prohibitions, too, are signs of mourning.

On the morning of Tisha B'Av, we do not wear tallitot (plural of *tallit*) or *tefillin* (phylacteries). Both are considered symbols of joy and beauty and hence are discordant with the mood. Work is permitted, but the day weighs heavily on those who observe it.

At *minhah,* the afternoon service, our spirits begin to lift. We put on tallitot and tefillin. The darkness begins to break. We read in the haftarah for that day, "'You shall go out with joy,' God says of Israel, 'and be led forth in peace. Before you the mountains and hills will break into song. All the trees of the field will clap their hands'" (Isaiah 55:12).We are promised that God will restore joy to Israel. And for the generations who have lived to see the founding of the State of Israel, Jerusalem rebuilt, Jews praying at the Western Wall, and hundreds of thousands of Russian and Ethiopian Jews living in safety and comfort in Israel, that promise has come true.

Messages of promise and comfort continue through the haftarot (plural of *haftarah*) for the next few weeks. The Shabbat immediately following Tisha B'Av is called Shabbat Naḥamu, Shabbat of Comfort. Its name comes from the first words of the haftarah, which also fortified the Jews of the first exile: "'Give comfort, give comfort to My people,' says your God. 'Tell her that the time of her punishment is done'" (Isaiah 40:1).

It is with this belief of new hope and eternal beginnings that we enter the month of Elul, listen to the sounds of the shofar, prepare for the High Holidays, and begin the cycle of time all over again.

Next Year in Jerusalem

In 1967, Israel miraculously won the Six-Day War and reunited the city of Jerusalem. Jews could once again pray at the Western Wall, one of the outer walls surrounding the Temple Mount and the only remnant of the Temple area. For 2,000 years, Jews have been turning their hearts and their eyes toward Jerusalem, toward the Temple, toward the wall, the resting place of the Shechinah, the earthly presence of God. By the way they have stood and the direction in which they have cast their eyes, they have felt closer to God and to one another. Every year since the reunification of Jerusalem, thousands of Jews from all over the world have gathered at the wall on Tisha B'Av to remember the Temple's glory and to celebrate the miracle of seeing Jerusalem and the Jewish nation rebuilt.

Unfounded Hatred

The rabbis of the Talmud tell us that the Second Temple was destroyed because of *sinat hinam*, unfounded hatred— hatred that festers between neighbor and neighbor; hatred that spews forth from the words we use to speak of one another; hatred that destroys the foundation of society. On November 4, 1995, the world again witnessed the truth of this sad wisdom. Prime Minister Yitzhak Rabin was gunned down by a Jew who

heeded the ugly words of some who opposed the peace process. For a moment, the modern Temple that is Israel was shaken.

Proverbs teaches us that "life and death are in the power of the word" (18:21). It is a lesson we cannot afford to ignore.

Other Days Commemorating the Loss of the Temple

Jerusalem was not destroyed all at once. A series of military setbacks (and internal disagreements) led to its collapse. Three special days recall those events. All are minor fast days, which means that their fasts last only from sunrise on one day to nightfall on the same day:

- Tzom Gedaliah (the Fast of Gedaliah). On 3 Tishre in 586 BCE, after the First Temple was destroyed, Gedaliah, the last Jewish governor of Judah, was assassinated by Jewish opponents.

- 10 Tevet. On this day, the Babylonians laid siege to Jerusalem in 588 BCE.

- 17 Tammuz. On this day in 70 CE, the Romans broke through the city walls of Jerusalem and, according to the ancient rabbis, so, too, did the Babylonians, in 586 BCE. That was the beginning of the end. The 17th of Tammuz begins the three weeks of semi-mourning that lead up to Tisha B'Av. During that season, traditional Jews

plan no weddings. Concerts and festivals are generally avoided. Wherever possible, moments that would otherwise be marked by the Sheheheyanu are postponed. From the 1st of Av until the 9th, traditional Jews serve meat and wine only on Shabbat. Liberal Jews, especially young people in Jewish camps or in Israel, focus on the observance of Tisha B'Av itself.

Personal prayers fill the crevices of the Western Wall.

Letters to God

Many people believe that God hears their prayers best when they pray at the Western Wall. It has become a tradition in modern times to write prayers on small pieces of paper and slip them into the small cracks in the huge stones of the wall. Years ago, if you could not go to the wall yourself, you would give your note to friends and ask them to place it high in the wall for you. Today technology reigns, enabling people to fax messages to the wall and to speak directly to the stones via cellular phones!

PART TWO

Jewish Life-Cycle Events

CHAPTER 17

Thresholds in Time

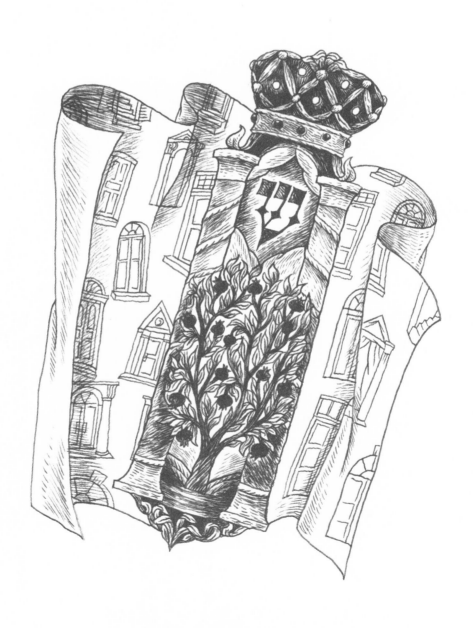

The rabbis tell us we should always carry two notes in our pockets.

In one pocket, the note should say, "For me, the world was created."

In the other, it should say, "I am dust and ashes."

—Hasidic saying

MY HUSBAND'S UNCLE SOL is the family's *simḥa* (celebration) man. If there is a wedding, bar mitzvah, bat mitzvah, baby naming or anniversary party—any family gathering of any significance—he is there. No matter the distance, the hardship or expense, he is there to celebrate, to enjoy and to dance—especially to dance. The rabbis of old said, "You have not seen joy until you have witnessed the joy of the water ceremony on Sukkot." Well, the Temple is gone, and the water ceremony is no more. But we have Sol, and I say to the rabbis, "You have not seen joy until you have seen Sol dance."

These young Scottish Jews are dressed up in kippot and kilts, ready to celebrate a family simḥa with a blend of klezmer and Celtic music.

Sol has seen many *simḥas*, and many sorrows. It is out of the depth of both that he dances. He makes the party richer, deeper, holier. He reminds those who might forget that a *simḥa* is different from a high school victory celebration or a block party. A *simḥa* is a religious pause along life's road, a joyous launching of a new part of one's life along a chosen path, witnessed and defined by a community of sojourners. That is why we celebrate in groups, and that is why the group celebrates. In Jewish life, the individual is most powerfully gifted with identity, purpose and support when accompanied by the group. And the group is renewed, rewarded and reaffirmed every time someone chooses to walk its paths.

Every culture and, even more, every religion recognizes that its members experience these moments of transition and transcendence, moments of release and reconnection, at times of celebration and at times of tragedy. Transitions are always unsettling, especially for the most settled among us. Life-cycle transitions, in particular, dislocate and often dismantle the carefully crafted order of our daily lives. To negotiate them well, to use them as opportunities for healthy and creative growth, we need help. We need help in mending and expanding the tapestry that reflects our lives. That is why every culture creates rites of passage.

We are guided across the thresholds of the most intimate passages of life—birth, coming-of-age, marriage, dying, mourning—by the company, rituals and values of our community. If we need ushers to guide us at theaters and place cards to guide us to our seats at dinners, how much more do we need help finding our way through the grand events of our lives.

These events are doorposts in time, and the rituals of our tradition become their mezuzot (plural of *mezuzah*). Just as a mezuzah marks (and, some say, protects) our passage from one domain to another, so do our rituals mark (and perhaps protect) our passage from one time of life to another. As a mezuzah designates the boundaries of sacred space, reminding us of who we are and where we belong, so the rituals focus our attention on who we are becoming and the place we now assume in the community. We are each celebrated for the individuals we are—unique and irreplaceable, with talents and loves, a name and a claim all our own—and for the Jewish citizens we are called upon to be.

Life-cycle events, such as weddings and baby namings, are for the celebrants *and* the witnesses alike. They reinforce meaning, reminding us of the paths we have chosen. They proclaim a change of status and offer us a guide to ease the way. They speak in ritual language, knowing that our hearts can receive what our heads might not. Life-cycle events give designated roles to both celebrants *and* community. When emotions threaten our behavior, boundaries and reason, we take refuge in acting according to the patterns of our age-old tradition. Rituals fill the space around us, asking us to do, recite and be. We give ourselves over to them, knowing they will keep us safe.

The second part of this book speaks about such passages, those that we experience and those that we witness. No individual traverses a life passage alone. We join and are joined by others, sometimes by invitation and sometimes by chance. We visit a friend in the hospital and are drawn into the drama of the patient in the next bed. We attend the wedding of our friends' daughter and review the joys and the pains of our own marriage. We go to the funeral of a colleague's mother, and upon returning home, we call our own mother, just to hear her voice.

How Judaism helps us negotiate the life passages—our own and those we witness—is the substance of this part of the book.

Jewish family life is so important that our tradition encourages us to actively rejoice with bridal couples.❧

CHAPTER 18

Birth

Affirming the Covenant

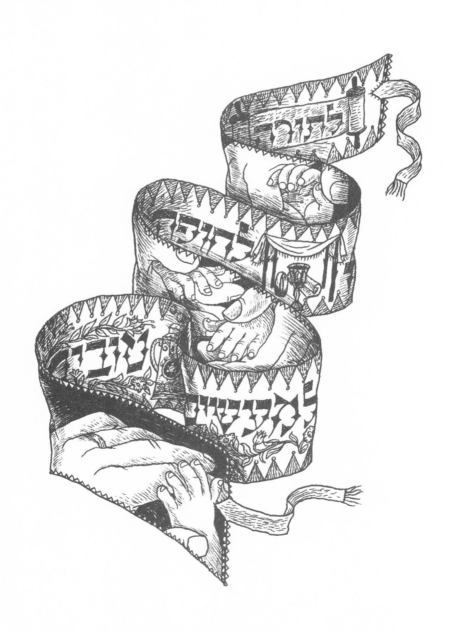

When Israel stood at Sinai to receive the Torah, the Holy One said, "I am prepared to give you My Torah, My prized possession. In return, you must give Me a guarantor."

Israel said, "Our ancestors are our guarantor."

The Holy One said, "Your ancestors are not suitable as a guarantor. Give Me a better guarantor."

Israel said, "The prophets are our guarantor."

The Holy One said, "The prophets too are not suitable as a guarantor. Give Me still a better guarantor."

Israel said, "Dear God, our children are our guarantor."

And the Holy One said, "Your children are a good guarantor. It is for their sake that I give the Torah to you."

—FROM SHIR HASHIRIM RABBAH

TO HOLD A NEWBORN IN OUR ARMS is to behold a miracle. "Where did you come from, little one?" we wonder as we gaze upon the face. "Where are you going? How long is your journey? What gifts do you carry? What songs will you sing?"

The Uniqueness of Every Child

The rabbis teach us, "When governments mint a coin, they use one mold, and all the coins come out the same. When God makes humans, God, too, uses the same mold, Adam and Eve, yet everyone is different. Therefore, each of us should say, 'For me, the world was created'" (*Mishnah Sanhedrin* 4:5).

To hold a newborn in our arms is to behold the power of life. How could such a tiny thing be so vigorous, so insistent? How can the mother's body be ripped apart and yet be whole moments later? How can life give forth life, changing from emptiness to fullness to emptiness? How can a process so carnal feel so divine?

To hold a newborn is to behold the birth of prayer. "You are so small and the world is so big," we say as our arms tighten around our child. "How can we help you find your way? There is so much left undone; the world is so needy; we are all still learning. What must we teach you? What will you teach us?"

We turn our eyes away, seeking the unseen presence that fills the room. "God, Parent of all, You know. Please, guide our steps. And protect our child throughout life."

Who Are the Parents?

"The one who raises a child, and not the one who merely begot him, is the one who is called father or mother" (*Exodus Rabbah* 46:5). Whether by infertility, happenstance or choice, many Jews are childless. But the now-famous African adage applies to all people: "It takes a village to raise a child." Never has this been truer than in modern-day America. Families are besieged by television, computers and video games, by overworked parents and underfunded schools, by client-saturated social service organizations and undersupervised children. Is it any wonder that our children are needy? Each of us can help a child. Our time and caring can guide them on the right path. Organizations in your community can use you. Make time. Get involved.

There are few pains or joys greater than those brought to us by our children. A steady hand, a stout heart and a sturdy compass are tools that serve a parent well. The stories and the rituals of Judaism—bolstered by the homespun wisdom of our families and friends—can provide us with other essential tools for building a home that gives our children roots and wings.

The Torah confirms how hard yet how sacred is the task of parenthood. God appears as the very first parent, struggling with children who are rebellious (Adam and Eve, the Israelites in the wilderness), skeptical (Lot, Jacob), challenging (almost all of the women), even too obedient (Abraham). We see that as the parent gives birth to the child, so, too, does the child give birth to the parent, teaching the parent new skills, opening the way to new experiences. The opening prayer of the Amidah reads, "Blessed are You, Adonai... God of Abraham, God of Isaac and God of Jacob," as if to remind

Each child brings his or her own blessing into the world.
—*Yiddish saying* ❧

us constantly that each child has a unique relationship with his or her parent. We are a different parent to each of our children. The Jewish people's relationship with God is reborn with each generation. We, too, are reborn as new parents with each child. If the Torah depicts parenting as a struggle and a joy for God, why should it not be for us?

Yet our tradition does not leave us bereft of guidance. When I was pregnant with my first child and working for a national Jewish organization, a co-worker asked me how I planned to make Judaism a part of my child's life. Married to a rabbi—though not yet a rabbi myself—I thought the question as odd as asking: How do you plan to bring a sense of gender to a locker room or a sense of curiosity to a reporter? Thinking there was some secret of parenthood I had not yet fathomed and at which I might therefore never excel, I hardly knew how to answer. I turned to her and said, "I will sing Hebrew songs to him, feed him Jewish foods, celebrate Shabbat with him."

"Is that all?" she sniffed.

And in that moment, I thought, "No, that is not all. That is everything."

Celebrating the Birth

We begin the journey of parenthood in celebration. There are foods to be prepared, people to be called, announcements to be made, invitations to be extended, religious leaders to be notified. The family is swaddled in attention and rituals. A private matter becomes a communal event, for at the celebration the child, the family and the people Israel are bound together as one. The congregation gathers, as friends and family but also as representatives of the community that the child will soon enter. The ceremony is twofold: covenantal and personal. It enacts the child's entry into the Covenant of Israel and it enables the parents to proclaim publicly the child's name.

Every child has at least two names: a first name, designating the child's uniqueness; and a second name, designating the child's family. The wisdom of conferring two names weaves the child within family and community from the earliest moments of life. It echoes the knowledge that sociologists impart: it is only within society that we

This birth announcement of Doriya Malkah (Leslie) daughter of Leah Pearl and Menuḥah was designed by Betsy Platkin Teutsch. ❧

"A person is known by three names: the one he is called by his father and mother, the one he is called by others, and the one that is recorded in the book of deeds" (*Kohelet Rabbah* 7:3).

Adoption

More and more Jews are adopting babies, some from Jewish birth parents, many not. In addition to being welcomed into the community with a covenant ceremony, children of non-Jewish birth parents undergo a conversion ritual—generally immersion in a *mikveh*, a ritual bath.

Adopted children are known by their adoptive parents' names. That is, a child named Joseph with adoptive parents Miri and Ben is known as Yosef ben Binyamin v'Miriam. Adopted children who are converted become Jews in all ways. This was established a thousand years ago, when a convert wrote to Maimonides and asked, "May I recite the opening blessing of the Amidah, which says, 'God of my ancestors,' for Abraham, Isaac and Jacob were not my ancestors?" And Maimonides responded that he could for they were. We all stood at Sinai; we all have the same ancestry.

achieve the fullness of personhood; it is only within relationships with others and through the norms and practices of our culture, whose performance confers meaning on the chaos of the cosmos, that we fully become ourselves.

Covenant in Hebrew is *brit*. While generically *brit* can be any promise or any agreement, in the Jewish tradition it has come to mean one special promise, the one that the Jews made to one another and to God at the foot of Mount Sinai 3,500 years ago. It was there that the Jews pledged—individually and together—to be God's people and God's partner in Creation.

Every Jew, tradition tells us, who has ever lived or is yet to be born was present that day at Sinai and was a partner in that promise. "It is not only with you that I make this Covenant," said the Eternal One, "but also with everyone here who stands before God this day and all those who are not with us here today" (Deuteronomy 29:13–14). Every Jew who is born, every child who is adopted into a Jewish family, and every person who converts to Judaism is formally inducted into the Covenant between God and the Jewish people, for they, too, are part of the Covenant of Sinai, made so many years ago.

The act of entering into the Covenant involves body as well as soul, so the ceremony is markedly different for boys and for girls.

Brit Milah: *Covenant of Circumcision*

Boys are brought into the Covenant today just as the first Jew, Abraham, was: through the ceremony of a *brit milah*, a covenant of circumcision.

Since the time of Abraham, *brit milah* has been the symbol marked on the bodies of Jewish males to reconfirm the eternal relationship between God and the Jewish people. On the eighth day after birth, as long as the baby is healthy, the circumcision is performed. Even if the eighth day is Shabbat, even if it is Yom Kippur, the *brit milah* is held. Family and friends come from all over to celebrate. A *mohel*, a Jew—male or female, not necessarily a rabbi—who has been trained in the ancient laws and in the modern methods of circumcision, performs the quick but delicate surgery.

The *brit milah* is a commandment, and tradition tells us that we should be eager to perform commandments. So, we perform them

A Prayer to Be Said upon Entering the Ninth Month of Pregnancy

When said as part of a traditional prayer service, this prayer—which comes from a prayer book that was written in Italy in 1786—is inserted after the Amidah and before May the One Who Makes Peace:

I thank the Lord with all my heart that I have carried the full nine months and that up to now God has spared me from all afflictions that could harm a pregnant woman and her child. Surely God's tenderness is unending. Again, I seek God's kindness so God will be with me and support me when my child is pressing to be born, and so that God will give me strength to bring forth my child....

—Out of the Depths I Call to You: A Book of Prayers for the Married Jewish Woman, edited and translated by Nina Beth Cardin

A Prayer to Be Said upon Entering Labor

Jewish women in Italy would recite the following prayer when labor pains began:

May the exalted, mighty, and awesome God, who in times of trouble answers those who fear You, accept my prayer and the pleas of Your entire people, the House of Israel. And amidst their company, may You remember and tenderly care for a woman, bound up and struggling as if bearing her first child. From within this struggle, through her pains and labor, her heart trembles and calls out. So it is with me today as I sit upon the birthing stool. My gaze is fixed on the Lord, my God. May You

see my pain and my tears, and grant my petition. May my prayer be welcome. In Your mercy, You will deliver me. In Your compassion, God, release me. Return my health and vigor and well-being. Restore my former strength. May my body once again be refreshed....

—Out of the Depths I Call to You: A Book of Prayers for the Married Jewish Woman, edited and translated by Nina Beth Cardin

Special Needs

Sometimes our dreams for a healthy child are not realized. Sometimes a child is born with disabilities. Too often we feel our tradition demands perfection and is less accepting of those who are different. But Jacob became lame when touched by the angel. Moses, we are told, was heavy of tongue.

All life is precious. All our children are children of Israel. Many synagogues and communities have programs that assist families whose children have disabilities. We have done much, and there is much more to be done. Local Jewish Federations are often good sources of information about relevant programs. They also can serve as advocates for the funding and creation of additional services.

A Prayer Recited at the Celebration of the Birth of a Child

May God give you eyes
    to see joy in the world,
Ears to hear the chirping
    of the birds,
A nose to smell the fragrance
    of the flowers,
A mouth to utter praises

and wonder,
Arms to embrace those you love,
Feet to run and jump and dance,
A heart to feel delight
    and love and hope,
And a soul to experience
    the world around you.

May God also grant you eyes
    that see the world's pain,
Ears that hear the cry
    of those in need,
A nose to sense the changes
    in the air,
A mouth to speak out
    both in protest and in support,
Feet to go quickly
    to the aid of others,
A heart to feel concern
    and commitment,
And a soul that seeks to better
    the world around you.

—Helise Lieberman

Among Sephardic Jews it is the custom to donate tzedakah at a brit. A tray with candles, called a saniyeh, is carried around the room and guests place a dollar on it in honor of the newborn. This contemporary saniyeh was made by Joseph Bibi, a Syrian Jew from Brooklyn, New York. ❧

Elijah

Some families set aside a chair at a *brit* ceremony for Elijah, the biblical prophet who lived in the ninth century BCE. Tradition has it that Elijah never died but, rather, was taken up to heaven in a chariot of fire. He comes back to earth, so we are told, disguised as a beggar or a wanderer to help Jews in need. He is said to visit every seder table and every *brit milah*. It is thought that Elijah will be the herald of the Messiah, the harbinger of peace and goodness. By setting aside a chair for Elijah at every *brit milah*, we are saying, "Maybe today Elijah will come; maybe this child is the one who will bring peace."

An embroidered cushion for a circumcision, Germany 1749. The empty chair is the chair of Elijah.

at the first possible moment. Although the first possible moment is the sunset that ushers in the eighth day (for the days of the Jewish calendar begin in the evening), Jewish law says a *brit* should not take place at night. (In olden times, it was often too dark to risk the procedure.) The first possible time, then, is early morning. (Morning is easier on the parents, too. The anxiety lasts only a few hours rather than all day.)

The *brit milah* ceremony is composed of two parts, the circumcision and the naming of the baby. Although the ceremony can be held anywhere, many people prefer holding it at the synagogue or at home. No matter where it is held, it always begins with the guests gathered in one room, the baby and his attendants in another. When everyone is ready, the baby makes his entrance, carried by the *sandeket*, or, in Yiddish, *kvaterin*, the godmother—a grandmother or other beloved woman. Everyone rises as if the baby were a king or a great scholar. They greet him by saying, "Blessed is the one who comes!"

Sometimes the baby is passed over the chair of Elijah. Other times the baby is placed directly on a table or on the lap of the *sandek*, the godfather, the person honored with holding the child during the ceremony. The mohel begins the ceremony with a prayer that designates the entrance into sacred time and with a blessing: "Blessed are You, Sovereign of the universe, who has sanctified us through Your mitzvot and commands us regarding circumcision." The circumcision, the cutting away of the foreskin in the ritually prescribed fashion, takes just a few seconds. Technically, it is the father who is responsible for circumcising his son, so many a mohel, in a grand and precise gesture, publicly asks the father whether he wishes to circumcise his son or delegate the mohel to act in his stead. The knife rarely changes hands. The parents recite, "Blessed are You, Sovereign of the universe, who has sanctified us through Your mitzvot and commanded us to enter this child into the Covenant of Abraham."

With the circumcision done, the naming ceremony immediately begins. A guest may be given the honor of reciting the blessing over the wine, the symbol of happiness and holiness. The prayers continue: "Blessed are You, our God, Sovereign of the universe, who sanctified this little one from the womb and had us mark the sign of the Holy Covenant on his flesh....Blessed are You, who established the Covenant."

The one who is given the honor of naming the child then recites:

Our God and God of our ancestors, protect this child and help his mother and father raise him well. Let his name be called in Israel..., son of... [the father's name] and... [the mother's name]. May his father be delighted with his offspring and his mother be overjoyed with her baby....Praise God, for God is good; God's kindness endures forever. May this little child one day be great.

The ceremony is concluded. The guests are invited to a *se'udat mitzvah*, the meal of celebration. The child snuggles in his parents' arms. The tension is broken and the Jewish people have grown by one.

Brit Banot: *Covenant of the Daughters*

The ceremony to welcome a daughter into the Covenant is relatively new. The Bible does not prescribe the way in which to celebrate the birth of a daughter or welcome her into the Covenant. The rabbis do not offer a way either. It has been only in the last century or so that Jewish parents have begun to develop ways to name a daughter. And it has been only since the 1970s that Jewish parents have developed ceremonies to welcome a daughter into the Covenant.

In recent centuries in Ashkenazic (eastern European) communities, a newborn daughter, if formally named at all, was named in the synagogue. Days after the baby's birth, often while mother and daughter were still indisposed, the father would be honored with an *aliyah*. Afterward a special blessing thanking God for God's kindness would be recited. The daughter's name would then be announced. The men of the community capped the celebration with *schnapps*—whiskey.

Sephardic Jews created a somewhat more elaborate and formal way of celebrating the birth of a daughter. (The ritual can be found in the Sephardic prayer books.) The family would convene a *zeved habat* (the gift of the daughter), with the community gathering at

Time Flies

Immediately after the circumcision, while the baby is being quieted with a pacifier soaked in wine, everyone present responds, "Just as this child has entered into the Covenant, so may he be blessed with entrance into a life of study, marriage and deeds of lovingkindness." In a gesture that reminds us that those events are not as far away as we think, my husband's family has a tradition of selecting an unopened bottle of whiskey from among those used to make a l'ḥayyim (a toast) at the *brit*, writing on the label, "for the bar mitzvah of ... [the name of the child]" and putting it aside to be opened 13 years later.

Although the ceremonies for welcoming a daughter into the Covenant may vary, they all serve to sanctify the occasion of a new life begun in the family and Jewish community.

Esther and Mordecai decreed the holiday of Purim. The Maccabees created the celebration of Ḥanukkah. The kabbalists created the liturgical tradition of *kabbalat Shabbat*, the Tu B'Shevat seder and *tikkun leil Shavuot*. The Israeli government added four new holidays to the calendar: Yom Hashoah, Yom Hazikaron, Yom Ha'atzma'ut, Yom Yerushalayim. The bar mitzvah celebration itself is probably not more than a few hundred years old. Today we live in one of the most fertile eras of Jewish ritual and liturgical creativity. Jewish girls and women are both the prime authors and the main beneficiaries of that creativity.

Raise the Cradle

In some towns, the neighbors would gather at the home of the newborn, encircle the cradle, raise it three times, and in unison ask, "What shall the baby be called?" The parents would then say the name of the baby, and sweets would be given out. That ceremony was called *hole kraasch*, a term generally thought to come from the French, *haute la crèche*, meaning "raise the cradle."

the baby's home. The daughter would be welcomed into the community, although not explicitly into the Covenant, with the coaxing, reassuring words from the Song of Songs: "Little dove hidden in the rocks of the cave, let me see your face, let me hear your voice, for your voice is sweet, and your face is lovely." Sweets would be eaten, and the baby would be blessed and given her name.

Today, many families are choosing to celebrate the birth of a daughter with a ceremony called *simḥat bat* (joy of a daughter) or *brit habat* (covenant of the daughter). Like a *brit milah*, the ceremony is composed of two parts: the covenant and the naming.

Many families choose to hold their *brit habat* ceremony in the synagogue on a Shabbat morning soon after the baby's birth. During the Torah reading, the parents are honored with an *aliyah*. The child is brought forward and held in front of the open ark. The rabbi or cantor recites the blessings of Covenant and gives the baby her Hebrew name. The parents may speak words of gratitude and hope. They may also sponsor the *kiddush*—often a buffet with *ḥallah* and wine, cakes, fish, cheeses and fruits—in honor of their child.

Some parents hold the ceremony at home on a Sunday or during the week. The women of the family may light candles in honor of the newborn and recite biblical verses that contain or spell out the child's Hebrew name. The parents may then save the candlesticks that are used at the candlelighting to give to their daughter upon her becoming a bat mitzvah. Other parents wrap their daughter in a tallit, to symbolize the comforting arms of God, and then save the tallit to give to the daughter upon her becoming a bat mitzvah. Still other parents pour water over the child's feet in a symbolic gesture of welcome and as a suggestion of the connection between women and the life-giving attribute of water.

Each of these ceremonies reflects the tastes of the family and the community but every one has several elements in common. Each is constructed like a drama, for that is what it is. The daughter is ceremoniously brought in by grandparents or friends, presented with pageantry to the *kahal*, the community. Her parents stand at the front of the room, eager to receive the precious child. A song or a prayer of welcome is recited by the community, often the same one found in the Sephardic tradition. As in the *brit milah*, so here the child is brought within reach of the parents, but they do not yet take her. First, she awaits her community's embrace.

My daughter assisted us at her covenant ceremony. When she was one month old, we gathered our community together for a ceremony that we called *hachnasat habat*. The sound itself is a poem, for all the vowels are pronounced "ah," the open sound of joy and amazement. The words mean "bringing in the daughter." More than just joy, they hint at the task of Covenant itself, for the Hebrew letters of *hachnasat* can also be read as *haknesset*, a reference to the gathering of Jews who welcomed our daughter into their covenant. The phrase also resonates with a phrase associated with Jewish women: The escorting and outfitting of a bride is called *hachnasat kallah*.

We chose to wrap our daughter in a tallit, believing that the transition into Covenant we wished to effect was best achieved by involving her whole body. From the moment she was brought into the synagogue by the *sandeket*, her godmother, to the moment before the final fold of the tallit was secured around her, she wailed. Through song and psalm, she wailed. But when the last fold of the tallit was around her, with the swaddling finally complete, when she was secure in the symbol that defines the Jewish people, she stopped crying. Here was a child with an inborn instinct for drama.

At any *brit habat*, after the covenanting, a guest is honored with the naming of the child. With a cup of wine in hand, the person recites words that declare the infant a participant in the pageantry of the matriarchs of Israel. This is one such blessing:

> May the One who blessed our ancestors, Sarah, Rebecca, Rachel and Leah, Miriam the prophetess, Deborah, Abigail and Queen Esther, grace this sweet child with good fortune and abundant blessings. And may her name be called among the daughters of Israel..., daughter of... [the father's name] and... [the mother's name]. May she be raised in good health, peace and tranquillity. Grant that her parents watch her grow in happiness, wisdom and prosperity. And may they be blessed with the merit of escorting her to her wedding canopy. May this be God's will, and let us say, "Amen."

Adding Drama

Many feel that despite the excitement of the birth of a daughter, the *simhat bat* ceremony often lacks the tension and the drama of a circumcision. Indeed, sometimes it does. When this rite was first performed, there was a suggestion to mark the sign of the Covenant on the body of the young girl, to bring parity to the two covenant ceremonies. Fortunately, those efforts failed. Still, some of the drama of the circumcision can be achieved through the use of music and song: A cantor or a lay musician can swell the emotions that are already present.

Choosing the Time

With no time-honored laws or traditions, the *brit habat* (singular of *brit banot*) is usually held anytime from eight days to a few months after birth.

Words may be spoken about her namesakes, the grandfathers or grandmothers, great-aunts or great-uncles, for whom she has been named and whose spunk or dignity or wit or graciousness the parents hope she may yet come to possess.

The moment is sealed with wine and blessings. These are some favorite blessings:

> Blessed are You, Sovereign of the universe, who continues the work of Creation. Blessed are You, Sovereign of the universe, who has created such beauty in the world. Blessed are You, Sovereign of the universe, for everything is created with Your glory.

Because the ceremonies are new and may be unfamiliar, families often prepare programs for the guests to encourage their participation. A few enterprising families append drawings and prayers of welcome written by the baby's siblings. Contact your rabbi or local chapter of Hadassah, Jewish Women International or National Council of Jewish Women for guidance.

The ceremony ends with the guests invited to join in a festive *se'udat mitzvah* as the daughter snuggles in the arms of her parents.

Pidyon Haben: Redeeming the Firstborn

THE ORIGINS OF THE TRADITION

For some firstborn sons, the celebration of their birth does not end with the *brit*. According to tradition, certain sons have an additional celebration, a *pidyon haben,* a ritual of redemption. They are the ones who are their mother's firstborn, are delivered through the birth canal, *and* are not grandsons of priests (*kohanim*) or Levites (*Levi'im*). If all these criteria are met, then when the son is one month old, he is to be "redeemed," that is, released from service to the Temple and the priests. Two reasons are offered for that tradition, and as is the case with the pilgrimage holidays, one is historical and one is agricultural.

According to the historical explanation, the final plague of the Exodus was the death of all firstborn sons in Egypt. The Israelite sons were saved, however, if their families dabbed the blood of a lamb on their doorposts. As a way of thanking God, all firstborn Jewish sons were to be dedicated to God. That means that they were to work at the Temple, in the service of the *kohanim*. It is likely that that never happened. Instead, the Torah required that the sons be redeemed, released from their service and returned to their families. In their place, money was given to the Temple.

According to the agricultural explanation, all life is a gift from God. In ancient times, Jews would offer their thanks for a year of bounty by dedicating to the Temple service the firstborn of their cattle, sheep and all other herds. Likewise, on the three pilgrimage holidays (Sukkot, Passover and Shavuot), they would take the first of their fruits to the Temple. Firstborn children are also special to God, but to dedicate them to the Temple service would have been to uproot them from their families and to fail to distinguish them from the rest of Creation. Instead, the Torah commands that they should be redeemed and their value in money be given to the Temple. Grandsons of priests and Levites are not redeemed, because they are forever in service to the Temple.

How We Celebrate

To mark the redemption of the firstborn, family and friends gather once again on the child's 31st day of life. This time it is not a *mohel* or a rabbi who leads the ceremony but a *kohen*, a priest. (If there is no priest to officiate, a rabbi may do so.)

The father approaches the *kohen* and says, "This is my firstborn whom God has commanded that I redeem."

The *kohen* asks, "Which would you prefer? To give me your first-born or to redeem him for five shekels?"

The father replies, "I would prefer to redeem my son."

Today the father gives the *kohen* five silver dollars in place of five shekels. And most often the *kohen* gives the money to tzedakah.

The parents then recite this blessing: "Blessed are You, Sovereign of the universe, who has sanctified us through Your mitzvot and who commands us to redeem our firstborn."

The ceremony ends with the reciting of the Sheheḥeyanu blessing and the blessing over wine.

New Traditions

Some Jews who are attracted to the agricultural aspect of the ceremony are developing redemption services for firstborn daughters, and egalitarian traditions involve both the mother and father in the act of redemption. Sometimes additional sums of money are dedicated to worthy causes in the child's name.

Each of Us Has a Name

This poem is by an Israeli poet, Zelda (1914–1984). It was translated by Marcia Falk.

Each of us has a name
given by God
and given by our parents.
Each of us has a name
given by our stature and
 our smile
and given by what we wear.
Each of us has a name
given by the mountains
and given by our walls.
Each of us has a name
given by the stars
and given by our neighbors.
Each of us has a name
given by our sins
and given by our longing.
Each of us has a name
given by our enemies
and given by our love.
Each of us has a name
given by our celebrations
and given by our work.
Each of us has a name
given by the seasons
and given by our blindness.

Each of us has a name
given by the sea
and given by
our death.

By sharing loving family stories of the past, memory is linked with hope. ❧

The Importance of Names

Last names are a window into the history of families. O'Donnell, Chung, Cohen, Giordano—all reveal a story about ethnic identity. First names also open a window into our past. They tell us something of our parents, their sense of identity, their memories and their hopes. Whether we name our sons Ashton or Joshua and our daughters Morgan or Elianna, we reveal a complex set of personal and social responses: memories of long-lost high school sweethearts, degrees of Jewish and American identity, the influence of the social icons of the day, our assessment of the future security of Jews in the Diaspora.

Most of that is unconscious. We are attracted to names that have meaning for us and whose sounds and associations we like. Ashkenazim have a tradition of naming their children after relatives who have died. Sephardim have a tradition of naming their children after living relatives. Sometimes a child is given two first names.

Wherever they come from, whatever they represent, names are sacred vessels. A most difficult part of parenting is choosing our child's name. It is much too awesome a task for mere humans. God named the patriarchs and Sarah in a primordial act of covenant. I always thought God should have named my children too. They should have come into this world with their names stamped on their feet, in ink that would rub off with the wear of my affection. And while we are at it, God should have included instructions on their care and insights into their souls: "Durable but sensitive; stroke gently to reveal full luster. Do not wring." Perhaps somewhere in the packaging that the doctors threw away after their birth were my children's names and handling instructions.

In the absence of divine guidance, we name our children as best we can with names that are witnesses to those who came before them or to dreams we have for their future. Children love hearing stories about relatives they were named after and what they were like when they were little. Shower your children with memories of the past, and they will grow to fill their names as only they can. For if we are blessed, the ceremony of birth is only a beginning. The best is yet to come.

A Prayer Written for Parents of a Child with Disabilities

This prayer was written by Rabbi Geoffrey Haber:

O God, from the depths I cry to you, help me to feel that the ways of Your providence are wise and good, though we understand them not.

In this moment, my full soul feels but little strength to pray. Yet You have given the miracle of life, and now we ask for the miracle of hope. Give us hope and strength that we may see the light at the end of this dark night. Give us the love and the commitment to advocate on behalf of our son's/daughter's… needs and provide for him/her the best care, a loving home, the brightest future that we can.

May the light of love that my child, … [child's name], son/daughter of … [name of father] and … [name of mother], kindled within my heart continue to burn brightly so that as I regain strength of soul, I may bring cheer unto all my dear ones. Praised are You, O God, who gives strength to the weak, who raises the lowly, who comforts the mourner, who gives hope to those in despair. Amen.

Yearning for a Child

The most famous matriarchs of the Bible suffered from infertility: Sarah, Rachel, Leah and Hannah. Yet the Bible leaves unrecorded their prayers beseeching God for a child and berating God for the condition visited upon them. The Talmud dares to imagine what Hannah said as she prayed to God during her desperate pilgrimage to Shiloh, the place of Eli the priest, before the establishment of the Temple in Jerusalem. The Book of Samuel tells us that Hannah fell upon the steps of the shrine in grief and moved her lips, but no sound came out. The rabbis filled in her words:

Sovereign of the universe, of all the parts of woman that You created, not one was made in vain. Our eyes You made for seeing; our ears You made for hearing; our noses, for smelling; our mouths, for eating and speaking; our hands, for working; our legs, for walking; our breasts, for nursing. But these breasts You gave to me, God, why do I not nurse with them? Give me a child, God, so that I may nurse.
—(*Brachot* 31b)

Prayer for an Adopted Child

Rabbi Sandy Eisenberg Sasso wrote a prayer that parents of an adopted child might add to the covenant ceremony:

Adonai is mindful of us, will bless us; will bless the house of Israel; will bless the house of Aaron; will bless those who revere Adonai, the little ones and the big ones together.
—After Psalm 115:12–13

We have been blessed with the precious gift of this child. After so much waiting and wishing, we are filled with wonder and gratitude as we call you our daughter/son. Our daughter/son, our child, you have grown to life apart from us, but now we hold you close to our hearts and cradle you in our arms with our love. We welcome you into the circle of our family and embrace you with the beauty of a rich tradition.

We pledge ourselves to the creation of a Jewish home and to a life of compassion for others, hoping that you will grow to cherish and emulate these ideals.

God of new beginnings, teach us to be mother and father, worthy of this sacred trust of life. May our daughter/son grow in health. May she/he be strong in mind and kind in heart, a lover of Torah, a seeker of peace. Bless all of us together beneath your shelter of *shalom* (peace), and grant our new family, always, the harmony and love we feel today.

A Prayer for Nursing

In Italy, when a mother would first bring her child to her breast to nurse, she would say:

May it be Your will, Lord my God and God of my forebears, that You provide nourishment for Your humble creation, this tiny child, plenty of milk, as much as [my child] needs.

Give me the disposition and inclination to find the time to nurse [my child] patiently until [my child] be satisfied.

Cause me to sleep lightly so that the moment [my child] cries I will hear and respond.

Spare me the horror of accidentally smothering my child while I sleep, God forbid.

May the words of my mouth and the meditations of my heart be acceptable to You, my Rock and my Redeemer.

—*Out of the Depths I Call to You: A Book of Prayers for the Married Jewish Woman,* edited and translated by Nina Beth Cardin

CHAPTER 19

Growing Up

Bar and Bat Mitzvah and Beyond

The whole world is kept alive by the breath of schoolchildren.

—Talmud

O UR PANTS GET TOO SMALL; our legs too long. Braces go on our teeth; baby fat disappears. We stay by ourself at night; we babysit for our brother. Step by step,

moment by moment, we grow from an infant into a child into a teenager into an adult. The

progression is never smooth, and some of us excel at one stage more than another. But sooner

or later, through the joy and the pain of daily experience, we learn
the most precious lessons of life: when to go it alone and when
to ask for help, when to be trusting and when to hold back, when
to stand firm and when to bend, when to take risks and when to
say "enough."

Growing up takes a lifetime, but there are milestones along the way and ceremonies to help us recognize those passages. There are sweet-16 parties and debutante balls, commencement exercises and housewarmings. These ceremonies mark moments of transition. They are dramas of change, carrying us across thresholds, declaring to one and all that what we once were, we no longer are. We are more, different, better. And the community that witnesses this declaration responds, "Amen."

One of the most festive rites of passage in the Jewish repertoire is the one that marks our children's coming-of-age, the bar and bat mitzvah celebration.

Coming-of-Age as a Jew

In every culture, there are two types of ceremonies, those that celebrate an event or an achievement and those that make it happen. A birthday party is of the first kind. It may be grand and public or small and intimate. Either way, it records the event and helps us manage, share or channel the emotions of the occasion. It may make us feel proud, pleased, noticed, cared for and loved. But it doesn't make us older. With or without the party, we are one year older.

A wedding is a ceremony of the second kind. No matter how much two people love each other, no matter how long they live together or how many engagement parties they throw, without a wedding they are not married.

Adult Bat and Bar Mitzvah Celebrations

Recently, women and men have begun experimenting with the joys of an adult bat or bar mitzvah celebration, sometimes because they never had one as a young adult, sometimes because they want to celebrate a milestone anniversary. Many women who came of age before the 1960s crossed over the threshold of adolescence without being offered the opportunity to celebrate the moment in a Jewish way. To mark their entrance into Jewish adulthood, albeit a bit after the fact, many synagogues hold adult bat mitzvah classes in which women learn to read Torah and haftarah, prepare to give divrei Torah (commentaries on the Bible) and lead services. They celebrate as one, giving one another strength and encouragement, often becoming an extended family, at least for the duration of their learning and celebration.

There are men who never marked their 13th birthday with a bar mitzvah. They, too, can now turn their attention to learning the skills of the service, sometimes along with their children. They may do so at the age of 60, when they become an "elder," or at any other significant time. And some Jews now celebrate a second coming of age at 83.

The bar and bat mitzvah celebration is of the first kind. With or without a ceremony, a boy becomes a bar mitzvah, a Jewish male who has attained the age of majority—13 years and one day—as reckoned by the Jewish calendar. With or without a ceremony, a girl becomes a bat mitzvah, a Jewish female who has attained the age of majority—12 years and one day—as reckoned by the Jewish calendar. (In liberal congregations, girls generally attain the age of majority at 13.) And yet the ritual is more than a celebration. It is a public demonstration of the mettle of the child. Pressure builds diamonds. And our children, through the pressure of public performance, emerge in their own eyes as much as in ours as the community's precious jewels. The ceremony opens the portal of adulthood through which the child now walks, and it reinforces the chosen identity of every Jewish adult in the room. Even if such ceremonies do not affect the child's legal status, they help express and define the emotions of a child's coming-of-age.

A bar mitzvah boy reads from the Torah as his parents look on. ❧

A Person, a Status, an Event

Bar mitzvah means "son of the commandment." (*Bar* means "son" in Aramaic, the language spoken by the Jews in the Land of Israel 2,000 years ago.) *Bat mitzvah* means "daughter of the commandment." There is no statute of limitations on being a bar or a bat mitzvah. Once achieved by virtue of age, it is a status we keep until we die.

In North America, the terms *bar mitzvah* and *bat mitzvah* are also used as verbs, as in "I was bar mitzvahed last year." And they have become terms for the celebration itself, as in, "My bat mitzvah will be next month."

The Power of Ritual

My daughter reminded me of the power of ritual one spring afternoon when she was in elementary school. Eager to raise money to buy a gift for a friend who was moving away, she sought ways to help around the house. She and I created a list of jobs for which I would pay her. After completing some of the designated chores, like folding the family's laundry and babysitting for her brother, she would come to me, announce the tasks completed and tote up the sum. In the beginning, I was enchanted by this game and marched promptly to my wallet to make good my debt. But once when I was deeply immersed in my work, my daughter came to me and presented me with her bill. I made the best semblance of a smile that I could and said, "Sweetheart, go to my pocketbook and take the money out of my wallet." She paused a moment and walked away. Not a minute later she was back. Looking a bit sheepish and hurt, she said simply, "I feel more honored when you give it to me."

The bar or bat mitzvah ceremony may not create our passage into adulthood, but it shapes the way we feel about it. Our children feel honored that we entrusted them with that sacred ritual and that we are present—heart and soul—to celebrate the passage with them.

Clearly the ceremony does not mean to suggest that—poof!—overnight a child has in every way become an adult. Rather, it affirms that, according to Jewish law, the child has crossed the threshold from the realm of youth into the realm of adulthood, that

Over the generations, the details of how a boy prepares for his bar mitzvah service may have changed but the intention has remained the same—to inspire him with sacred purpose. ❧

the child has lived long enough to appreciate and benefit from the wisdom of his or her first hard-won experiences in life. The ceremony recognizes and celebrates the child's growing talents and skills, ambitions and responsibilities. And it proclaims that the child's achievements and potential are noticed and cherished by the community of Israel.

The History of the Celebration

The celebration of a Jewish child's coming-of-age is relatively new. The Bible does not speak of it. The Talmud hardly mentions it. There is one brief note found in a little-traveled part of the Talmud that mentions the tradition of elders blessing children who complete their first Yom Kippur fast at the age of 12 (if a girl) or 13 (if a boy).

Only sometime in the Middle Ages did coming-of-age come of age. The ritual hinges on the defining symbol of Jewish adulthood: entering the circle of public prayer. That permits the child to be counted in the *minyan* (the group of ten adults that constitutes a public quorum) and to be called for an *aliyah* (the privilege of reciting the blessings over the reading of the Torah). The acts symbolize the child's ability to stand with adults, to be a steward of our tradition and to be entrusted with our most sacred possession.

These remain the two standard ritual elements found in almost every bar mitzvah celebration today: the child of honor joins in a community prayer service (generally on Shabbat), recites the blessings of his *aliyah,* recites some or all of the weekly Torah portion and chants the *haftarah* (the weekly reading from the Prophets).

The bat mitzvah ceremony developed centuries later. In the late 1800s, in response to the accessibility and seductiveness of secular education for Jewish daughters in particular, the Jewish communities of France and Italy determined that their girls needed a way to formally receive some Jewish education and publicly mark their coming-of-age. Those communities created group bat mitzvah celebrations, designed to be held when the girls were 12 years of age. The celebrations were preceded by a period of intense study. Upon the conclusion of the course of study, the whole congregation would gather to witness, with song and ceremony, the scripted catechismlike performance by the girls.

But it was in New York City in 1922 that the first individual bat mitzvah ceremony was held. Twelve-year-old Judith Kaplan, daughter of Rabbi Mordecai Kaplan, founder of the Reconstructionist movement, stood before the congregation—all by herself. Her father had just completed reading the Torah portion and the haftarah. She stood at a lectern, recited the opening blessing accompanying an *aliyah* and read from her *ḥumash,* the printed volume of the Five Books of Moses. It was a daring moment for a daring father and daughter, decided upon only the night before. The ceremony changed forever the way girls would enter Jewish adulthood. Since then, in synagogues and homes around the world, girls are choosing to celebrate their coming-of-age publicly. Although the form of the celebration may differ in Reform, Reconstructionist, Conservative and Orthodox congregations, almost every group in Judaism has designed some formal, public way of welcoming Jewish girls into the world of adulthood.

Judith Kaplan Eisenstein celebrating the 70th anniversary of her bat mitzvah. ❧

When a Child Grows Up, The Parents Must Learn to Let Go

"Blessed are You, O God, who has released me from the obligations of this child."

That is a blessing that was traditionally recited immediately after a child's aliyah. At first glance, it seems harsh and uncaring. And in fact, the blessing is only partially true. For as parents, we continually care about, stew about, fuss and fret over the well-being of our children. But during the time of the Talmud, when that blessing was created, it helped parents publicly acknowledge that their children were on their own and that despite the parents' desire to hold on, it was time to let go.

It is not so different today. Although parents of a bat or bar mitzvah do not—in fact, cannot—give up legal responsibilities for their 12- or 13-year-old child, they must remember that their child is growing more independent every day. By reciting that blessing, the parents are reminded that little by little they must learn to let go.

How We Celebrate

Today, a bar or bat mitzvah ceremony is the highlight of years of elementary Jewish education and the culmination of a year-long course of study in which the children hone their Hebrew skills, are initiated into the ancient ways of chanting the Torah and haftarot, and explore the spiritual message of these texts.

The celebration usually takes place in the synagogue during a Shabbat morning service. Depending on the bat or bar mitzvah's

At simhas, such as wedding and bar and bat mitzvah celebrations, it is a tradition to raise the celebrants on chairs and dance to the beat of freilich (joyous) music. ⬿

Families Come in All Shapes and Sizes

Families today are often much more than mother, father, brother or sister. There may be birth parents, adoptive parents, stepparents or same-sex parents. There may be sisters, half brothers and stepbrothers. There may be Jews and non-Jews, exes and in-laws and many grandparents. We may get along well together; we may not. Whatever our families look like, they are ours. And we have to make the day work with, or despite, them. The child's teachers and rabbi can help design a way for the family to celebrate the day appropriately. Our job, as ones who love the child, is to transcend our discomfort or anger with another member of the family and not let the spotlight be moved away from our child.

abilities and desires, as well as the synagogue's traditions, the honoree may lead part or all of the service. The young person almost always receives an *aliyah* called the *maftir,* usually the seventh (the last one). Then he or she stands alone at the pulpit to read the *haftarah,* a designated selection from a book of the Prophets.

Young voices in small bodies fill an adult role. The chant the children have practiced for so long is no longer a melody to be memorized but a sacred, ancient message to be shared. The children proclaim it to the community, assuming the voice and the role of the prophets. They are taking their place among millions of children who preceded them and millions who will follow them. They become the transmitters of the ancient text for the entire congregation. And in some congregations, when they are done and the last note has faded, the child is pelted with candies and chocolates, thrown from every corner of the congregation, giving flight to the joyous emotions that fill the room.

Through their encounter with the Torah, the children are transformed, if only for a moment. They grow before our eyes (and we, their parents and grandparents, age). Their fine suits or dresses seem to fit them even better when they descend from the *bimah* than when they ascended.

The bar or bat mitzvah does not celebrate alone. Other members of the family may also be honored at the service. Father and mother, uncles and aunts, grandfathers and grandmothers, are honored. Some may be called up for an *aliyah.* Some may be asked to open and close the ark or dress the Torah after it is read. Others may be asked to read a special prayer, to offer the child words of admiration and advice or to speak about the family's history.

The family usually invites the entire congregation to continue celebrating with them at a *kiddush* immediately following the service. The *kiddush*—often a buffet with ḥallah and wine, fish, bagels, cheeses, fruits, cake and a sampling of the child's favorite foods—is a time of happiness, laughter and relief. The trial by ordeal is over, and every survivor is a victor. Now is the time for fun. But the *kiddush* is only the beginning of the celebration. So much energy has gone into planning the event, so much hope and tension and work.

Many of the celebrants have come from far away to dance at this *simḥa*, this joyous occasion. The bar or bat mitzvah's friends and parents' friends might have words they want to share, blessings they want to offer and hugs (and presents!) they want to give. All this energy must be focused and released somewhere, and that somewhere is usually a splendid party.

Beyond the Party

Simḥas are best celebrated with festive meals, *se'udot mitzvah*. As it is with weddings and covenant ceremonies, where the meal is an integral part of the celebration, so it is with bar and bat mitzvah celebrations. Often the parents put as much effort into planning the party as the child puts into learning the haftarah. In its own way, the party is the adult component of the child's rite of passage, for it is part of that publicly performed sacred moment, a letting go of the person who was once their baby, an acknowledgment of the birth of a young man or a young woman. For some families, the party is the parents' first formal ritual act as "elders," their coming-out as leaders in their community. It is a time for them to shine as they, too, move a notch up the generational ladder.

Amid the whirlwind of invitations, menu, guest list, band and party, many families build in opportunities to turn their celebration into a blessing for others. The party can become the young adult's first formal act of *gemilut ḥasadim,* hands-on deeds of lovingkindness.

For example, the family might ask guests to bring cans of food or donations of clothing as their ticket of admission to the celebration. (Such instructions can be printed on the invitation.) Or instead of purchasing expensive but short-lived floral centerpieces, the family might place baskets of potted plants at the center of each table, accompanied by cards explaining that a donation on behalf of the guests was made to a hunger-relief organization. The baskets can then be given to the oldest guest at each table or to the person who has the next *simḥa.*

At the end of the celebration, some families announce that left-over food will be donated to a soup kitchen or a shelter, thereby fulfilling the mitzvot of feeding the hungry and avoiding waste.

Setting Limits

Officials at some day schools and synagogues, in an effort to avoid the upward spiral of competition in which each party has to be bigger and better than the last, meet with the parents of each year's bar and bat mitzvah class and with them establish rules to limit conspicuous consumption. To ease the burden of selecting and buying dozens of gifts, some bar and bat mitzvah classes agree that each family will contribute a set amount of money for a class gift to be given to each bar or bat mitzvah student. At the beginning of the year, each child chooses his or her favorite from a list of gift options.

These teens dressed up as tzedakah boxes to raise money for the United Jewish Fund. ☙

Some generous bat and bar mitzvah celebrants even slip a note into their invitations requesting that instead of bringing gifts, the guests make a donation in their honor to a particular charity, cause or organization.

Sometimes the celebrants announce that they have designated a portion of their gifts to be given to tzedakah or that, to mark their growing responsibilities, they have pledged to spend 10 hours working for a charity. Sometimes the entire party is transformed into an opportunity for *gemilut hasadim*. There is no band, no dee-jay, no kitschy theme. Instead, an invitation is extended to friends and family members to help repair an old synagogue, fix bicycles for needy children or make toys for homeless children.

Just the Beginning

Coming-of-age is just the beginning of a future of possibilities and achievements. If we imagine that our lives are works of art, then every deed is a brushstroke, every word a color. We paint our grandest masterpieces in the medium of the everyday. At the bar or bat mitzvah celebration, the frame is set, the canvas drawn tight. And so the adult artwork begins.

Menarche

The onset of menstruation, which roughly coincides with the age of bat mitzvah, has almost always been a quiet affair in Judaism. Modesty shields the community and the young woman from unwanted public celebration. One classic ritual of recognition of the milestone among Ashkenazic Jews is for the mother to slap her daughter across the face, a tradition with few adherents today. And yet menarche is a milestone. Almost every woman can remember the day and the place of that experience. Some contemporary mothers have struggled to create menarche ceremonies for their daughters. Often such ceremonies resonate more powerfully for the mother than for the daughter, and they have yet to ignite the popular imagination.

So what are we to do? Borrowing images and ideas from a menarche ritual created by Judy Petsonk, an activist in the search for modern rituals, perhaps we can imagine a modest ritual such as this:

Participants: mother and daughter. Place: the daughter's room. Items: a rose and a piece of the mother's or grandmother's jewelry. The mother speaks words that welcome the daughter into the circle of womanhood. She may speak of her hopes for her daughter and the pride she has in her.

The mother hands her daughter the rose, a symbol of the daughter's flowering and beauty. She then gives her a piece of jewelry, telling her why she chose it for this moment.

Gila Gevirtz, a Jewish artist and educator, reminds us about the connection between Jewish women and jewelry. The Midrash tells us that the Israelite women refused to give their jewelry to build the golden calf, but freely gave of it to build the Tabernacle. Our jewelry thus can symbolize our faithfulness to God, our family, our people and our beloved. Our heirloom jewelry can bind us to the wisdom and love of all the women who came before us and remind us that we can become women like them, in our own right.

The ceremony may end with the mother reciting a prayer adapted from the covenant ceremony: "Just as you entered the world of womanhood, so may you enter the world of Torah, marriage and the pursuit of kindness and justice."

The rose petals may be dried and made into spices for havdalah, a reminder of the beauty of the daughter's body as it matures and ages.

On Learning to Drive

When the car from the driver's ed school honked outside our door, indicating that the instructor was waiting to pick up my son for his first driving lesson, I realized that now was the moment. My oldest was crossing the threshold into a world of newfound freedom. I had only a second to catch him before he bolted, and I wanted to offer him a blessing. I looked up—for he was already half a head taller than I—held his shoulders and recited the traditional prayer: "In the name of God, the Protector of Israel: Michael will escort you on your right. Gavriel will accompany you on your left. Uriel will be in front; Rephael, behind. And above you always will be Shechinat El, the Loving Presence of God." As is often the case, my son graciously, if somewhat bemusedly, tolerated the moment—and me. And then he was out the door.

The text was one that came naturally to me. Every night I offer that blessing to those of my children who will bear it. (The superrationalists in my family have no truck with angels.) It comes from the longer version of the bedtime Shma.

Who Is a Jew?

In the early 1980s a Jewish educator visited a bar and bat mitzvah class at a liberal synagogue on Long Island, New York. She asked the children to draw a picture of a religious Jew. Almost every one of them, girls and boys alike, children from suburban America, drew a picture of an elderly man with a long beard, sideburns (payot) and a kippah or a hat. The exception was a child who was born of Korean parents and adopted at a young age by an American Jewish family. She drew herself standing on the bimah in front of a Torah scroll.

Who are the authentic Jews? All those who grasp the Torah and say, "It is mine."

CHAPTER 20

Marriage

The Sanctification of Love

And God said, "It is not good for the human to be alone. I will make a partner

for him…." So God cast a deep sleep upon the human, and while he slept, God

took one of his ribs and closed up the flesh on that spot. And God fashioned that

rib into a woman and brought her to the man. And the man said, "This is bone

of my bone and flesh of my flesh." Therefore, a man leaves his parents and joins

with his wife, and they are as one flesh.

—Genesis 2:18, 21–24

W E NEED ONE ANOTHER. We crave the company of family and friends, a place that is ours where people love us and understand us. We seek the safety of a strong home, where we can make mistakes and not be mocked; get angry and know we will be forgiven, test our beliefs, change our minds, sulk, strut, sing and still have a place waiting for us at the dinner table.

As young adults, home is our private training ground. It is our first mediator and teacher of culture, the place that tames the chaos of the world with words and stories and dreams. It is the place that protects us from all that lies beyond the front door, and the place that readies us to meet it. It is where we are given space in which to prepare ourselves for the world each day, where we rehearse our personalities, trying out the different people we imagine ourselves to be, where we sharpen our ways of negotiating, learn the proper etiquette of winning and losing, where we are loved and accepted unconditionally in exchange for giving our love unconditionally. When it comes time to leave, it is that sense of love and shelter that we seek to build into a home of our own.

We rehearse the creation of such a place throughout our young lives—in our supersecret clubs as kids, in our sport teams in high school, in the Greek clubs in college, in study groups in law school, in lunch groups at work. If we are lucky, we create several such places throughout our lives, and a bit of the warmth of each one stays with us even after we grow apart from them. But the most important place of love and shelter is the place we call home.

Finding the Beloved

Home begins with one. But family begins with two. How does one become two? How do we find the one who completes us, the one who picks us up at the station, has the other key to our car, uses our toothbrush by mistake and we don't care? "Upon my couch at night, I sought the one I love; I sought, but did not find him....I rise and roam the town, through the streets and squares.... I met the watchman and asked, 'Have you seen the one I love?'" (Song of Songs 3:1–3).

Once it was a lot easier. "And God fashioned that rib into a woman and brought her to the man." Forget the hunt. This is God's dating service, special delivery. But if God was worried that even the first man and the first woman might not have found each other on their own (why else would God have brought her to him?), how much harder is it for us? We read books offering us advice; go to coffee shops, lectures and tzedakah programs; allow friends to set us up on blind dates. After a while, birth seems a lesser mystery than finding our beloved. We become comfortable buying single-serving frozen-food packages at the supermarket.

Then at work, at the gym, in class, at a wedding, or in the new way we look at an old friend, love seems to find us. Our world contracts and expands all at the same time. The poet Ḥayyim Naḥman Bialik expresses the intensity of the moment in his poem "Ayech": "In the innocence of my prayers and the purity of my thoughts, in the meditations of my mouth and the depths of my suffering, my soul sought only one thing: knowing you, just you, you, you."

Yet in exploring every movement, every inch of the one we love, we discover ever so much more about the world around us: the way things smell, the way people walk, the expressiveness of eyes, the arcs of eyebrows. Time itself becomes almost palpable, heavy and labored when we are away from our beloved, buoyant and eternal when we are together.

All of a sudden so many things that are good seem to be ours: comfort, joy, growth, desire, passion, love. We do not know how we lived without our beloved before, but we are certain we never want to be parted again. Our devotion can only be contained, our fear of loss can only be soothed by a promise that says "forever." The promise of marriage—with its constancy and its commitment—spreads a blanket of calm and serenity across our world. In the midst of this sprawling, disorderly universe, we have a center. So awesome is that feeling that it became a metaphor for the relationship between God and the people Israel. In the words of Hosea (2:21): "I betroth you to Me forever. I betroth you in righteousness and justice, kindness and compassion. I betroth you in faithfulness. And you shall know your God."

Weaving the Bonds of Marriage

No matter how many times people have fallen in love, each time it is new. Though billions of men and women inhabit this planet, Judaism lets us imagine that each couple is a reflection of that first couple, as much the center of the world as were Adam and Eve. The sixth blessing of the wedding ceremony speaks to God about the bride and the groom, saying, "Open the floodgates of happiness for these two lovers, just as You brought joy to Your

The Key to the Power of Marriage Is Its Exclusiveness

"I am my beloved's, and my beloved is mine," says the poet of the Song of Songs. Perhaps for the first time ever in our lives, we don't have to share. Even more, we are not permitted to share. To know that our beloved is pledged to us alone, that our beloved loves us fully and unlike any other, and that we faithfully and exclusively devote ourselves to our beloved in return is to know peace.

A Hidden Sorrow

Perhaps there is no loss carried more privately than the loss of a mate. The one we would turn to for comfort in our sorrow is the very one for whom we mourn. An empty place greets us in bed each morning and lies beside us every night. Home, once our fortress of comfort, is now a field of memories. Old routines have been broken; new ones must be created. Widows and widowers are remarkable and dignified in the ways they bear their sorrow and learn to remake their lives. Wherever and whenever we can, we should try to ease their way by including them in our holiday plans and our social lives.

The Story of Eve's Birth

We can read the story of Eve's "birth" as a lesson to men and women alike about making sacrifices for love: We can achieve completeness only when we are willing to surrender a part of ourselves for the one we love. As in the mystics' tale of Creation, in which God contracted, withdrawing a part of God's self to make room for the creation of the world, we, too, must withdraw a bit from our universe of self to make room for the one who will join us. In becoming less, we become complete.

A Dwelling Place for God

In Hebrew, the words for *man* and *woman* differ only by two letters, *yod* and *hay*. Together those letters form the name of God. The rabbis tell us that means that when a man and a woman make a home together, they create another dwelling place for God on earth.

A Day for Weddings

The Torah tells us that twice on the third day of Creation, God said, "It is good." Therefore, some couples choose to get married on Tuesday, for it is the one day of the week that was twice blessed.

Creation in the garden of Eden long ago. Blessed are You, God, who gladdens the hearts of groom and bride."

Bringing joy to newlyweds is a mitzvah that surpasses that of study. The Talmud tells us that if a student is studying and a bridal party passes in the street, he should put aside his books and join the entourage. The learned rabbis, to whom all the community turned for models of modesty and propriety, would themselves shamelessly and with abandon dance before the bride and the groom. The Midrash tells us that in the absence of any friends or extended family in the garden of Eden, God served as a *shushbin* (a member of the wedding party) to Adam and Eve.

A joyous marriage is the foundation of the world. We celebrate first-time marriages and second-time marriages. We celebrate weddings at which parents escort their children down the aisle and weddings at which children escort their parents down the aisle. Whether individuals are barren or fertile, young or old, bringing them together is a holy task. The Talmud records that a woman once asked a rabbi, "What has God been doing since Creation?" "Making marriages" was the reply. Why? It is an extension of Creation. We are created the first time at birth. We are created anew through marriage.

Beyond weaving together two lives, marriage allows us to build a home for ourselves and for our children, safe and secure and full of love. To feel little arms around our necks, to have a child pull us excitedly by the hand, to watch our children achieve or stumble and pick themselves up again, to watch them fall in love and build a home of their own—these are among the greatest joys of our lives. "To see the children of your children, that is called peace within Israel." These are the words we sing at wedding feasts. These are the gifts and the dreams that marriage gives us.

How We Celebrate

Hundreds of years ago a Jewish wedding had two parts. The first was the engagement ceremony (*kiddushin* or *erusin*); the second, the wedding itself (*nisu'in*). For the *kiddushin*, the families of the bride and the groom would come together to sign a contract in which they promised that their children would be wed. That

Circling the Groom

In most Jewish weddings, the groom goes up to the *huppah* (wedding canopy) first, escorted by his parents. The bride follows, escorted by her parents. At some weddings, when the bride reaches the *huppah*, she walks around the groom, sometimes three times, sometimes seven. Several reasons are suggested: that the center of her world now moves from her parents' home to her new home, symbolized by her husband; that just as her husband gives her a wedding ring, so the circling is the wedding ring she gives him; that since the *huppah* represents her new home, she walks around it as if to define its walls and its boundaries. At some weddings, the bride and the groom take turns walking three times around each other and once around the *huppah* together.

The Ritual Bath

A *mikveh* is a natural or human-made gathering of waters used as a ritual bath by women— and men, at times—in order to bring about heightened spiritual awareness and to prepare for the renewal of sexual relations.

A bride may choose to go to a mikveh after her last period before her wedding. She may invite her mother and mother-in-law, her sisters and some of her closest friends to celebrate this crossing of a threshold.

Three days before a dear friend was to be married, a group of us gathered with her at a mikveh. It was the official start of her wedding festivities. Before she entered the room where she would bathe and ready herself for the waters, we gathered in a circle around her and showered

her with gifts: bath oils, fragrant shampoo, pearly conditioners, loofah sponges, creams and soaps. To mark her transition from woman to bride, we covered her face with a mud mask made from the nutrients of the Dead Sea. The more artistic among us painted designs. The rest of us smudged. Our bride was a very good sport.

When she came out from her immersion in the mikveh, all dried and dressed, we gave her a gift of a bloodstone, a symbol of woman's strength and our love. We each held the stone as we offered her our blessings for a fulfilling and loving life with her beloved. As self-conscious and clumsy as we all were at this attempt at a new ritual, in truth, when the laughing subsided, the tears flowed. And the bride was ready for marriage.

When a Marriage Ends

Sometimes no matter how hard people try, their marriage doesn't work. Both the Bible and the Talmud understood that when love is gone and tension is in the home, the marriage should end. So Judaism provides for divorce. No court sits in judgment of the merits of the case; no judge determines whether or not to grant a divorce. Rather, at the couple's bidding, they appear before the rabbi, the scribe and witnesses. The scribe writes the divorce document, called a *get*, which ends the marriage. The wife cups her hands together in front of her, and the husband places the folded document in them. As if to seal the point, the rabbi then cuts the document, legally showing that it has been delivered and symbolically rending what had once been joined.

This 18th-century engraving shows the mikveh in Amsterdam, Holland. The three women who are portrayed are likely to represent the bride, her mother, and an attendant.

A Woman Who Is "Chained"

According to classical Jewish law, a husband can divorce his wife, but a wife cannot divorce her husband. If the husband were to become mentally incompetent, disappear or refuse to divorce her when she wanted out of the marriage, she would become an *agunah*, a woman "chained" to a man she no longer took as her husband.

In modern times, although a couple may receive a civil divorce, the husband may refuse to give his wife a *get*. The various religious denominations offer different solutions to such a situation. The Reform movement accepts the civil divorce in place of the religious divorce; the Reconstructionist movement allows a similar remedy but prefers and encourages a Jewish divorce, with the adaptation of making it egalitarian, or, if necessary, permitting women to initiate the divorce. The Conservative movement and, most recently, segments of the Orthodox community, have established courts of law that, if the circumstances allow, are able to annul the marriage and free the woman—and the man.

A Premarital Aliyah

Aufruf is a Yiddish word meaning "call up." On Shabbat a week or two before the wedding, the groom and, in some communities, the bride as well are honored with an *aliyah*. Generally the families of the couple gather to celebrate the occasion, and a festive luncheon is held afterward for family and friends. Sometimes after the final blessing of the *aliyah*, the congregants throw candy at the bride and the groom, as they do at a bar or bat mitzvah celebration, and the children of the congregation scurry to gather up the goods.

Yom Kippur Katan

The day of the wedding is like a little Yom Kippur for the bride and groom. In traditional communities, the bride and the groom fast and recite prayers that help them focus on what is to come and how they hope to be. They ask God to forgive their past mistakes and to help them start a new life together.

A Ḥuppah at Home

Often couples who have a personalized *ḥuppah* display it in their home. Sometimes they hang it in the living room. Sometimes they hang it over their bed. Sometimes they choose to make it into a quilt for the babies they hope to have.

agreement meant that the bride and the groom were legally bound to each other. Although not yet married, they would need a *get*, a Jewish divorce document, if they wanted to end the engagement, and the one who broke that promise would have to pay a cash penalty. But since the wedding had not yet taken place, the bride and the groom still lived apart, with their parents, while the families prepared for the wedding.

There was much to be done. Bedding—mattresses, blankets, sheets and pillows—needed to be sewn; a house had to be bought or built; kitchen utensils and furniture had to be prepared. When the time of the marriage arrived, the families came together for the *nisu'in*, the long-awaited wedding ceremony and feast. The bride and the groom would be escorted into their new home, and the feasting and the celebrating continued for another six days.

Today the two ceremonies are held at the same time. When the wedding ceremony begins, the community is assembled, and the *ḥuppah*, the wedding canopy, symbolizing the couple's new home, stands empty at the front of the room. With music to guide their steps, the groom and the bride are escorted by their parents to the *ḥuppah*. Sometimes the *ḥuppah* is a family *tallit*. Sometimes it is a cloth specially embroidered by the bride, her mother, her mother-in-law or friends. Most often it is a satin or velvet cloth—much like a Torah mantle, only much bigger—provided by the synagogue or caterer. The *ḥuppah* is supported by friends and family specially chosen for the honor. The groom arrives first, the bride second. When all are settled in their places under the *ḥuppah*, the ceremony begins.

THE BETROTHAL

The first part of the ceremony is the *kiddushin*, the engagement, also called betrothal. *Kiddushin* means "to make holy," and refers specifically to holiness through separation from other people. Through the ritual of *kiddushin*, the bride and the groom promise themselves to each other. They are made holy to each other and to no one else, just as the Jewish people were made holy to God at Mount Sinai when they promised they would have no other god.

Kiddushin is performed with a blessing over a cup of wine, an engagement blessing and a ring:

> Blessed are You, God, Sovereign of the universe, Creator of the fruit of the vine.

> Blessed are You, God, Sovereign of the universe, who has sanctified us through Your mitzvot and commands us regarding sexual relations, that we should refrain from the forbidden and be devoted to the one we have chosen through the acts of *ḥuppah* and *kiddushin*. Blessed are You, God, who has sanctified the people Israel through the rituals of *ḥuppah* and *kiddushin*.

The groom then presents the bride with a gold ring and, while placing it on her right index finger, proclaims, "Behold you are consecrated to me with this ring according to the laws of Moses and Israel."

Today most brides give their grooms a ring as well, either during the ceremony or after, and may recite a verse from the Bible's love poem, the Song of Songs, or a favorite passage from another source, or a pledge that they wrote.

The ceremony continues with the reading of the *ketubah*, the wedding document that provides written proof that these two people got married on such and such a day in such and such a place. It records the groom's promises to care for his bride, to feed her, provide for her and love her "as do all Jewish husbands." Whereas the traditional *ketubah* speaks only of the groom's responsibilities to the bride, today many Jewish brides add to it their own declaration of commitment, promising to love, care for and provide for their husbands. Some brides and grooms write their own wedding document, declaring in their own words their love and expectations, their dreams and commitment. As with any Jewish legal document, the *ketubah* is signed by two reliable witnesses—in this case, unrelated to either bride or groom. It is then given to the bride to keep. Years ago it was her protection. In case of divorce or her husband's death, she would claim financial support according to the terms of her *ketubah*.

Two wedding rings from Venice, Italy. Traditionally, the ring given to a Jewish bride at the wedding ceremony is without ornamentation or jewels. Afterwards, a more decorative wedding ring may be worn.

An Illuminated Ketubah

Judaica shops are good sources for *ketubot* (plural of *ketubah*). There are many texts with a variety of decorations available. Some rabbis may be more comfortable with certain texts, so it is always helpful to consult the rabbi before purchasing a *ketubah*. Many couples choose to work with a calligrapher and design the *ketubah*—both the text and the illumination—according to their own specifications.

A Bride's Prayer

Two hundred years ago, brides in Italy used to say this blessing: "*Ribono Shel Olamim,* Ruler of the universe, may it be Your will that You cause my husband to love me with a perfect love. Place shalom, wholeness and peace, love, tenderness, harmony and fulfilling companionship between me and my beloved. So may we always be."

A Household of Peace

Sh'lom bayit, peace and wholeness within the household, is one of the greatest blessings that families can provide. *Sh'lom bayit* gives us the surety and the security that allows us to unload, regroup and recharge after the onslaughts of the day's events. But *sh'lom bayit* must be worked on constantly, shored up, for it can be subject to erosion over time. Before the marriage, couples often create a bridal registry, eager to outfit their house with objects of loveliness. Perhaps on the first wedding anniversary and on others thereafter, couples can turn to their *sh'lom bayit* registry asking, What are the daily acts we do for each other that reinforce our love? What habits should we try to overcome? What do we resolve never to say in an argument? What can I do to make you happier?

THE WEDDING

Now the second part of the ceremony, the wedding itself— *nisu'in*—begins. It is composed of seven blessings, called, appropriately, *sheva brachot* (seven blessings), which include the blessing over the ceremony's second cup of wine.

The blessings speak of the creation of life, of man and woman: "Blessed are You, Source of Life, Sovereign of the universe, who created humankind."

They recall the two ways in which the Torah speaks of the creation of woman and man: both together, created as one, made in the image of God (Genesis 1) and woman built up as the perfect, eternal match for Adam (Genesis 2). Each wedding is a renewal of Creation.

They continue by speaking of the joy of the people: "May the barren one, Zion, rejoice with the ingathering of her children. Blessed are You, the One who makes Zion happy with her children."

And they speak of the joy of the couple:

Open the floodgates of happiness for these two caring lovers just as You brought joy to Your creation in the garden of Eden long ago. Blessed are You, God, who gladdens the hearts of groom and bride.

Blessed are You, Compassionate One, Sovereign of the universe, who created joy and gladness, bride and groom, rejoicing and celebration without end, love and devotion, serenity and commitment. Speedily, God, may there again be heard in the cities of Judah and in the streets of Jerusalem the sounds of joy and laughter, the voice of the bride and the voice of the groom, the noise of young people feasting and singing. Blessed are You, God, who brings joy to the bride and the groom.

The final act of the wedding is the traditional breaking of the glass. Many explanations for it are offered: to scare away the evil eye that always threatens to undo our happiness; to symbolize an irreparable break with the past; to indicate the end of the bride and groom's virginity; to represent the parents' breaking hearts—amid their joy—as they give away their children. But the most common reason offered is that even at the moments of our greatest personal joy we remember that Jerusalem and the Temple were twice destroyed and that until a true peace comes to Israel and all the world our happiness is incomplete. The glass reminds us that our destinies are not ours alone. We are bound to one another in an eternal covenant.

With the wedding complete, the celebration begins. Helping the couple rejoice on the day of their wedding is a mitzvah that was enhanced in many European communities by a professional *badhan,* a jester, whose services would be hired just for the occasion. He would juggle bottles on his chin or hat, compose poems and songs for the bride and the groom and entertain the guests with dances and stories. Today friends and family members sometimes bring masks and streamers, confetti and jump ropes, all sorts of carnival games, to amuse the couple.

In more observant communities, the wedding celebration lasts seven days. The bride and the groom are invited to the homes of friends and family members for a whole week's worth of lunches and dinners, each meal followed by the seven blessings, *sheva brachot,* as long as a minyan is present. After the *sheva brachot* festivities, the couple leave for their long-awaited honeymoon.

When the week of *sheva brachot* ends and the honeymoon is over, after the presents have all been put away, when routine settles in, the bride and the groom begin their new life together. Those who are young and able build a home, work at their jobs, raise their children, coach Little League games, volunteer at book fairs, have dinner with their grandparents, support favorite candidates, go on vacation and organize the synagogue's Purim carnival. Their children grow up, and so do they. And the circle of life continues.

For every bride and groom, young or old, marrying for the first time or not, the wedding is magic: The air bears the fragrance of the poet's apple orchards, youth is recaptured, and life is renewed. No wonder everyone loves a wedding.

When the groom breaks the glass, the guests call out, "Mazal Tov!" and the celebration begins ❧

An Anniversary Prayer

How do we bless those who are already blessed with a loving marriage? The Talmud answers with a story: A man is crossing the desert. He is hungry and tired and terribly thirsty. Suddenly he happens upon a tree whose fruit is sweet and whose shade is pleasant and beside which is flowing a cool brook. So he eats of the fruit and drinks of the water and rests in the comfort of the shade. When it is time to leave, he says, "Dear tree, how can I bless you? If I were to say 'May your fruit be sweet,' behold, your fruit is already sweet. If I were to say 'May your shade be pleasant,' behold, it is already pleasant. If I were to say 'May you be blessed with a flowing brook,' behold, you already have one. Rather, I will say, 'May it be God's will that all that shoots forth from you be as blessed as you.'"

CHAPTER 21

Death and Mourning

A Life to Be Remembered

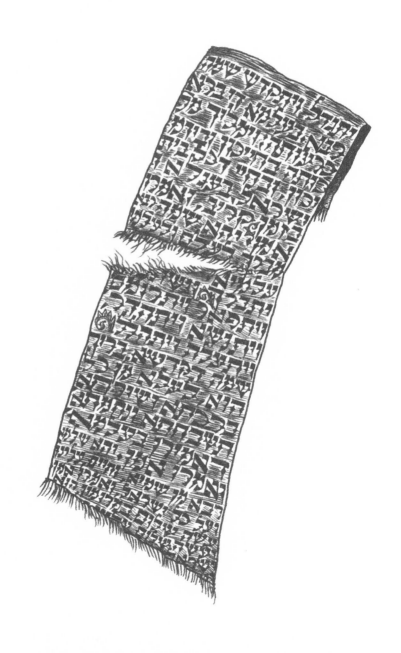

A visitor came to see the Ḥafetz Ḥayyim, a rabbi well-known for his piety and

simplicity. When the visitor arrived, he was surprised at what he saw: a table,

a chair, a bookcase, a closet, a bed, a desk. "Where are all your possessions?" he asked.

"Where are yours?" the rabbi replied.

"What do you mean," the visitor protested. "I am just a visitor."

"So am I," the Ḥafetz Ḥayyim answered.

—Martin Buber, Tales of the Hasidim

WE ALONE OF ALL CREATURES know that one day we and each of our loved ones will die. Yet we dare open ourselves to others, to trust them and love them, knowing that eventually they will leave us. And we dare to let other people love us, knowing that we will leave them. How wonderful that we are so courageous, and so irrational, for life would be pale, empty and lonely without such love.

Knowing that life ends heightens the value of each moment we live. The day after sickness lifts, our world may seem fresher and more vibrant than before. Our home may appear like the garden of Eden when we return from the hospital. And some who are diagnosed with an oppressive and life-threatening disease say that their lives are richer now than they were before. Could there have been another way to teach us such awareness, such appreciation? After all, dying is a high price to pay for the joy of living.

What Is Death?

What happens to us after we die? Is it an end or a beginning? a reunion or separation? Should we be afraid or not? No one knows. Many Jews throughout the centuries and up to this day have believed that life continues after death. Judaism even has a name for the afterlife, *Olam Haba*, the World to Come. The rabbis imagined this world as a paradise, *gan Eden,* the place where it is always Shabbat. It is the place with no hatred, sickness or poverty. It is the place that can know no more death, where we sit with crowns on our heads, delighting in the splendor of God's glory.

The second paragraph of the Amidah, the prayer that forms the center of every service, speaks of God vanquishing death: "You sustain the living with lovingkindness; You bestow eternal life upon the dead....You keep faith with those who sleep in the dust.... Blessed are You, God, who restores the dead to life." Just as God heals and comforts those who are sick in body or broken in spirit, God restores the dead. Talmudic theology holds that there will be a resurrection of our bodies and a return of our souls at the end of days.

Still, death is fearsome, for it threatens to snuff out our consciousness and remove us from the presence of God. The early-morning prayers comfort us with visions of immortality:

> The soul which You have given me, God, is pure. You created it; You formed it; You breathed it into me. You keep watch over it while it is in me. You will take it from me in time to come and return it to me at the end of time. All the while it is in me I will praise You, God, Protector of the souls.

The prayer seeks to assure us on both counts: that we, in our individuality, will endure and that we will never cease to be embraced by God.

The Lessons of Death

In Italy 200 years ago, Jewish mothers used to recite a special prayer when handing over their sons to be circumcised. They would pray that God give their eight-day-old baby an honorable life, a long life and a good death. That sounds odd, even morbid to our ears. Today we shun talk of death when celebrating the start of life. But those mothers knew that life was precarious. Mortality was an ever-present guest; they might carry their children to the graveyard just as they now carried them to the Covenant. So they asked for the best a parent could ask for, that their children die peacefully after a full life, in old age, without pain and without violence.

We also know that ultimately we cannot defeat death. We can use our great technological advances to save people's lives. We can pray for them to live, recite psalms for them and dedicate sacred learning to them; we can visit them, cajole them to eat, to hang on and pull through. But there are times when it is a *tefillat shav*, a petition recited in vain, an unfair and unachievable expectation of God to pray that our loved ones not die. Rather, we should pray as those mothers did, that our loved ones die a good, peaceful, natural death.

The Talmud (*Ketubot* 104a) records the story of Rabbi Judah, who was deathly ill and racked with pain. His disciples, desperate to keep him alive, recited prayers constantly for him. The prayers worked and he remained alive, but in unbearable pain. At last, Rabbi Judah's handmaiden, taking pity on her master, climbed to the roof of the house and threw a jug hard toward the ground. At the sound of the shattering jug, the disciples paused in their prayers, and at that moment, Rabbi Judah's soul was released.

Our task is not to defeat death. Our task is to be certain that death does not defeat us. We are called to live our lives with passion and caring so that death cannot erase our legacy or our quest. A life devoted to family and friends, a life devoted to discovery and awareness, a life devoted to building community, a life devoted to

Visiting the Sick

It is a great mitzvah to visit someone who is sick. There is something in it for both the visitor and the one who is visited. One-sixtieth of the illness goes away, according to one Talmudic tradition, every time someone comes to visit. And visiting the sick, *bikkur holim*, is counted as one of the few mitzvot for which a person receives reward both in this world and in the world to come.

A Blessing to Be Recited upon Hearing of a Death

When we hear that someone has died, we say this blessing: Blessed are You, our God, Sovereign of the universe, the One True Judge.

raising the young—all those are good lives whose achievements can never be erased.

Honoring the Dead

Death is a threshold we cross alone, but it makes profound claims on those who are left behind. Judaism teaches us that tending immediately to the deceased shows honor to the one who died and offers comfort to those who mourn. As a member of a community faced with a death, the first thing that we must do, then, is take care of the body. It is to be handled with the greatest respect and dignity, carefully and modestly, with an attitude of reverence and awe.

Between death and burial there is much to do. The rabbi and the Jewish funeral home guide the mourners through the necessary steps and arrange for the body to be tended. Almost every city with a sizable Jewish community has within it a *hevrah kaddisha* (fellowship of holiness). These volunteers are specially trained to tend to the bodies of the deceased. Men take care of men, and women take care of women. They carefully wash the body according to the ways of tradition and dress it in its burial clothes. In more traditional communities, these clothes are white shrouds. In other communities, they are clothes selected by the family. Men (and perhaps one day, women) may be draped in tallitot, one corner of which has been cut.

While the body is in the funeral home awaiting burial, members of the *hevrah kaddisha* or members of the family or the broader community sit with the body and recite psalms, for the body is not to be left alone. One of the greatest fears of those who are dying is that they will be abandoned. The laws of caring for the critically ill, as they evolved in the Jewish tradition, tell us that we are to visit the sick regularly and may not leave the side of someone who has begun the final stages of dying. Family members and friends may take turns sitting with their loved one through those difficult hours. Our commitment to offering comfort and a presence to those who are dying extends even to death. We do not abandon the body until it is returned to the earth. At that point, our attention turns to those who mourn.

This late-18th-century picture from Prague, Czechoslovakia, shows a shroud being sewn.

The Gift of Life

All branches of Judaism encourage organ donation. The Torah tells us: "Do not stand idly by the blood of your neighbor." When someone needs us, and we are in a position to save them, we must respond, using all appropriate measures available to us. After death, when we no longer need our bodies, it is a *mitzvah shel hesed*, a most sacred and generous act, to give our organs to those who will die without them. "Choose life" (Deuteronomy 30:19).

Kayla's Prayer

Judaism encourages us to make a final confession before dying. One woman, Kayla, found the traditional words of confession, the Vidui, lacking. They did not say what she needed to say. So, with her rabbi, Lawrence Troster, she composed the following personal confession:

Listen to my voice
O Lord our God,
And God of my ancestors.

I lie here on the brink of life,
Seeking peace, seeking comfort,
   seeking You.
To You O Lord I call and to You
   O Lord I make my supplication.
Do not ignore my plea.
Let Your mercy flow over me
   like the waters,
Let the record of my life
   be a bond between us,
Listen to my voice when I call,
Be gracious to me and answer me.

I have tried O Lord to help You
   complete creation,
I have carried Your yoke
   my whole life.
I have tried to do my best.
Count my effort for the good
   of my soul,
Forgive me for when I have
   stumbled on Your path.
I can do no more, let my family
   carry on after me,
Let others carry on after me.

Protector of the helpless,
   healer of the broken-hearted,
Protect my beloved family
   with whose soul my own soul
   is bound.
Their hearts depended
   upon mine,
Heal their hearts when they
   come to depend on You.

Let my soul rest forever under
   the wings of Your presence,
Grant me a share
   in the world to come.
I have tried to love You with all
   my heart and with all my soul,
And even though You come
   to take my soul,
Even though I don't know why
   You come,
Even though I'm angry
   at the way You take me
For Your sake I will still proclaim:
Hear O Israel, the Lord
   is our God, the Lord alone.
The Lord is with me,
   I shall not fear.

Hospices

Increasingly, Jewish communities and synagogues are becoming involved with hospice care, bringing the comforts of Jewish beliefs, sacred time and holy community to those who are dying and to their families. It is an art at which the Jewish community once excelled. In the 17th century, Rabbi Aaron Berechiah ben Moses of Modena wrote the definitive Jewish book of prayers and rituals dealing with illness and dying. Titled *Ma'avar Yabok*, it proved a bit inaccessible to the general public. Less than a century later, Rabbi Simon Frankfurter wrote *Sefer Hahayyim—The Book of Life—* a popular Hebrew-language guidebook to the rituals and prayers of illness and dying. Because Rabbi Frankfurter believed that women also needed to know how to die well and that they certainly needed to know how to tend to the sick and the dying, and because he knew that most women did not understand Hebrew, Rabbi Frankfurter translated large sections of his book into Yiddish. Neither of these books is currently available in English. Perhaps with the renewed interest in hospices, that empty space on our bookshelves will soon be filled.

This prayer, from *Sefer Hahayyim*, is to be recited in a hushed voice by one attending the very ill. And when it appears that the ill are in their last moments, one must stay with them, and not leave, so that they do not die alone. It is a mitzvah to tend to people at the moment of death. And it is a mitzvah to pray that they die if it is clear that they are suffering greatly in their last moments:

Adonai, Adonai, God of mercy and kindness, long-suffering, gracious and truthful, be merciful to … [the person's name], who is sick, and to all those who are deathly ill among Your people, those who lie upon their beds with their souls struggling in them to leave. In Your hands is the power of eternal life and the ability to heal and restore the ill to health. Please, remove the harsh decree; allow Your mercy to reign over Your people.

But if the decree will not be changed, and You will gather to You the soul of this one, save his/her soul, and gather it to You, pure and holy. Let it be joined to the light of the Shechinah. May the four angels stand beside him/her, and may his/her soul depart with a kiss and the embrace of the spirit of all spirits. Guard its going in all ways. May it go out in peace and travel in peace; may its journey be in peace and its resting be in peace.

While one person's death can sadden many people, only members of the immediate family are considered mourners: mothers, fathers, spouses, sisters, brothers, sons and daughters. Grandchildren, in-laws, and other close relatives often observe some or all of the requirements of mourning. Converts, adopted children and stepchildren can choose to observe the laws of mourning for those who bore or raised them.

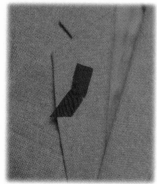

A kriah ribbon. The tradition of kriah, rending one's clothing as a sign of grief, stems from the biblical story of Jacob. When Jacob's sons brought him Joseph's bloodstained robe telling him that his favorite son had been killed by a wild beast, Jacob responded by tearing his own garment.

Mourning, Steps Toward Healing

When a loved one dies, no matter what the person's age or circumstances, the family is often in shock. Their lives have been turned upside down. They may cry. They may shout. Or they may just sit, silent and still. It is as if a part of them had died as well. Their hurt is too fresh, their wound too deep for healing to begin. Judaism understands that mourning—which is the beginning of healing—cannot be forced too quickly. "Do not comfort the bereaved while their dead lie before them," the rabbis tell us. Healing happens slowly, over the course of time. So Judaism offers a guide to healing, step-by-step.

The first step is called *aninut.* It spans the period from death to burial. During this time, the mourner is called an *onen* and is released from the obligation to perform the positive mitzvot. For example, mourners do not have to pray, cannot be counted in a minyan and do not have to recite any of the blessings of gratitude, such as the blessing over bread. Their thoughts are elsewhere. They are occupied with their loss and with making plans for the burial. They may be too angry, too full, too empty or too stunned to talk to God. How unfair it would be to burden them with those obligations at such a time. The rituals of mourning are designed to be a gift, a release, and not a burden. Jewish law surrenders some of its normal claims before the power of grief.

The Funeral

Jewish burials generally take place the day after death. There are two reasons that a burial can be postponed: if family members coming from afar would otherwise miss the funeral or if the day is Shabbat or a *Yom Tov,* a holiday on which no work may be done. In such cases, the burial is scheduled as soon thereafter as possible.

On the day of the burial, the mourners gather at the funeral home or graveside and perform the ritual of *kriah,* in which they cut or tear a portion of their clothes (often a sweater, a scarf, a vest or a tie). That symbolizes in deeds what our words cannot adequately express. Sometimes when we grieve, we feel as if our hearts were ripping. Sometimes when a loved one dies, we want to rage— at God, at our loved one, at ourselves—and to tear something to shreds. Past cultures indulged in mortification of the flesh. *Kriah* provides a safer way to express these primal urges. It helps us safely act out these emotions. We neither ignore nor succumb to our feelings of pain, anger, frustration, guilt, fear, loss. We wear them on our clothes.

Some people today do not cut their clothes. They feel more comfortable wearing a torn black ribbon provided by the rabbi or the funeral home. Those who have lost a parent wear the ribbon (or the tear) on their left side, above the heart. All other mourners wear the ribbon (or the tear) on the right.

At the funeral, the rabbi, cantor or friends offer prayers, recite psalms (especially Psalm 23) and speak words of comfort to the mourners. They speak of the one who died, what that person loved, accomplished, hoped for; they talk of his or her signature ways, favorite sayings, best recipes. Sometimes the speakers tell stories that make us smile; sometimes they tell stories that make us cry. Both have a place at a funeral.

The funeral ends with a special prayer, El Malei Rahamim, God, Full of Compassion:

> God, who is full of compassion, the Divine Presence who lives on high, grant a perfect rest, nestled under Your protective wings, to the soul of… [name of the deceased]. Let his/her place be in the garden of Eden…, and bind his/her soul in the bond of life. Grant that he/she rest in peace. Amen.

After a funeral that is not conducted at the graveside, the family and friends accompany the body to the cemetery. At the graveside, those present may want to recite one or two more psalms. The body is lowered into the grave, and the graveside Kaddish, which speaks of eternal life, is recited. The act of burying the dead is the greatest act of *hesed*, lovingkindness, that anyone can perform, both because it is so very hard to perform, and because there can be no expectation of reward or repayment. It is called *hesed shel emet*, pure kindness.

Judaism offers everyone present the opportunity to participate in the mitzvah of burying the dead. All are invited to take a bit of earth and throw it on the coffin. The dull thud of the soil hitting the hard wooden coffin in which lies a grandfather, a mother or a

A Plain Pine Box

Long ago, wealthy families would spend extravagant amounts of money on expensive caskets and funerals. The poor would see that and be disturbed, even offended. Were they not more important than the dead? Why would the wealthy spend their money on aesthetics for the dead rather than on tzedakah for the living? And in death, did not the poor deserve as fine a funeral as the wealthy? So the rabbis ruled that every Jew, rich or poor, should be buried in simple garments and in a plain pine box.

Escorting the Dead

It is a great mitzvah to accompany the dead to the grave. But it is not always possible to do so. One tradition teaches us, therefore, that if we cannot go to the cemetery, we should line up behind the hearse and walk behind it for a short way. Thus, we perform the mitzvah of accompanying the dead, even if only part of the way.

Cremation

Judaism frowns on cremation and on above-ground burial, unless high water tables make in-ground burial impossible. We are taken from the earth, according to the Creation story of the second chapter of Genesis, and it is to the earth that we are to return. Cremation, like tattoos, is considered a desecration of the gift of our bodies. Burial aesthetics are often determined more by our culture than by personal taste. Why not, then, allow Jewish aesthetics to guide our way?

The Signs of Mourning

There are many traditional laws of mourning to help us grieve. Just as it is not healthy to mourn too much, it is also not healthy to mourn too little. So Judaism offers us a guide to mourning during the week of shiva. The mourners are to sit on low chairs, close to the ground. They should bathe only when absolutely necessary. Men do not shave. Women do not put on make-up. Neither do they cut their hair. Mourners should not worry about how they look. It is for that reason that mirrors in houses of shiva are covered with cloths or sheets or streaked with soap. Mourners should be spared any concerns about business. They have but one job that week: grieving and being comforted.

friend is one of the sharpest sounds on earth. It pierces our hearts and opens the floodgates of grief. And yet it also comforts, because we know we are tending to the needs of our loved one. We know we are giving the last shelter he or she needs here on earth. And we are reminded that our love cannot be vanquished by death.

Shiva

After the burial, the mourner becomes an *avel*. The period of mourning is called *avelut*. It is distinguished by three divisions: the 7 days immediately following the burial, the remainder of the first 30 days after the burial, and the first full 11 months.

The first week is called *shiva*, meaning "seven." It is a time when the mourner sits at home. The mourner does no work—no laundry, no shopping, no cleaning, and with the help of the extended family and friends, no cooking—and engages in no form of entertainment. There are to be no distractions from the matter at hand—mourning. Most family members in mourning choose to sit together in the same house for at least part of the week.

Upon arriving home from the cemetery, the family may find that friends have put a bowl, a pitcher of water and a towel at the front door. Many people like to rinse their hands upon returning from the cemetery. It is a symbol that they have left the world of the dead and are reentering the home of the living.

The first meal is prepared by friends who stay behind to tend to the details of the homecoming while others go to the cemetery. It is called *se'udat havra'ah* (meal of healing) and helps remind the mourners of two things: that although a loved one has left them, they are not alone—the community is with them, to care for them and comfort them—and that although a part of their lives has ended, the next part, a new part, will soon begin. Round foods, such as bagels, hard-boiled eggs, lentils and grapes, are often served, symbolizing the circle of life.

A full shiva lasts seven days and seven nights. Many sit the full seven days; others sit for three. Throughout shiva, a candle burns, as if to say, "Though the body of our loved one has left us, the soul and the memory continue to light our lives." All week people continue to send or bring food, a sign of physical and spiritual nourishment offered by the community. Close friends continue to prepare the meals, set the table and clean up. During that week, the community tends to the needs of the mourners, even laundering their clothes for them if necessary. The mourners are not hosts—they do not greet us at the door when we come in, or show us where to sit, or offer us food and drink.

All the signs and the rituals of mourning reinforce the rupture of home: the lack of boundaries (people walk in without knocking, putter around the kitchen without supervision), the inversion of roles (the host becomes the one who is waited upon), the seating on low chairs. They reflect the feelings of the mourner: The world is topsy-turvy; the home and family that once were are no more. Yet even in the symbolic destruction, Jewish tradition begins to lead the mourners to the next stage: a rebuilding and a reintegration into the community. And it does that through the tradition of visiting, or paying a shiva call.

To be sure, one of the most important parts of shiva is the visiting. People visit morning, noon and night, trying to bring comfort to the mourners. The door to a shiva home is unlocked. Visitors do not knock or ring the bell. They let themselves in and join the mourners. They may talk of memories they have of the one who died or bring pictures to share. If they did not know the deceased, they may ask questions about the person. When they don't know what to say, they can simply say, "I am so sorry." They can ask about the person's life. They may even sit with the mourners in silence; the most important thing is just to be there.

Except on Shabbat, the mourners traditionally do not leave their home, not even to go to synagogue. Instead, the synagogue comes to them. Their rabbi and friends gather in their home once or twice a day, in the early morning for *shaḥarit* (the morning service) and around sunset for *minḥah* and *ma'ariv* (the afternoon and evening services). It is at those services that the mourners recite the Mourners' Kaddish, which is said only in a *minyan,* a group of ten or more adults gathered as a community in prayer.

On Friday evening there is a pause in the shiva. The power and the promise of Shabbat, a taste of the world to come, override the mourners' sadness and remind them that their grief will not last

Saying Goodbye

Throughout the week of shiva, people who visit the mourners say goodbye by reciting the same words: "May God who is everywhere comfort you along with all those who mourn in Israel."

Standing Alone

Traditionally, only the mourn-ers stand for the Mourners' Kaddish. Today more and more synagogues are encouraging the entire con-gregation to stand as well. Some do it as a gesture of comfort to and solidarity with those who mourn. Some do it as a defiant and loving demonstration of remember-ing all the victims of the Holocaust who have no one to recite the Kaddish for them. Both are noble gestures.

Yet a powerful moment is lost in that tradition. Though we turn to the community to soothe our pain, in truth we each mourn alone. We need to be able to stand alone in our loss even while we seek support from our friends and our loved ones. When we stand alone for Kaddish, we show—ourselves as much as others—that we can stand through this loss, too.

And often we want to be recognized for our loss. Although we cover ourselves with community, as we cover a wound with balm, we don't want our loss to blend into the loss of the whole. Our loss is unique. When we hurt, something inside us wants to say, "Look at me! Care for me! Hold me!" To stand alone in the midst of com-munity allows the congrega-tion to look around and say, "Oh, yes, I see where the pain and the memories are sharpest this week." To allow such a public display of personal vulnerability also strengthens the ties of community, builds trust and union and allows the comfort to flow where it must.

forever. The family goes to the synagogue. The evening service, *kabbalat Shabbat,* begins with the mourners outside the sanctuary. Toward the end of *kabbalat Shabbat,* the mourners are ushered into the sanctuary, and the rabbi leads the congregation in greeting them with these words: "May God who is everywhere comfort you along with all those who mourn in Israel."

The days come and go. Shiva ends on the seventh day, with the morning prayers. Friends who have come to make the minyan leave for work. The family members put away their black ribbons and torn clothes. They pack up the siddurim, the prayer books, and clear the house of signs of mourning. Then together they take a short walk around the block, showing that they are ready to reenter the world and begin the next stage of mourning—and living.

The Remainder of the Mourning Period

The next period of mourning is called *shloshim,* meaning "thirty," for it lasts until 30 days after the burial. During that month, the mourners begin to return to life. For those who lived apart from their loved one, the routines of the day can provide escape and comfort. For those who lived with the one who died, the days themselves can be an enemy. Routines bring pain instead of dis-traction. The structure of the days must be made anew.

The pain of the loss is never far beneath the surface and can well up unexpectedly anytime. Our tradition recognizes that and wants mourners to know that they are not yet expected to be healed and that their loss has not been forgotten by the community. So for that first month, while the mourners are trying to balance grieving and living, Judaism suggests that they do things that help them express their continued sense of loss. They go to the synagogue and recite the Mourners' Kaddish. Men do not yet shave. The mourners do not buy new clothes or go to the theater or hear live music. Some people do not even watch television during that month.

The mourning period for one's parents, according to Jewish law, is 11 months. For all other members of the immediate family, including a spouse, it is one month. The difference is not a matter of love or devotion. It is, rather, an acknowledgment of a basic truth: With the death of our parents, our threshold of this life has closed; those who brought us into this world have left it. Children say Kaddish for their parents and limit the entertainment they allow themselves for the full 11 months of mourning. For all others for whom we mourn, we say Kaddish for 30 days. Should we be overcome with the desire to say it more often, we can. But whether for parent or other loved one, the mourning period should end after 11 months.

The Unveiling

At the end of 11 months of mourning (or earlier), the family returns to the cemetery to dedicate a stone carved with the name of the deceased and the birth and death dates to mark the site of the grave permanently. The stone is set in the ground before the family arrives and is draped with a cloth. The family gathers round. Some psalms are recited; some words about the loved one are spoken; family and friends often share stories, memories or thoughts. Then the stone, with the name upon it, is unveiled. This brief service does not require a rabbi and usually can be conducted by family members.

Remembering the Dead

After 11 months, the period of mourning is officially over. But memories and feelings of loss never die. So every year, tradition gives the mourners several opportunities to express those feelings.

One such opportunity is the anniversary of the loved one's death according to the Jewish calendar. That day is called a *yahrtzeit*. At sundown on the night of the *yahrtzeit*, the relatives light a *yahrtzeit* candle, designed to burn for 25 hours. They may go to the synagogue and recite the Mourners' Kaddish. Many synagogues send *yahrtzeit* reminders, telling the family on what day of the secular calendar the *yahrtzeit* falls.

On designated days of the festivals of Passover, Shavuot and Sukkot, and on Yom Kippur, *yahrtzeit* candles are also lit. A memorial service, called *yizkor* (which means "may God remember") is recited for loved ones who have died. The prayers are simple, and are concluded by the El Malei Rahamim, the classic memorial prayer that asks God to be kind to the deceased. In many

Visiting the Cemetery

Although Jews visit their loved ones' graves all year round, right before the High Holidays is an especially popular time. In times past, the dead were thought to be able to intercede on behalf of the living. No doubt the living, at the time of repentance and anxiety, sought comfort and aid from those in the other world. Women often saw themselves as especially capable of reaching the dead and serving as intercessors between this world and the next. Today we go as a gesture of love and devotion, to tend the grave, to be close to those who were close to us. And before we leave, we place a stone on the top of the headstone, a visual reminder that the one who rests there is not alone.

Jewish cemetery in New Delhi, India. Jewish gravestones can be identified by the symbols on them, such as a Magen David (Shield of David), Lion of Judah and eternal light.

One way to make a loved one's memory "be for a blessing" is to give tzedakah. This Israeli ambulance was donated by an American couple to the Magen David Adom, the Red Shield of David, in memory of their beloved aunt. The Red Shield of David is the Israeli equivalent of the American Red Cross.

synagogues, children whose parents are alive leave the service while the *yizkor* prayers are being recited.

A Yahrtzeit Memorial

After my grandmother died, we found in the back of her closet a pen-and-ink drawing of a fantastic wild animal surrounded by two decorative pen-and-ink frames. The animal, front paw extended toward the observer, stands under Hebrew writing that says, "A Yahrtzeit Memorial: My mother, Ḥaya Michalya bat R' Moshe, died on the 12th day of Shevat 5686." At the top of it all is a rhyming quotation in Hebrew, which roughly means, "People hoard every nickel and dime but do not fret over wasting time." We had discovered my grandmother's homemade *yahrtzeit* memorial, an example of a form of Jewish folk art popular about a century ago. I never knew my great-grandmother Ḥaya Michalya, but her presence—in the form of an animal with a fearsome body and friendly face—keeps me company as I work at my desk.

Healing a Broken Heart

The death of a loved one leaves us wounded. Sometimes we fear we will never heal. But with time, we do. Sometimes we fear that the darkness will overwhelm us. But with time, it lifts. We can help ourselves by speaking of our loved ones, tending to their possessions, performing acts of lovingkindness in their name and teaching others the precious lessons of their legacy. And we can help heal the hurt of others who mourn by listening to their stories, sitting with them when they cry, entering the world of their loved ones and bringing them closer to us. As long as our loved ones are remembered, as long as they remain a part of us, they can never die.

May their memory be a blessing.

Ethical Wills

Even as we are bidden to leave detailed wills to promote the peaceful disposition of our earthly possessions, so we are blessed with a tradition of writing ethical wills. Ethical wills are documents that parents write to their children in which they attempt to state in a few words the values by which they tried to live their lives, and the values they hoped to instill in their children.

Summing up one's philosophy of life in a brief missive is a challenge for most people. There is no one way to do it.

In his book *So That Your Values Live On*, Jack Reimer includes the following two approaches to writing an ethical will.

On the eve of the Holocaust, a mother wrote:

"Judaism, my child, is the struggle to bring God down upon earth, a struggle for the sanctification of the human heart. This struggle your people wages not with physical force but with spirit, with sincere, heartfelt prayers and by constant striving for truth and justice.…This is your mission, your purpose on earth."

Rabbi Herbert Friedman, a national leader in the Jewish Federation and philanthropic communities, began his will by saying, "In this eighth decade of my life, let me start to leave my legacy of opinions and conclusions, beginning with four subjects: what I believe, what I have done, what I have learned, and what my dream is for you." Not a bad outline.

The end of one's life is a good time for creating an ethical will. But other times are also good. When we are about to embark on a new journey, when we find ourselves at a crossroads, when we wonder about our future, we can sit down and write a will. We can write about our beliefs and our dreams, where we want to be and how we want to be. For every bit as important as our goals are the ways in which we choose to achieve them. If we create a strong and noble vision of where we want to go, we have a better chance of being satisfied on the day we look back to survey where we have been.

A Prayer of Trust

Sometimes we must make the difficult decision of removing our loved one from life support, either in keeping with their end-of-life wishes, or because their brain has ceased to function. Navah Harlow, a patient advocate in New York City, wrote the following prayer for children to say when they give the order to turn off the life support machines for their parents:

Aveenu sheh-ba-sha-mayim— Our Father in Heaven—

Today is the day that I have spoken for my beloved mother/father even as she/he spoke for me when I was a child without words, without understanding. He/she anticipated my needs and protected me from harm when I was yet unable to negotiate my life independently.

Today she/he is no longer capable of speech, of comprehension, of expressing his/her love for me as she/he has always done through words and through actions.

Today I have spoken as I promised I would. I have articulated his/her wishes as she/he has articulated them to me over these past few years. We both hoped that this day would never come. We both hoped that Your will would be done quietly, peacefully. But that was not meant to be. The inevitable outcome of his/her illness was postponed by hopes and dreams and medical technology. We know today that nothing can help. The life that was acceptable to him/her is no longer accessible. The process of dying is being prolonged.

Today I have spoken as I promised. I have fulfilled the mitzvah, the commandment, of honoring my father/mother.

He/she lived with integrity, has acted righteously and has spoken truthfully. Take her/him, then, unto Your sanctuary, let her/him repose upon Your holy mountain.

Epilogue
The Journey Continues

In this direction you shall find a way home,

THE BIBLE—a compilation of 39 books from Genesis to the Second Book of Chronicles —ends with Cyrus, the king of Persia, freeing the Jews from exile and calling upon all who so desire to return to Israel and rebuild the land: "Those of you who heed this call, God is with you. And you shall go up" (36:23).

It is a timeless call, reminding us that we each experience a time of exile in our lives. We leave the garden of our parents' home, searching for ourselves, searching for a love, searching for a new way home. In the beginning, it can be very good. We camp a bit here and tarry a bit there. We enjoy a first touch, a daring new thought, and we push our boundaries with a nudge or a thump, strengthening the skins of our younger selves. Wonder covers our fears, and desire fuels our movement onward. Yet when newness fades or pain sets in, or when we just get tired, we seek comfort in something greater than adventure. We long for a sign, a sense that somehow we are on the right path. In a song, a face, a belief, a place, we seek a meaning and a purpose beyond ourselves.

We Are Different Now

In *Tales of the Hasidim,* Martin Buber recounts this story:
> Without telling his teacher anything of what he was doing, a disciple of Rabbi Barukh inquired into the nature of God. He penetrated further and further into the secret until he was tangled in doubts, and what had been certain up to this time became uncertain. When Rabbi Barukh noticed that the young man no longer came to him as usual, he went to the city where he lived, entered his room unexpectedly, and said to him: "I know what is hidden in your heart. You have passed through the fifty gates of reason. You begin with a question and think, and think up an answer—and the first gate opens, and to a new question! And again you plumb it, find the solution, fling open the second gate—and look into a new question. On and on like this, deeper and deeper, until you have forced open the fiftieth gate. There you stare at a question whose answer no man has ever found, for if there were one who knew it, there would no longer be freedom of choice. But if you dare to probe still further, you plunge into the abyss."
> "So, I should go back all the way, to the very beginning?" cried the disciple.
> "If you turn, you will not be going back," said Rabbi Barukh. "You will be standing beyond the last gate: you will stand in faith."

There are times in our life's journey when we need to turn, to reverse course. When we do, we are going not back but ahead, in a different direction. The place where we once stood and now stand again is not the same as before because we are not the same as before.

Without such a seeking, our travels in exile turn to wandering. They may be unrestrained and pleasurable at first, but they often leave us empty and despairing later on. With a guide and a goal, however, our wandering becomes a journey, a purposeful adventure that takes us from here to there. And it is not just any adventure, but a way upward. As Cyrus said, "And you shall go up." To go up in Judaism is to get closer to the center of all things, to reach toward the source of ultimate meaning and desire. To go up is to go home, to be in the company of one's people and one's God.

Judaism offers itself as that guide to going up. Judaism offers itself as that calling, that map that says, In this direction you shall find a way home, to your people, to your God, to yourself.

And way before we reach our destination, we begin the ascent. Our rise begins with our very first step. That is the nature of climbing. We simply must point ourselves in the right direction and lift our feet—and we have begun. Perhaps that is why we Jews always face Jerusalem when we pray. For once we face the heights of the Judaean hills, everything we do afterward is a step upward.

But what of our destination? Moses lived a life of holiness always traveling to, but never entering, the Holy Land. We, too, can never know whether we will enter our promised land. But our prize is not just our arrival there. Our prize is also found in living a life of ascent.

Many of us wait for a call from our Cyrus, an invitation to begin our journey. Sometimes that call comes to us in joy—a first love, a new child, a job promotion. Sometimes it comes to us in pain—a divorce, a layoff, an illness. Sometimes it comes to us from within. Whenever and however it comes, we can heed it by turning our sights to the place of ascent that we call Jerusalem. And then it can be said of us, "And we will go up."

This book is designed to be a map for such a journey. Let it be your companion. Let it grow dog-eared with use, and let it be trained to open to your favorite parts. Write in it; write on it. Add recipes and shopping lists, insights and arguments, commentary and personal history. Let it become one of the volumes that chronicles your journey. And may your journal find a place of honor on your family bookshelf, a guide for the loved ones who come after you.

Now there is only one thing left for me to do before we each go on our way: offer the prayer for all those who journey:

> May it be Your will, our God and God of our ancestors, that You watch us leave in peace and guide our steps in peace. Bring us to our desired destination, whole in life and in joy. Save us from the hands of all enemies and dangers that lurk along the way. May we be received with grace, kindness, and generosity by You and by all who greet us. Listen to our prayers, for You are the God of prayer and supplication. Blessed are You who listens to our prayers.

A Taste of Arrival

Despite the essential nature of a journey, one without end grows tedious and troublesome. We begin to despair of ever reaching our goal. Eventually hope and passion and purpose die. That is why there is Shabbat. Shabbat is a taste of arrival. It offers us the experience and the promise of getting there. It is the day when all has been done, the day on which we come home. We rest and enjoy and reflect on where we have been. And then, after 25 hours, we are off on another leg of the journey.

A Traveler's Prayer

Rabbi Sheila Peltz Weinberg has written an everyday traveler's prayer for this generation.

A prayer for the journey
We could say it every day
When we first leave the soft warmth of our beds
And don't know for sure if we'll return at night
When we get in the trains, planes & automobiles
And put our lives in the hands of many strangers.
Or when we leave our homes for a day, a week, a month or more—
Will we return to a peaceful home? Untouched by fire, flood or crime?
How will our travels change us?
What gives us the courage to go through that door?

A prayer for the journey.
For the journey we take in this fragile vessel of flesh.
A finite number of years and we will reach
The unknown, where it all began.
Every life, every day, every hour is a journey.
In the travel is the discovery,
the wisdom, the joy.
Every life, every day, every hour is a journey.
In the travel is the reward, the peace, the blessing.

צֵאתְכֶם לְשָׁלוֹם.

Tzeitchem leshalom.

Go in peace.

Prayers and Rituals
for the Home

EACH OF JUDAISM'S FOUR MAJOR DENOMINATIONS and some synagogues have their own unique prayerbook that reflects the community's particular traditions retained from "the old country," even as it has been molded by the trends, tastes and beliefs of modernity.

While these and yet other siddurim are largely the same, they also bear witness to the differences among the communities they represent. It is part of the adventure of exploring Judaism to encounter this diversity and to find the book, and thus the community, that suits one best.

What follows is not a prayerbook, nor meant to replace the search for a prayerbook, but rather serves as a quick reference to a starter set of prayers, some of which are presented in an abbreviated form.

DECLARATION UPON RISING IN THE MORNING

We awaken, stretch and take a quick accounting of our body. Our thoughts begin to lumber toward the promises and possibilities that await us this day. Yet it is only in the next moment, when we become aware of our awareness, that we become fully human once again. And so it is then that we pause and thank the Creator for this day's gift of our life.

Note that the first word of the declaration is gender-specific. Men say *"modeh,"* women say *"modah."*

מוֹדֶה\מוֹדָה אֲנִי לְפָנֶיךָ

מֶלֶךְ חַי וְקַיָּם

שֶׁהֶחֱזַרְתָּ בִּי נִשְׁמָתִי בְּחֶמְלָה

רַבָּה אֱמוּנָתֶךָ.

I thank You, God,

Eternal One,

for lovingly restoring my soul to me,

filled with Your eternal trust.

Modeh/Modah ani l'fanecha melech ḥai v'kayam sheheḥezarta

bi nishmati b'ḥemlah rabah emunatecha.

❧

BLESSING FOR PUTTING ON A TALLIT

In the morning, before formal prayer, we wrap ourselves in a tallit,
as if we are draping the soft presence of God close around us.

בָּרוּךְ אַתָּה יהוה
אֱלֹהֵינוּ מֶלֶךְ הָעוֹלָם
אֲשֶׁר קִדְּשָׁנוּ בְּמִצְוֹתָיו
וְצִוָּנוּ לְהִתְעַטֵּף בַּצִּיצִית.

Blessed are You,

our God, Creator of time and space,

who enriches our lives with holiness,

commanding us to wrap ourselves in the tallit.

Baruch atah adonai eloheinu melech ha'olam asher kid'shanu

b'mitzvotav v'tzivanu l'hitatef batzitzit.

SHMA

Deuteronomy 6:4–9

The Shma is a daily declaration that reminds us of who we are and Whose we are. When we say these words, we see that wherever we are, and wherever we go, we remain in constant touch with God and the Jewish people. And should we but desire it, we can become a sacred threshold that joins this world and God.

The Shma is said once in the morning, again in the evening, and once more upon going to bed.

שְׁמַע יִשְׂרָאֵל יהוה אֱלֹהֵינוּ Hear, O Israel, Adonai, our God,

יהוה אֶחָד. Adonai is One.

בָּרוּךְ שֵׁם כְּבוֹד Blessed be the Name of God's glorious

מַלְכוּתוֹ לְעוֹלָם וָעֶד. majesty forever and ever.

Shma yisrael adonai eloheinu adonai eḥad.

Baruch sheim k'vod malchuto l'olam va'ed.

(Continue on page 251)

וְאָהַבְתָּ אֵת יהוה אֱלֹהֶיךָ	You shall love Adonai your God
בְּכָל לְבָבְךָ וּבְכָל נַפְשְׁךָ	with all your heart, with all your soul,
וּבְכָל מְאֹדֶךָ	and with all your might.
וְהָיוּ הַדְּבָרִים הָאֵלֶּה	And these words
אֲשֶׁר אָנֹכִי מְצַוְּךָ הַיּוֹם	which I command you today
עַל לְבָבֶךָ	shall be in your heart.
וְשִׁנַּנְתָּם לְבָנֶיךָ	You shall teach them diligently to your children
וְדִבַּרְתָּ בָּם	and you shall speak of them
בְּשִׁבְתְּךָ בְּבֵיתֶךָ	when you are sitting at home
וּבְלֶכְתְּךָ בַדֶּרֶךְ	and when you go on a journey,
וּבְשָׁכְבְּךָ	when you lie down
וּבְקוּמֶךָ.	and when you rise up.
וּקְשַׁרְתָּם לְאוֹת עַל יָדֶךָ	You shall bind them as a sign on your hand
וְהָיוּ לְטֹטָפֹת בֵּין עֵינֶיךָ	and they shall be jewels between your eyes.
וּכְתַבְתָּם עַל מְזֻזוֹת	You shall inscribe them on the doorposts
בֵּיתֶךָ וּבִשְׁעָרֶיךָ.	of your house and on your gates.

V'ahavta eit adonai elohecha bechol l'vav'cha

uv'chol nafsh'cha uv'chol m'odecha.

V'hayu had'varim ha'eileh asher anochi m'tzav'cha hayom al l'vavecha.

V'shinantam l'vanecha v'dibarta bam b'shivt'cha b'veitecha uv'lecht'cha

vaderech uv'shochb'cha uv'kumecha.

Uk'shartam l'ot al yadecha v'hayu l'totafot bein einecha.

Uch'tavtam al m'zuzot beitecha uvisharecha.

BLESSING OVER BREAD

The creation of food is a partnership between God and humanity.
This partnership is reflected in the unusual wording of the blessing
recited before eating bread, the staple of life and first food to be
eaten at every meal.

בָּרוּךְ אַתָּה יהוה
אֱלֹהֵינוּ מֶלֶךְ הָעוֹלָם
הַמּוֹצִיא לֶחֶם מִן הָאָרֶץ.

Blessed are You,

our God, Creator of time and space,

who brings forth bread from the earth.

Baruch atah adonai eloheinu melech ha'olam

hamotzi lehem min ha'aretz.

❧

GRACE AFTER MEALS

In addition to offering a blessing before eating, we also offer a longer prayer of thanks after the meal. Below is the first paragraph of the Birkat Hamazon, the series of blessings that is recited at the conclusion of a meal.

בָּרוּךְ אַתָּה יהוה	Blessed are You,
אֱלֹהֵינוּ מֶלֶךְ הָעוֹלָם	our God, Creator of time and space,
הַזָּן אֶת הָעוֹלָם כֻּלּוֹ בְּטוּבוֹ	who feeds the entire world through Your goodness,
בְּחֵן וּבְחֶסֶד וּבְרַחֲמִים.	with kindness and graciousness.
הוּא נוֹתֵן לֶחֶם לְכָל בָּשָׂר	You give bread to every creature,
כִּי לְעוֹלָם חַסְדּוֹ.	for Your beneficence is unending.
וּבְטוּבוֹ הַגָּדוֹל	And through Your great goodness,
תָּמִיד לֹא חָסַר לָנוּ	never have we been
וְאַל יֶחְסַר לָנוּ	and never shall we be
מָזוֹן לְעוֹלָם וָעֶד	in need of food;
בַּעֲבוּר שְׁמוֹ הַגָּדוֹל.	great is the glory of Your name.
כִּי הוּא אֵל זָן וּמְפַרְנֵס לַכֹּל	For You, God, feed the world,
וּמֵטִיב לַכֹּל	bringing goodness to all,
וּמֵכִין מָזוֹן לְכָל בְּרִיּוֹתָיו	preparing food for all
אֲשֶׁר בָּרָא.	Your creations.
בָּרוּךְ אַתָּה יהוה	Blessed are You,
הַזָּן אֶת הַכֹּל.	who feeds the world.

(Transliteration on page 254)

Baruch atah adonai eloheinu melech ha'olam

hazan et ha'olam kulo b'tuvo b'ḥein uvḥesed uvraḥamim.

Hu notein leḥem l'chol basar ki l'olam ḥasdo.

Uvtuvo hagadol tamid lo ḥasar lanu v'al yeḥsar lanu

mazon l'olam va'ed ba'avur sh'mo hagadol.

Ki hu eil zan umfarneis lakol umeitiv lakol

umeichin mazon l'chol b'riyotav asher bara.

Baruch atah adonai hazan et hakol.

～ﾟ

ALTERNATIVE GRACE AFTER MEALS

For those who are truly pressed for time, there is a short version of
the Birkat Hamazon. It is better to recite the fuller array of blessings,
if one can. But the shorter one also gets the job done.

בְּרִיךְ רַחֲמָנָא   Blessed are You, Merciful One,

מַלְכָּא דְּעָלְמָא   the one who is everywhere, always,

מָרֵיהּ דְּהַאי פִּתָּא.   Creator of this bread.

B'rich raḥamana malka d'alma mareih d'hahy pita.

～ﾟ

SHEHEḤEYANU

The world is full of routine, which is often a blessing in its own
right. But when exciting events happen—the purchase of a car; the
celebration of an anniversary; a child's first day of school—tradition
provides us with a way to celebrate. We recite this blessing.

בָּרוּךְ אַתָּה יהוה
אֱלֹהֵינוּ מֶלֶךְ הָעוֹלָם
שֶׁהֶחֱיָנוּ וְקִיְּמָנוּ
וְהִגִּיעָנוּ לַזְּמַן הַזֶּה.

Blessed are You,

our God, Creator of time and space,

who has supported us, protected us,

and brought us to this moment.

Baruch atah adonai eloheinu melech ha'olam

sheheḥeyanu v'kiy'manu v'higiyanu lazman hazeh.

CANDLELIGHTING FOR SHABBAT

We celebrate Shabbat with candles, wine and bread—the basics of an elegant, graceful meal.

Tradition asks us to light the Shabbat candles no later than 18 minutes before sunset. We place them on the dining table, breakfront or other surface where we can see them while dining. We light them, encircle them with our hands three times, cup our hands in front of our eyes and say:

בָּרוּךְ אַתָּה יהוה
אֱלֹהֵינוּ מֶלֶךְ הָעוֹלָם
אֲשֶׁר קִדְּשָׁנוּ בְּמִצְוֹתָיו
וְצִוָּנוּ לְהַדְלִיק
נֵר שֶׁל שַׁבָּת.

Blessed are You,

our God, Creator of time and space,

who enriches our lives with holiness,

commanding us to kindle

the Shabbat lights.

Baruch atah adonai eloheinu melech ha'olam asher kid'shanu

b'mitzvotav v'tzivanu l'hadlik neir shel shabbat.

KIDDUSH FOR SHABBAT EVE

We use wine (or grape juice) to help us celebrate the sacredness of
the day. So we raise the filled Kiddush cup and say:

וַיְהִי עֶרֶב וַיְהִי בֹקֶר	It was evening and morning:
יוֹם הַשִּׁשִּׁי.	the sixth day.
וַיְכֻלּוּ הַשָּׁמַיִם וְהָאָרֶץ	Now the heavens and the earth were completed
וְכָל צְבָאָם.	with all they contained.
וַיְכַל אֱלֹהִים בַּיּוֹם הַשְּׁבִיעִי	On the seventh day God completed
מְלַאכְתּוֹ אֲשֶׁר עָשָׂה	all the divine labor of Creation,
וַיִּשְׁבֹּת בַּיּוֹם הַשְּׁבִיעִי	and ceased on the seventh day
מִכָּל מְלַאכְתּוֹ אֲשֶׁר עָשָׂה.	from all the divine labor which God made.
וַיְבָרֶךְ אֱלֹהִים	Then God blessed
אֶת יוֹם הַשְּׁבִיעִי	the seventh day
וַיְקַדֵּשׁ אֹתוֹ	and sanctified it,
כִּי בוֹ שָׁבַת מִכָּל מְלַאכְתּוֹ	for on that day God ceased from all the work
אֲשֶׁר בָּרָא אֱלֹהִים לַעֲשׂוֹת.	of Creation which God had made (Genesis 2).

Vay'hi erev vay'hi voker yom hashishi.

Vay'chulu hashamayim v'ha'aretz v'chol tz'va'am.

Vay'chal elohim bayom hash'vi'i m'lachto asher asah

vayishbot bayom hash'vi'i mikol m'lachto asher asah.

Vay'varech elohim et yom hash'vi'i

vay'kadeish oto ki vo shavat mikol m'lachto

asher bara elohim la'asot.

(Continue on page 258)

בָּרוּךְ אַתָּה יהוה
אֱלֹהֵינוּ מֶלֶךְ הָעוֹלָם
בּוֹרֵא פְּרִי הַגָּפֶן.

Blessed are You,

our God, Creator of time and space,

who creates the fruit of the vine.

Baruch atah adonai eloheinu melech ha'olam borei p'ri hagafen.

Blessed are You, our God, Creator of time and space, who enriches our lives with holiness, and who delights in us. With love and desire You have given us the holy Shabbat, a taste of the days of Creation. For it was the first among Your sacred days, a reminder of our liberation from Egypt. For You chose us from among all the nations, and You made us holy. With love and pleasure You gave us the holy Shabbat. Blessed are You, who hallows Shabbat.

Drink the wine.

We bless our children and our guests (see page 259), either now or before Kiddush.

Before the meal is served—on Friday night and Saturday lunch—we recite the blessing over bread (see page 252) over the ḥallah.

Note: At lunch on Saturday, before reciting the blessing over the ḥallah, the bless-
ing over wine may be recited. (See the blessing above that praises God "who
creates the fruit of the vine.")

A BLESSING FOR CHILDREN

It is customary for parents to bless their children at the Shabbat dinner table. Traditionally, they lightly place their hands on the child's head while reciting the following blessing:

For Sons

יְשִׂמְךָ אֱלֹהִים
כְּאֶפְרַיִם וְכִמְנַשֶּׁה.

May God make you
like Ephraim and Menasseh.

Y'simcha elohim k'efrayim v'chim'nasheh.

May God bless you
    with the strength and faithfulness of Ephraim
    and the wisdom and kindness of Menasseh.

For Daughters

יְשִׂמֵךְ אֱלֹהִים
כְּשָׂרָה רִבְקָה רָחֵל וְלֵאָה.

May God make you like
Sarah, Rebecca, Rachel and Leah.

Y'simeich elohim k'sarah rivkah raḥel v'lei'ah.

May God bless you
    with the strength and vision of Sarah,
    with the wisdom and foresight of Rebecca,
    with the courage and compassion of Rachel,
    with the gentleness and graciousness of Leah,
    and with their faith in the promise of our people's heritage.

(Continue on page 260)

For All Children

יְבָרֶכְךָ יהוה וְיִשְׁמְרֶךָ.
יָאֵר יהוה פָּנָיו
אֵלֶיךָ וִיחֻנֶּךָּ.
יִשָּׂא יהוה פָּנָיו אֵלֶיךָ
וְיָשֵׂם לְךָ שָׁלוֹם.

May God bless you and keep you.

May God's presence radiate upon you
and grant you graciousness.

May God's presence be with you
and grant you peace.

Y'varech'cha adonai v'yishm'recha.

Ya'eir adonai panav eilecha vihuneka.

Yisa adonai panav eilecha v'yaseim l'cha shalom.

❧

Hosts may also offer their guests the following blessing: "May you
find peace within these walls and seek goodness far beyond them."

HAVDALAH SERVICE

After the sun has set and three stars appear in the sky, Shabbat is escorted out with wine, candles and scents.

In preparation for the ritual, fill a Kiddush cup with wine or grape juice; place at least two kinds of spices in a spice box; light a braided *havdalah* candle—if none is available, use two ordinary candles with their flames touching; and prepare a plate in which to douse the flame with wine or grape juice.

Kiddush

Raise the filled Kiddush cup and say:

בָּרוּךְ אַתָּה יהוה
אֱלֹהֵינוּ מֶלֶךְ הָעוֹלָם
בּוֹרֵא פְּרִי הַגָּפֶן.

Blessed are You,

our God, Creator of time and space,

who creates the fruit of the vine.

Baruch atah adonai eloheinu melech ha'olam borei p'ri hagafen.

Set the cup down without drinking from it and recite the blessing over the spices.

Blessing over the Aromatic Spices

בָּרוּךְ אַתָּה יהוה
אֱלֹהֵינוּ מֶלֶךְ הָעוֹלָם
בּוֹרֵא מִינֵי בְשָׂמִים.

Blessed are You,

our God, Creator of time and space,

who creates a potpourri of spices.

Baruch atah adonai eloheinu melech ha'olam borei minei v'samim.

Pass the spice container around so that each person can inhale the scent. Continue with the blessing over the *havdalah* candle.

(Continue on page 262)

Blessing over the Havdalah Candle

בָּרוּךְ אַתָּה יהוה
אֱלֹהֵינוּ מֶלֶךְ הָעוֹלָם
בּוֹרֵא מְאוֹרֵי הָאֵשׁ.

Blessed are You,

our God, Creator of time and space,

who creates the light of fire.

Baruch atah adonai eloheinu melech ha'olam borei m'orei ha'eish.

All present raise their hands, noticing the light of the flame through their fingernails and the play of shadow and light on their hands. Continue with the final blessing.

בָּרוּךְ אַתָּה יהוה
אֱלֹהֵינוּ מֶלֶךְ הָעוֹלָם
הַמַּבְדִּיל בֵּין קֹדֶשׁ לְחֹל.

Blessed are You,

our God, Creator of time and space,

who separates the holy from the mundane.

Baruch atah adonai eloheinu melech ha'olam

hamavdil bein kodesh l'ḥol.

Take a sip of the wine or juice, then pour the remaining liquid onto the plate you have prepared and douse the flame in it.

BLESSING FOR AFFIXING A MEZUZAH

The mitzvah of attaching a mezuzah to the doorposts of one's home is based on the first paragraph of the Shma. In fact, the mezuzah is merely the container which holds a parchment on which the first paragraph of the Shma is written. It is the parchment that is the essence of what is attached to the door.

The mezuzah is positioned two-thirds of the way up on the right doorpost as you enter the house or room. The top of the mezuzah should point slightly in the direction of the room that is about to be entered.

With hammer in hand, mezuzah poised and ready, friends and family gathered, the following blessing is recited:

בָּרוּךְ אַתָּה יהוה
אֱלֹהֵינוּ מֶלֶךְ הָעוֹלָם
אֲשֶׁר קִדְּשָׁנוּ בְּמִצְוֹתָיו
וְצִוָּנוּ לִקְבֹּעַ מְזוּזָה.

Blessed are You,

our God, Creator of time and space,

who enriches our lives with holiness,

commanding us to attach a mezuzah to our homes.

Baruch atah adonai eloheinu melech ha'olam asher kid'shanu

b'mitzvotav v'tzivanu likbo'a m'zuzah.

CANDLELIGHTING
FOR FESTIVALS AND ROSH HASHANAH

On the three pilgrimage holidays (Passover, Shavuot and Sukkot) as well as on Rosh Hoshanah, we light holiday candles and recite the following blessing. When the holiday falls on Shabbat, we recite the words in parentheses.

בָּרוּךְ אַתָּה יהוה
אֱלֹהֵינוּ מֶלֶךְ הָעוֹלָם
אֲשֶׁר קִדְּשָׁנוּ בְּמִצְוֹתָיו
וְצִוָּנוּ לְהַדְלִיק נֵר
שֶׁל (שַׁבָּת וְשֶׁל) יוֹם טוֹב.

Blessed are You,

our God, Creator of time and space,

who enriches our lives with holiness,

commanding us to kindle

the (Shabbat and) holiday lights.

Baruch atah adonai eloheinu melech ha'olam

asher kid'shanu b'mitzvotav v'tzivanu

l'hadlik neir shel (shabbat v'shel) yom tov.

❧

A special Kiddush for the holidays is also recited. It is included in most Shabbat and holiday prayerbooks. The Sheheḥeyanu (see page 255) is recited either after the candles are lit or at the dinner table right after Kiddush.

CANDLELIGHTING FOR YOM KIPPUR

Yom Kippur has its own candlelighting blessing. If the holiday coincides with Shabbat, we add the words in parentheses.

בָּרוּךְ אַתָּה יהוה
אֱלֹהֵינוּ מֶלֶךְ הָעוֹלָם
אֲשֶׁר קִדְּשָׁנוּ בְּמִצְוֹתָיו
וְצִוָּנוּ לְהַדְלִיק נֵר
שֶׁל (שַׁבָּת וְשֶׁל) יוֹם הַכִּפּוּרִים.

Blessed are You,

our God, Creator of time and space,

who enriches our lives with holiness,

commanding us to kindle

the (Shabbat and) Yom Kippur lights.

Baruch atah adonai eloheinu melech ha'olam

asher kid'shanu b'mitzvotav v'tzivanu

l'hadlik neir shel (shabbat v'shel) yom hakippurim.

The Sheheḥeyanu (see page 255) is recited after the candles are lit.

BLESSING UPON WAVING A LULAV

Every morning of Sukkot, except Shabbat morning, it is the custom
to perform the following ritual. Hold the lulav in the right hand and
the etrog in the left. Bringing the lulav and etrog together (with the
pitam, the stem, of the etrog pointing downward), recite this blessing:

בָּרוּךְ אַתָּה יהוה
אֱלֹהֵינוּ מֶלֶךְ הָעוֹלָם
אֲשֶׁר קִדְּשָׁנוּ בְּמִצְוֹתָיו
וְצִוָּנוּ עַל נְטִילַת לוּלָב.

Blessed are You,

our God, Creator of time and space,

who enriches our lives with holiness,

commanding us to take the lulav and etrog.

Baruch atah adonai eloheinu melech ha'olam asher kid'shanu

b'mitzvotav v'tzivanu al n'tilat lulav.

Before shaking the lulav for the first time during the holiday, we recite
the Sheheḥeyanu (see page 255) immediately after saying the blessing above.

Turn the etrog over so that the *pitam* is facing up, and still holding
your hands together, shake the lulav and the etrog in front, to the
right, in back, to the left, up and down.

BLESSING UPON SITTING IN A SUKKAH

The following blessing is recited when eating a meal in a sukkah.

בָּרוּךְ אַתָּה יהוה
אֱלֹהֵינוּ מֶלֶךְ הָעוֹלָם
אֲשֶׁר קִדְּשָׁנוּ בְּמִצְוֹתָיו
וְצִוָּנוּ לֵישֵׁב בַּסֻּכָּה.

Blessed are You,

Our God, Creator of time and space,

who enriches our lives with holiness,

commanding us to dwell in the sukkah.

Baruch atah adonai eloheinu melech ha'olam

asher kid'shanu b'mitzvotav v'tzivanu leisheiv basukkah.

CANDLELIGHTING FOR HANUKKAH

Hanukkah candles are placed in the *hanukkiyah* from right to left, and lit from left to right following the blessings.

Because of the law prohibiting the lighting of a fire on Shabbat, on Friday, Hanukkah candles are lit before lighting the Shabbat candles; on Saturday night they are lit after *havdalah*.

בָּרוּךְ אַתָּה יהוה
אֱלֹהֵינוּ מֶלֶךְ הָעוֹלָם
אֲשֶׁר קִדְּשָׁנוּ בְּמִצְוֹתָיו
וְצִוָּנוּ לְהַדְלִיק נֵר שֶׁל חֲנֻכָּה.

Blessed are You,

our God, Creator of time and space,

who enriches our lives with holiness,

commanding us to kindle the Hanukkah lights.

Baruch atah adonai eloheinu melech ha'olam asher kid'shanu

b'mitzvotav v'tzivanu l'hadlik neir shel hanukkah.

(Continue on page 269)

בָּרוּךְ אַתָּה יהוה
אֱלֹהֵינוּ מֶלֶךְ הָעוֹלָם
שֶׁעָשָׂה נִסִּים לַאֲבוֹתֵינוּ
בַּיָּמִים הָהֵם בַּזְּמַן הַזֶּה.

Blessed are You,

our God, Creator of time and space,

who performed miracles for our ancestors,

in the days of long ago. And in this time.

Baruch atah adonai eloheinu melech ha'olam she'asah nisim

la'avoteinu bayamim haheim baz'man hazeh.

On the first night of Ḥanukkah, the Sheheḥeyanu (see page 255) is
also recited.

Personal Weavings

Each month of the Jewish calendar has its own personality

J UST AS THE PAGES OF THIS BOOK reflect the collective diary of the Jewish people, so the pages in this section can become a diary for you. It is my hope that you will freely record your comments and insights in the margins throughout the book. But it is here, in "Personal Weavings," that I turn the book fully over to you.

Each two-page spread is devoted to one month, beginning with Tishre. Return to these pages, year after year, to record the traditions, anecdotes, holiday guest lists, recipes, questions and musings that mark your personal and communal life, for they will help fashion the stories that become the next chapter of the Jewish people. And once a year—perhaps during the Days of Awe, or on a birthday, or in a house of shiva—open these pages and discover again the wisdom, humor and comfort you have recorded.

Personal Weavings

TISHRE

ROSH HASHANAH

FAST OF GEDALIAH

YOM KIPPUR

SUKKOT

HOSHANA RABBA

SHEMINI ATZERET

SIMḤAT TORAH

BIRTHDAYS

ANNIVERSARIES

YAHRTZEITS

SIMḤAS

REMEMBRANCES

May the new
year be full
of sweetness
and goodness.

Personal Weavings

ḤESHVAN

ROSH ḤODESH

BIRTHDAYS

ANNIVERSARIES

YAHRTZEITS

SIMḤAS

REMEMBRANCES

like the moon,
the Jews will
always come bac
shining bright,

Personal Weavings

KISLEV

ROSH ḤODESH

ḤANUKKAH (DAYS 1–6)

BIRTHDAYS

ANNIVERSARIES

YAHRTZEITS

SIMḤAS

REMEMBRANCES

A great miracle
happened there

Personal Weavings

TEVET

ROSH HODESH

HANUKKAH (DAYS 7–8)

FAST OF THE
10TH OF TEVET

BIRTHDAYS

ANNIVERSARIES

YAHRTZEITS

SIMHAS

REMEMBRANCES

Just as white
space frames the
letters of the Po
so intervals of
frame our celebr

Personal Weavings

SHEVAT

ROSH HODESH

TU B'SHEVAT

BIRTHDAYS

ANNIVERSARIES

YAHRTZEITS

SIMHAS

REMEMBRANCES

...and God planted a garden in Eden...

Personal Weavings

ADAR

ROSH ḤODESH

FAST OF ESTHER

PURIM

SHUSHAN PURIM

BIRTHDAYS

ANNIVERSARIES

YAHRTZEITS

SIMḤAS

REMEMBRANCES

And Esther sent
word to Mordecai:
"Go assemble the
Jews of Shushan...

Personal Weavings

NISAN

ROSH HODESH

FAST OF THE
FIRSTBORN

PASSOVER

YOM HASHOAH

BIRTHDAYS

ANNIVERSARIES

YAHRTZEITS

SIMHAS

REMEMBRANCES

Passover is the
story of freedom
defiance, hope
and renewal.

Personal Weavings

IYAR

ROSH ḤODESH

YOM HAZIKARON

YOM HA'ATZMA'UT

LAG BA'OMER

YOM YERUSHALAYIM

BIRTHDAYS

ANNIVERSARIES

YAHRTZEITS

SIMḤAS

REMEMBRANCES

From Zion sha
come the To
the word of Go
from Jerusa

Personal Weavings

SIVAN

ROSH ḤODESH

SHAVUOT

BIRTHDAYS

ANNIVERSARIES

YAHRTZEITS

SIMḤAS

REMEMBRANCES

When God spoke on
Mount Sinai, the
world became silent
so that all the
might know that
is none beside You

Personal Weavings

TAMMUZ

ROSH HODESH

FAST OF THE 17TH
OF TAMMUZ

BIRTHDAYS

ANNIVERSARIES

YAHRTZEITS

SIMHAS

REMEMBRANCES

We are a union

of weavers.

Personal Weavings

A V

ROSH ḤODESH

TISHA B'AV

BIRTHDAYS

ANNIVERSARIES

YAHRTZEITS

SIMḤAS

REMEMBRANCES

"When God returned
our exiles to Zion,
it was like a
dream. Our mouth
were fitted with
laughter, our tongue
sang with joy..."

Personal Weavings

ELUL

ROSH HODESH

SELIHOT

BIRTHDAYS

ANNIVERSARIES

YAHRTZEITS

SIMHAS

REMEMBRANCES

To speak of time
is to enter the
language of stor

Calendar of Jewish Holidays

A Twenty-Year Listing

Jews are united

by the Torah,

Sinai, Israel and

the Calendar.

O UR CALENDAR DISPLAYS THE ETERNAL and portable geography of our people. No mat-ter where in the world we may find ourselves, if we hang our calendar on the wall, we are home. Though a place may be new and different, it takes on an old familiarity through the

names of time. Shabbat is Shabbat whether in the United States or Australia. We can find Passover and Ḥanukkah where they have always been. Calendars make visible the ground that travels with us and that is always there to hold the footfalls of our lives.

As Jews, however, we live in two calendars, the Hebrew calendar superimposed upon the Gregorian, or secular, calendar. A Jewish holiday falls on the same day of the Jewish calendar year after year. It is the secular date that varies. On the following pages, for your convenience, is a 20-year calendar that shows the secular date on which each Jewish holiday falls.

Each holiday begins at sunset on the previous day of the secular calendar.

JEWISH YEAR Secular Year	5760 1999/2000	5761 2000/2001	5762 2001/2002	5763 2002/2003
Rosh Hashanah 1 Tishre	Sept. 11	Sept. 30	Sept. 18	Sept. 7
Yom Kippur 10 Tishre	Sept. 20	Oct. 9	Sept. 27	Sept. 16
Sukkot 15 Tishre	Sept. 25	Oct. 14	Oct. 2	Sept. 21
Shemini Atzeret 22 Tishre	Oct. 2	Oct. 21	Oct.9	Sept. 28
Simhat Torah * 22/23 Tishre	Oct. 2/3	Oct. 21/22	Oct. 9/10	Sept. 28/29
Hanukkah 25 Kislev	Dec. 4	Dec. 22	Dec. 10	Nov. 30
Tu B'Shevat 15 Shevat	Jan. 22	Feb. 8	Jan. 28	Jan. 18
Purim 14 Adar	March 21	March 9	Feb. 26	March 18
Passover 15 Nisan	April 20	April 8	March 28	April 17
Yom Hashoah 27 Nisan	May 2	April 20	April 9	April 29
Yom Hazikaron 4 Iyar	May 9	April 27	April 16	May 6
Yom Ha'atzma'ut 5 Iyar	May 10	April 28	April 17	May 7
Lag Ba'omer 18 Iyar	May 23	May 11	April 30	May 20
Yom Yerushalayim 28 Iyar	June 2	May 21	May 10	May 30
Shavuot 6 Sivan	June 9	May 28	May 17	June 6
Tisha B'Av 9 Av	Aug. 10	July 29	July 18	Aug. 7

*Many Reform and Reconstructionist Jews celebrate Shemini Atzeret and Simhat Torah on the same day, 22 Tishre. Other Jews celebrate Shemini Atzeret on 22 Tishre and Simhat Torah on 23 Tishre.

JEWISH YEAR Secular Year	5764 2003/2004	5765 2004/2005	5766 2005/2006	5767 2006/2007
Rosh Hashanah 1 Tishre	Sept. 27	Sept. 16	Oct. 4	Sept. 23
Yom Kippur 10 Tishre	Oct. 6	Sept. 25	Oct. 13	Oct. 2
Sukkot 15 Tishre	Oct. 11	Sept. 30	Oct. 18	Oct. 7
Shemini Atzeret 22 Tishre	Oct. 18	Oct. 7	Oct. 25	Oct.14
*Simḥat Torah** 22/23 Tishre	Oct. 18/19	Oct. 7/8	Oct. 25/26	Oct. 14/15
Ḥanukkah 25 Kislev	Dec. 20	Dec. 8	Dec. 26	Dec. 16
Tu B'Shevat 15 Shevat	Feb. 7	Jan. 25	Feb. 13	Feb. 3
Purim 14 Adar	March 7	March 25	March 14	March 4
Passover 15 Nisan	April 6	April 24	April 13	April 3
Yom Hashoah 27 Nisan	April 18	May 6	April 25	April 15
Yom Hazikaron 4 Iyar	April 25	May 13	May 2	April 22
Yom Ha'atzm'aut 5 Iyar	April 26	May 14	May 3	April 23
Lag Ba'omer 18 Iyar	May 9	May 27	May 16	May 6
Yom Yerushalayim 28 Iyar	May 19	June 6	May 26	May 16
Shavuot 6 Sivan	May 26	June 13	June 2	May 23
Tisha B'Av 9 Av	July 27	Aug. 14	Aug. 3	July 24

JEWISH YEAR Secular Year	5768 2007/2008	5769 2008/2009	5770 2009/2010	5771 2010/2011
Rosh Hashanah 1 Tishre	Sept. 13	Sept. 30	Sept. 19	Sept. 9
Yom Kippur 10 Tishre	Sept. 22	Oct. 9	Sept. 28	Sept. 18
Sukkot 15 Tishre	Sept. 27	Oct. 14	Oct. 3	Sept. 23
Shemini Atzeret 22 Tishre	Oct. 4	Oct. 21	Oct. 10	Sept. 30
*Simhat Torah** 22/23 Tishre	Oct. 4/5	Oct. 21/22	Oct. 10/11	Sept. 30/ Oct. 1
Hanukkah 25 Kislev	Dec. 5	Dec. 22	Dec. 12	Dec. 2
Tu B'Shevat 15 Shevat	Jan. 22	Feb. 9	Jan. 30	Jan. 20
Purim 14 Adar	March 21	March 10	Feb. 28	March 20
Passover 15 Nisan	April 20	April 9	March 30	April 19
Yom Hashoah 27 Nisan	May 2	April 21	April 11	May 1
Yom Hazikaron 4 Iyar	May 9	April 28	April 18	May 8
Yom Ha'atzma'ut 5 Iyar	May 10	April 29	April 19	May 9
Lag Ba'omer 18 Iyar	May 23	May 12	May 2	May 22
Yom Yerushalayim 28 Iyar	June 2	May 22	May 12	June 1
Shavuot 6 Sivan	June 9	May 29	May 19	June 8
Tisha B'Av 9 Av	Aug. 10	July 30	July 20	Aug. 9

JEWISH YEAR Secular Year	5772 2011/2012	5773 2012/2013	5774 2013/2014	5775 2014/2015
Rosh Hashanah 1 Tishre	Sept. 29	Sept. 17	Sept. 5	Sept. 25
Yom Kippur 10 Tishre	Oct. 8	Sept. 26	Sept. 14	Oct. 4
Sukkot 15 Tishre	Oct. 13	Oct. 1	Sept. 19	Oct. 9
Shemini Atzeret 22 Tishre	Oct.20	Oct. 8	Sept. 26	Oct. 16
*Simḥat Torah** 22/23 Tishre	Oct. 20/21	Oct. 8/9	Sept. 26/27	Oct. 16/17
Ḥanukkah 25 Kislev	Dec. 21	Dec. 9	Nov. 28	Dec. 17
Tu B'Shevat 15 Shevat	Feb. 8	Jan. 26	Jan. 16	Feb. 4
Purim 14 Adar	March 8	Feb. 24	March 16	March 5
Passover 15 Nisan	April 7	March 26	April 15	April 4
Yom Hashoah 27 Nisan	April 19	April 7	April 27	April 16
Yom Hazikaron 4 Iyar	April 26	April 14	May 4	April 23
Yom Ha'atzma'ut 5 Iyar	April 27	April 15	May 5	April 24
Lag Ba'omer 18 Iyar	May 10	April 28	May 18	May 7
Yom Yerushalayim 28 Iyar	May 20	May 8	May 28	May 17
Shavuot 6 Sivan	May 27	May 15	June 4	May 24
Tisha B'Av 9 Av	July 29	July 16	Aug. 5	July 26

JEWISH YEAR Secular Year	5776 2015/2016	5777 2016/2017	5778 2017/2018	5779 2018/2019
Rosh Hashanah 1 Tishre	Sept. 14	Oct. 3	Sept. 21	Sept. 10
Yom Kippur 10 Tishre	Sept. 23	Oct. 12	Sept. 30	Sept. 19
Sukkot 15 Tishre	Sept. 28	Oct. 17	Oct. 5	Sept. 24
Shemini Atzeret 22 Tishre	Oct. 5	Oct. 24	Oct. 12	Oct. 1
Simḥat Torah* 22/23 Tishre	Oct. 5/6	Oct. 24/25	Oct. 12/13	Oct. 1/2
Ḥanukkah 25 Kislev	Dec. 7	Dec. 25	Dec. 13	Dec. 3
Tu B'Shevat 15 Shevat	Jan. 25	Feb. 11	Jan. 31	Jan. 21
Purim 14 Adar	March 24	March 12	March 1	March 21
Passover 15 Nisan	April 23	April 11	March 31	April 20
Yom Hashoah 27 Nisan	May 5	April 23	April 12	May 2
Yom Hazikaron 4 Iyar	May 12	April 30	April 19	May 9
Yom Ha'atzma'ut 5 Iyar	May 13	May 1	April 20	May 10
Lag Ba'omer 18 Iyar	May 26	May 14	May 3	May 23
Yom Yerushalayim 28 Iyar	June 5	May 24	May 13	June 2
Shavuot 6 Sivan	June 12	May 31	May 20	June 9
Tisha B'Av 9 Av	Aug. 14	Aug. 1	July 22	Aug. 11

Index

THE AUTHOR GRATEFULLY ACKNOWLEDGES PERMISSION TO REPRINT THE FOLLOWING:

"Jonah, Son of Truth," Devorah Steinmetz, appeared in *Beginning Anew: A Woman's Companion to the High Holy Days,* ed., Judith A. Kates and Gail Twersky Reimer (New York: Simon & Schuster, 1997) reprinted with permission of the author.

"Warsaw Ghetto Uprising," *The New American Haggadah,* ed., Gila Gevirtz (New Jersey: Behrman House, 1999), reprinted with permission of the publisher.

"The Tear," excerpt from *The Book and the Sword: A Life of Learning in the Shadow of Destruction* by David Weiss Halivni. Copyright © 1996 by David Halivni. Reprinted with permission of Farrar, Straus & Giroux, LLC.

"Kayla's Prayer," by Lawrence Troster, reprinted with permission of the author.

"A Traveler's Prayer," Sheila Peltz Weinberg, reprinted with permission of the author.

"A Prayer Recited at the Celebration of the Birth of a Child," Helise Lieberman, printed with permission of the author.

"A Prayer Written for Parents of a Child with Disabilities," by Geoffrey Haber, printed with permission of the author.

"A Prayer of Trust," by Navah Harlow, reprinted with permission of the author.

"Each of Us Has a Name," by Zelda, trans., Marcia Falk, 1996, reprinted with permission of the translator.

"Prayer for an Adopted Child" by Sandy Sasso. Excerpted from *Lifecycles, Volume 1: Jewish Women on Life Passages and Personal Milestones.* Copyright © Debra Orenstein. (Woodstock, VT: Jewish Lights Publishing, 1997). Permission granted by publisher.

THE PUBLISHER GRATEFULLY ACKNOWLEDGES THE COOPERATION OF THE FOLLOWING SOURCES OF PHOTOGRAPHS AND GRAPHIC IMAGES:

Bill Aron: 9, 24, 25, 41, 50, 72, 209, 213; Beth Hatefutsoth: 76; Creative Image Photography: 14, 38, 44, 56, 63, 65, 92, 104, 108, 125, 133 (top), 136, 140, 141, 168, 210; Joyce Culver: 4; Gustav Doré: 8, 79, 98, 99, 101, 109 (right), 130, 169, 177, 181; Stanley Friedman: 30; Gila Gevirtz: 70, 117, 238; Hebrew Union College-Jewish Institute of Religion: 144; Israel Government Tourist Office: 161; Israel Ministry of Tourism: 162, 174, 183; Israel Museum: 223; The Jewish Museum: 171; Jewish National Fund: 115; Francene Keery: 57, 59, 109, (center) 112, 131, 204; Richard Lobell: 33, 43, 61, 77, 185, 190, 197, 237; Bill Mitchell Photography: back cover flap; Beth Shepherd Peters: 23, 66; Eric Pollitzer: 149; Rembrandt/ The Jewish Museum: 123; April Saul: 7; Clare Sieffert: 15, 41, 62, 87, 107, 120, 124, 139; SPL/Photo Researchers: 48; Union of American Hebrew Congregations: 221; Therese Wagner: 191, 225; Sunny Yellen: 26, 85, 121, 127, 160 (bottom); Alan Zale/New York Times Pictures: 211; Zionist Archives and Library: 114, 158.